GUERRILLA MARKETING FOR FINANCIAL ADVISORS

Secrets For Making Big Profits From Your Financial Advisor Business

By Jay Conrad Levinson
and
Grant W. Hicks, CIM, FCSI

D0249923

© Copyright 2003 Grant Hicks and Jay Levinson. All rights reserved.

No part of this publication may be reproduced, stored in a retrieval system, or transmitted, in any form or by any means, electronic, mechanical, photocopying, recording, or otherwise, without the written prior permission of the author.

Printed in Victoria, Canada

National Library of Canada Cataloguing in Publication Data

Hicks, Grant, 1967-
     Guerilla marketing for financial advisors / Grant Hicks and Jay Conrad Levinson.

Includes bibliographical references.
ISBN 1-4120-0399-7

     1. Financial planners—Marketing.   2. Investment advisors—Marketing.   I. Levinson, Jay Conrad   II. Title.

HG179.5.H52 2003   332.6'068'8   C2003-902876-3

TRAFFORD

This book was published *on-demand* in cooperation with Trafford Publishing.
On-demand publishing is a unique process and service of making a book available for retail sale to the public taking advantage of on-demand manufacturing and Internet marketing.
On-demand publishing includes promotions, retail sales, manufacturing, order fulfilment, accounting and collecting royalties on behalf of the author.

Suite 6E, 2333 Government St., Victoria, B.C. V8T 4P4, CANADA

Phone	250-383-6864	Toll-free	1-888-232-4444 (Canada & US)
Fax	250-383-6804	E-mail	sales@trafford.com
Web site	www.trafford.com	TRAFFORD PUBLISHING IS A DIVISION OF TRAFFORD HOLDINGS LTD.	
Trafford Catalogue #03-0768	www.trafford.com/robots/03-0768.html		

10   9   8   7   6   5   4   3

GUERRILLA MARKETING FOR FINANCIAL ADVISORS

MARKETING STRATEGIES FOR SUCCESS AS A FINANCIAL ADVISOR–FOR STOCKBROKERS, INSURANCE AGENTS, INVESTMENT PROFESSIONALS, AND THEIR ASSISTANTS

BY
THE AUTHOR OF THE BEST–SELLING GUERRILLA MARKETING SERIES, JAY CONRAD LEVINSON, AND
GRANT W. HICKS, CIM, FCSI

No matter what business you're in, Jay Conrad Levinson shows you how to grow sales and profits beyond your wildest dreams—without spending an extra penny on marketing costs!
-Robert Allen, Best-selling author and world-renowned lecturer

In the marketing world, no one knows how to use the weapons of the trade better than industry expert Jay Levinson. He is living proof that his unconventional marketing ideas work.

-*Entrepreneur* Magazine

Guerrilla Marketing books are among the best marketing books our reviewer has ever read.

-*Seattle Times*

Every book by Jay Levinson is worth reading.
-Jane Applegate, author of *Succeeding in Small Business*

Dedications

Grant:
Kim, Madison, and Austin. For their love and support.

Jay:
Bill Shear for doing what it took to build a brand.

Acknowledgements

I could not have completed this if my wife, Kim, didn't support me 100%. The roadblocks disappeared once I teamed up with Jay. His encouragement to get it done was nothing short of inspirational; he is a great author, guerrilla marketer, and person. To Denis Rochon, who believed in me when I entered the investment industry. To individuals along the way who helped me and gave me inspiration and ideas, including Michael Wolfond of Partners in Planning and Carol Hagel, my assistant. To Bruce Batchelor and Trafford publishing, an awesome person and company to work with. To my clients, for placing their trust and confidence in me to manage their financial goals and dreams. A special thanks to my top client supporters, Bob and Sheila Smith, for their help at seminars and referrals and for their genuine business support. To my parents for their confidence in me. To the fund companies and wholesalers for their support and teamwork. And finally, a big thanks to you, the reader, who is like me and wants to learn more to earn more in this great industry for years to come.

About Jay Conrad Levinson

Jay Conrad Levinson is the author of the best-selling marketing series in history, *Guerrilla Marketing*, and 29 other business books. His books have sold 14 million copies worldwide. His guerrilla concepts have influenced marketing so much that his books appear in 39 languages and are required reading in many MBA programs worldwide.

Jay taught guerrilla marketing for ten years at the extension division of the University of California in Berkeley; he was a practitioner in the United States as Senior Vice-President at J. Walter Thompson and in Europe as Creative Director and Board Member at Leo Burnett Advertising.

He has written a monthly column for *Entrepreneur*, articles for *Inc.*, and on-line columns published monthly on the Microsoft web site–in addition to occasional columns in the *San Francisco Examiner*. He also writes on-line columns for several Internet web sites, including Netscape, America Online, Fortune Small Business, and Hewlett-Packard.

He is the Chairman of Guerrilla Marketing International, a marketing partner of Adobe and Apple. He has served on the Microsoft Small Business Council and the 3Com Small Business Advisory Board. His *Guerrilla Marketing* is a series of books, audiotapes, videotapes, an award-winning CDRom, an Internet web site, and a breakthrough on-line marketing advancement called The Guerrilla Marketing Association, a marketing support system for small business, a way for business owners to spend less, get more, and achieve substantial profits.

Visit *www.gmarketing.com* for more information.

About Grant W. Hicks, CIM, FCSI

Grant Hicks has been successfully selling business-building ideas since 1989. These ideas are based on his everyday experiences as a financial advisor and business builder. He managed a financial planning firm and built it up over 3 years from 20 advisors to more than 70 advisors. That firm was successfully merged into Partners in Planning Financial Services.

He then went back to managing clients and as a Retirement Planning Specialist rapidly built up his business from $1 million to more than $40 million under management in just over two years. His innovative marketing ideas won the best ideas for Canadian financial advisors contest in 2001, and he was featured across Canada at the Advisors Forums and in *Advisor's Edge*, Canada's magazine for financial professionals. His ideas have also appeared on *www.advisor.ca*, a Canadian advisors' marketing and business-building web site. Grant speaks to audiences of financial advisors, mutual fund wholesalers, and insurance professionals on a regular basis about how to build business through his marketing ideas. His promotional web site, *www.financialadvisormarketing.com*, is a virtual search engine for marketing for investment professionals and the financial industry with hundreds of links to the best marketing ideas and speakers in the industry today. He holds the Canadian Investment Manager (CIM) portfolio management designation from the Canadian Securities Institute and is a Fellow of the Canadian Securities Institute (FCSI), the highest mark of professionalism in the Canadian Securities Industry. Grant is a long-standing member of the Canadian Association of Financial Planners (CAFP), The Canadian Association of Insurance and Financial Advisors (CAIFA, now called Advocis), and the Federation of Independent Deposit Brokers (FCIDB). He is a shareholder of Partners In Planning Financial Services, Canada's largest independent financial advisory firm. He owns Hicks Financial, a fixed-income-management company.

He is also President of Hicks Financial Consulting, a marketing and consulting firm to the financial services industry. Grant writes a weekly column on financial topics in his hometown newspaper in Parksville, British Columbia. He is married with two children. Grant played professional hockey in Europe before starting his career in the financial services industry.

Visit *www.financialadvisormarketing.com* for more information and email Grant at *ghicks@financialadvisormarketing.com*.

Chapter Summary Quick Reference

Chapter 1
Build a Better Business And Marketing Plan

Chapter 2
Getting New Clients from Outside Sources

Chapter 3
Getting New Clients from Internal Marketing

Chapter 4
Welcoming New Clients

Chapter 5
Wowing Clients

Chapter 6
Mastering Service for All Clients

Chapter 7
Taking Your Business to the Next Level

Chapter 8
Marketing Principles for Financial Advisors

Chapter 9
Guerrilla Marketing Tools and Marketing Action Plan Worksheet

Foreword

I'm amazed when I meet savvy financial advisors who know all there is to know about the world of high finance but know hardly anything about the world of marketing. In the current and future business environments, every financial planner must realize that he or she is actually in four businesses at once.

The first, of course, is the financial advising business, just as it says on your business card. The second, and commit this one to memory, is the marketing business—because your financial advice must be marketed in order for your prospects to benefit from it and for you to profit from it.

The third business you're in is the service business because that's really what you're marketing in the first place and what your clients will increasingly expect from you. And the fourth business you're in all along is the people business, for it's people who will be your prospects, your clients, your representatives, and your staff. The lifeblood of any business is people. The vitality of a business is service. The fire that fuels the profits is marketing.

Guerrilla Marketing for Financial Advisors tells you how to be a Rembrandt in the art of marketing. It covers both the crucial and the overlooked methods of marketing. Grant W. Hicks takes you by the hand and leads you safely through the minefields of marketing to the achievement of your goals—and beyond, if you so desire. The power of well-planned marketing is awesome—as those of you who plan financial futures are well aware.

Guerrilla Marketing means striving for conventional objectives and attaining them with unconventional methods. It means making your primary marketing investment not money, but time, energy, imagination, and information. Grant W. Hicks has packed these pages with the exact information you should have—better suited to your specific needs than an MBA in Marketing from any institution of learning on earth.

His wisdom covers all the details of successful marketing for financial advisors. Overlooking any of them can make the difference between gliding and struggling. Best of all, he does it in true guerrilla fashion—pointing out the ways to market first-class while paying less than economy fare.

As I'm privileged to be associated with this book, you're blessed to have the opportunity not only to soak up its wisdom, but also to act on its insights. Action is the purpose of the exercise. Guerrilla Marketing is not a spectator sport.

After you've completed this book and you've recovered from the onslaught of common sense and brilliance on every page you read, you're going to feel more optimistic about your future than ever. I don't blame you. Now, you've got the acumen of a guerrilla.

What is Marketing in the First Place?

Marketing is absolutely every bit of contact any part of your business has with any segment of the public. Guerrillas view marketing as a circle that begins with your ideas for generating revenue and continues on with the goal of amassing a large number of repeat and referral clients. The three keys words in that paragraph are EVERY, REPEAT, and REFERRAL. If your marketing is not a circle, it's a straight line that leads directly into Chapters 7, 11, or 13 in the bankruptcy courts.

How is Guerrilla Marketing Different from Traditional Marketing?

Guerrilla marketing means marketing that is unconventional, non-traditional, not by-the-book, and extremely flexible. Ten factors make it different from old-fashioned marketing:

1. Instead of investing money in the marketing process, you invest time, energy, and imagination.

2. Instead of using guesswork in your marketing, you use the science of psychology, laws of human behavior.

3. Instead of concentrating on traffic, responses, or gross sales, profits are the only yardstick by which you measure your marketing.

4. Instead of being oriented to companies with limitless bank accounts, guerrilla marketing is geared to small business.

5. Instead of ignoring clients once they've invested, you have a fervent devotion to client follow-up.

6. Instead of intimidating small business owners, guerrilla marketing removes the mystique from the entire marketing process, clarifies it.

7. Instead of competing with other businesses, guerrilla marketing preaches the gospel of cooperation, urging you to help others and let them help you.

8. Instead of trying to make sales, guerrillas are dedicated to making relationships, for long-term relationships are paramount.

9. Instead of believing that single marketing weapons such as advertising work, guerrillas know that only marketing combinations work.

10. Instead of encouraging you to advertise, guerrilla marketing provides you with 100 different marketing weapons; advertising is only one of them.

These are ten very critical differences and are probably the reasons that the concept of guerrilla marketing has filled a void in the world's economy, explaining why the guerrilla books (GUERRILLA MARKETING, GUERRILLA MARKETING ATTACK, GUERRILLA MARKETING WEAPONS, GUERRILLA MARKETING EXCELLENCE, GUERRILLA FINANCING, GUERRILLA SELLING,

GUERRILLA ADVERTISING and GUERRILLA MARKETING HANDBOOK are among 30 books in the series) have been translated into 33 languages, sold over one million copies, are required reading in most MBA programs, are available in audiotape and videotape versions, as computer software, as a nationally-syndicated column, as a newsletter, and are the most popular and widely-read marketing books in the world.

Jay Conrad Levinson
Marin County, California, 2003

The information in this book does not constitute a recommendation for the sale or purchase of any securities or insurance.

Contents

Chapter 2   83

Getting New Clients from Outside Sources

Chapter 3   **153**

Getting New Clients from
Internal Marketing

Chapter 4   **184**

Welcoming New Clients

Introduction

This has been a fourteen-year journey—fourteen years of collecting notes at seminars, trade shows, courses, meetings, and conferences. In listening and in writing the notes I had one goal in mind, to share my experiences with other financial advisors and educate them about marketing. With this book my goal is to become an educator and to speak and write of the marvelous ideas I have been fortunate to collect over the years from industry experts, managers, marketing experts, and exceptional financial advisors sharing their experiences. The members of this financial community are proud to share their ideas and help their fellow advisors build their businesses.

This book is written for the dedicated financial advisor who is developing his or her career and has the desire to go to THE NEXT LEVEL. The next level, however, needs to be defined. This is not a book that will take you from a $50,000 annual income to a $2,000,000 annual income instantly. It will increase your potential in the industry, it is intended to make you decide what is the next level for you and your business, and it will provide ideas to help you get there faster and easier. It will add value to your business, make you think of marketing, and help you develop great relationships. Relationships with your clients, their friends, and their families that will last decades. Relationships with colleagues, marketing and support people, competitors, and head offices. Networks of industry associates that you see at conferences, road shows, and luncheons. Friendships that go beyond work—to social events, movies, your children playing together, and other memorable occasions. In the end, your business is the relationships that you have built in the business, not just production, production, production. It is a people business and it is these relationships that will be remembered, not just your production numbers.

Financial advisors are constantly bombarded by ideas from sales literature, conferences, colleagues, managers, industry publications, wholesalers, or head office. We collect the information, assemble it, and sometimes put it to use. Then next week, month, year, we change our business because we have heard another great idea. At the end of five years in this business we come to realize that nothing is new; there are different spins on old ideas. We then go about creating a campaign or marketing plan. This seems to work well so we stick to it and reap the benefits. Two years later, sitting on a beach in Maui, we realize that those plans really helped business. Successful financial advisors realize the power of marketing and are devoted to improving their business plans. Soon they find themselves at the top of the field. These advisors are seen as leaders in the industry and sought for their expertise.

The simple truth is that it all starts with an idea. The idea is expanded, researched, customized, and formulated into a plan; then the plan is put into motion. Results soon follow, thus that simple idea creates wealth for the advisor's clients and brings value to the world. Because of that simple idea, many people may be able to retire earlier or send their children to a choice college. Amazingly, this single, simple idea creates a spark that grows into a ball of fire that the advisor had never imagined.

Each strategy holds several key ideas to help your business. At the end of each strategy is an action summary that asks you if you should add that strategy to your marketing plans and whether you require additional information. At the back of the book, using the Guerrilla Marketing Action Planning Worksheet, you can record your summary action plans for all strategies. I have also included some extra questions to ask yourself about your business. Use the worksheet and questions to develop your business and take action to achieve the success you truly desire.

The ideas are simple and a dime a dozen, but put one into action and see what can happen. Think big and you will be surprised by the results.

While there are hundreds of ideas in this book, we have organized it for you so that at the end of the book is a summary list of ideas to develop and implement over time. Use this as a worksheet for your marketing plan in progress. Rome wasn't built in a day, but look at the great job they did!

Explore the ideas in this book. Risk conventional wisdom and challenge yourself to new heights of success. See yourself on that beach in Maui (where I started writing this book) and enjoy your fruits of your success. Dare to turn your practice up a notch. I challenge you to improve yourself as well as your business.

Go for it and good luck.
Enthusiastically yours,
Grant

P.S. Important Compliance Note Please Read

How's that for an attention-grabber? As advisors we know that all marketing must adhere to company and industry policies and compliance. Make sure that any marketing idea or activity is cleared through your firm and its compliance department before proceeding. All securities and insurance industry rules and regulations must be followed. We must hold ourselves high in the public eye, so compliance with all of your marketing standards is a key to future success.

Chapter 1
Build a Better Business
and
Marketing Plan

What lies behind you and what lies ahead of you pales in comparison with what lies within you.

-Ralph Waldo Emerson

Build A Better Business Plan–Your Ten-Year Vision

Concept:

Writing out your goals is one thing. Establishing a system and framework for accomplishing your goals is crucial to your success. Working on your business on a regular basis will create results that are dramatically better than working in your business. I guarantee that working harder in this business will not make you more successful. Working on your business and regularly developing ideas for success will. Why do the greatest athletes such as Tiger Woods keep practicing on a regular basis? Each day they are trying to get a little better. They are working on their game, not playing the game.

Objective:

As financial advisors we plan our clients' long-term financial futures every day. So why do we neglect to do it for ourselves and for our businesses? I have asked several financial advisors what "long-term" means. They usually answer that they develop five-, ten-, or fifteen-year plans for clients. Then I ask, "How long is your business plan?" If it is not ten years, maybe you don't plan on being in the business that long. I dare you to look at your financial plan and share it with your peers. Then look at your long-term business plan. If you have one, congratulations! You're in the top 20% of financial advisors in the world. If you're like most financial advisors, however, you wrote it a few years ago and never updated it. As advisors, we develop long-term financial plans, yet the average business plan for financial advisors is one to three years. Develop your plans as one-year (must-do), three-year (achievable), five-year (goal-oriented), and ten-year (long-term vision).

To sell you on the benefits of the business plan, I would show you that projections into the future based on what you know today would be of huge benefit to your success. The challenge is to think how you can grow and do things differently to achieve higher goals. Start by thinking what your ideal business plan would look like, if you could design amazing financial targets and goals, then think of a business or advisor that you would like to emulate. Think of the possibilities. The only limit is how much you can imagine. Challenge yourself to become the most successful financial advisor you know, not because of the money you will earn but because of the person and advisor you will become.

Strategy:

Start today to develop one-year (short-term), three-year, five-year, and ten-year (long-term) written business plans for success. Most advisors love to feel they are independent and work for themselves, yet they lack the discipline to run a successful business. If you work for a firm, structured goals and targets are set for you and followed up on a regular basis. As an independent financial advisor, I know that it is one thing to write a business plan, but to be disciplined and accountable for it is another. Make yourself accountable to someone and share your business plan. This may be a spouse, an associate financial advisor, a wholesaler, or someone in your peer group (discussed in a later chapter). A business plan has the benefit of creating a blueprint for even greater success.

Grant's Tip:

Review each section of your plan every month and set goals for certain dates in each category.

When you review each month, make sure you revisit and check off completed goals. Have a place to keep ideas to review and develop. For example, I keep a folder with business planning ideas that I pick up. Each month when I review, I also review these ideas so that I might implement them into my business (with a time frame for completion). If I see a new software program, I keep the idea for review at the time I planned to spend working on my business, not in my business.

Review the ideas with your peer group or people who help you be accountable in the business. Have you ever spoken with someone who said they are busy because it's month-end? Why don't you have a month-end where you review production, business planning ideas, your business and marketing plans and goals? Do you think this exercise each month will bring greater results?

One idea to use when you are developing your plan is to find a boardroom-type space where you can take each section of your business plan and freely write out the benefits. Do this exercise with someone else (or your peer group) to make yourself accountable and to give you feedback on your process. Remember, success leaves clues. Ask other successful advisors for their business plans and invite them to a strategy session. Surround yourself with literature on building business plans. Our web site has hundreds of successful sites devoted to developing business plans and marketing plans. Hundreds of books are written on this topic. Ask the wholesalers or marketing representatives with whom you work, or even your company, for help on this area.

At the end of this strategy is a sample confidential business plan. If you want to see what other companies do with business plans, check out corporate annual reports. Usually a company's vision and plan are there. Questions I receive from audiences are, "What is included in a business plan?" or "How much time does it take to prepare a business plan?" The answers are simple and straightforward. An effective business plan holds the fundamental information to manage your business as it will look five years from now. Then start working backwards. What will you need to have in place when the business is successful? What business is successful now and how is its business plan laid out?

The easiest way to build a business plan is to start by writing down your goals. Take a blank pad of paper and start writing. Combine business goals, family goals, spiritual goals, lifetime goals, travel goals, etc. Write them all down, then break them down into time segments—per year, per month, per week, and per day. For example, if your goal is to have 30 new clients this year with average investable assets of $300,000 for a total of $9 million new assets, how much per month and per week do you need to achieve the goal? Do this with all of your goals.

More importantly, activity drives production. What activities do you need to do to arrive at those numbers? Some experts suggest you make your numbers based on three assumptions—best-case scenario, likely numbers, and worst-case scenario. After you have completed your business plan, the key area should be a one-page summary of key objectives and key actions you need to take to follow up and complete your plans. One tip I will give you is to review your results for the past week every Monday morning, rewrite your one-page summary of goals and plans, and plan your week. One definition of insanity is doing the same things over and over and expecting different results. Each month and year, what are your targets for improvement? Would you invest in a business that targets growth of 5% per year? Not likely; you want businesses that target plus-10% to plus-20% growth per year. What is your target for growth per year?

A final note: Work on your vision. Here is a story from Michael Gerber's book, *The E-Myth Revisited* (HarperBusiness; 1995), that tells you why we ask ourselves these questions. Tom Watson, the founder of IBM, was asked to what he attributed IBM's phenomenal success. He is said to have answered:

IBM is what it is today for three special reasons. The first reason is that, at the very beginning, I had a very clear picture of what the company would look like when it was finally done. You might say I had a model in my mind of what it would look like when the dream—my vision—was in place.

The second reason was that once I had that picture, I then asked myself how a company that looked like that would have to act. I then created a picture of how IBM would act when it was finally done.

The third reason IBM has been so successful was that once I had a picture of how IBM would look when the dream was in place and how such a company would have to act, I then realized that, unless we began to act that way from the very beginning, we would never get there.

In other words, I realized that for IBM to become a great company it would have to act like a great company long before it ever became one.

From the very outset, IBM was fashioned after the template of my vision. And each and every day we attempted to model the company after that template. At the end of each day, we asked ourselves how well we did, discovered the disparity between where we were and where we had committed ourselves to be, and, at the start of the following day, set out to make up for the difference.

Jay's Comments:

The first insight is that guerrillas plan backwards, beginning with the attainment of their loftiest goals in the future, then working back to the present. If you can allow yourself to visualize success, the path to it will be easier to find. Most companies see the beginning of the path in front of them, but don't see where it leads in the distance. Their short-sightedness gets them in trouble when change or unforeseen circumstances occur.

The hardest job in the planning of marketing is seeing the target. You must remove the shackles of insecurity and fear in order to travel to your final destination. So you've got to think as though you've been attaining your goals all along as you plan for your distant future. You must see your company at its finest in 20 years in order for it to operate at its peak in ten years. By knowing what must be accomplished for such optimum performance, you can see where you must be in five years. That helps you concentrate upon what must be done by the end of one year. And that points the way to what you've got to do tomorrow, to do today, to do now.

When the golf ball is in the middle of the fairway and the green 200 yards away, the great golfers don't aim for the green. They aim for the cup. How do you come up with a successful business plan? As Grant suggests, you evolve it over time. Revise and revise it until it is a powerful plan packed with enthusiasm and excitement about the future. You put it to work and then you stay with it no matter what (in most cases). You watch it slowly take effect, rise and falter take a bit more effect, hold on even more, stumble, then finally grab on and soar, taking you with it. Your plan is working. Your bank account is growing. And it all happens because you were committed to your business plan.

What usually happens if you weren't patient enough during the time your plan slowly took effect? You might have changed the plan. Many entrepreneurs do. What if you dropped the plan the moment it faltered? You would have lost out. What if you lost your cool when your sales slid backwards? You might have scrubbed the plan. Suppose you dropped the plan when you stumbled, as virtually all marketing and business plans do. You tell your clients to be patient when the market changes and stick to their plan. If you change your plan what will happen? Disaster may have ensued. But because you stayed with the plan, because you were committed to it and believed in the long-term benefits, it finally took hold and did what you wanted it to do. Your success was very much due to your understanding of the concept of commitment. If you had not been in touch with the essence of the concept, you probably would have taken one of many tempting opportunities to kill the plan and would have killed your chances along with it. However, you understood what commitment means, and it paid off for you.

Additional Resources:

Web site: Visit "Business Planning" on *www.financialadvisormarketing.com.*

Examples:

See the following Sample Confidential Business Plan.

Action Summary:

To add to my marketing plans:	Yes _____	No _____
Additional information required:	Yes _____	No _____

You'll go out on a limb sometimes because that is where the fruit is.

-Will Rogers

Sample Confidential Business Plan For Grant Hicks

Contents

1. Business Philosphy
2. Mission And Vision Statement
3. Marketing Statement
4. Strategies/Goals
5. Targets
6. Technology Strategies
7. Support Staff
8. Professional Development
9. Business-building Ideas to Review
10. Measuring Success

1. Business Philosphy

- Kindness–Work with nice people.
- Interest–Work with clients who want help and advice.
- Referable–Clients who work in a team environment with accountants and lawyers, not "do-it-yourselfers."
- Conservative–Clients who are conservative in nature when investing.
- Quarterbacks–Clients who want us for all of their financial needs–for tax, estate, and investment management.
- Independent Thinkers–Clients who can make a decision and stick to it and trust in their decisions.
- Family–Clients who have strong family values.
- Personal–Building client relationships one family at a time. Relationship-oriented–*Thinking of You*–Using our slogan to think of ways we can help our clients.

2. Mission And Vision Statement

Mission:
Helping Canadians achieve financial security and peace of mind through sound financial planning since 1989.

Vision:
- To be the best team of retirement planners on Vancouver Island, Canada (population approximately 1 million).
- To have a highly specialized education focusing on retirement planning, estates, and inheritances.
- To have a team managing $500 million-plus assets for retirees.

- To be a known source for retirement advice and planning on Vancouver Island in the accounting, legal, and retirement communities.
- To focus on the benefits for our clients including unbiased advice, helping them increase their retirement income, planning their estates and inheritances, and adding value to their personal lives.
- To have one of the best client communications systems in the industry.

3. Marketing Statement

The goal is to develop a memorable trademark or slogan that will be remembered for generations.

Grant Hicks personal marketing slogan is: *Thinking of you.*

Additional slogan: *Helping you achieve financial peace of mind through sound retirement planning since 1989.*

Future Ideas: Focusing on maximizing your retirement income with tax-efficient investment solutions and preserving wealth for your family

Sweat Focus:

S–See a vision of 500 million under administration.

W–Work effectively not efficiently.

E–Expect clients will invest with us.

A–Achieve great results from our marketing.

T–Thanks: always thank clients for business and referrals.

4. Strategies–Goals

Goal 1: Be a quality organization–client-focused service for all levels, with one of the best follow-up systems in the industry, and with one of the best client communications systems in the industry.

Goal 2: Be a diversified financial services organization–team up with the best products and services and build successful relationships within the industry.

Goal 3: Be a dynamic marketing organization, be known for retirement planning, and be known for resource partners.

5. Targets

One-year target–$50 million under administration.

Start-of-year database–Clients, 268; centers of influence, 20; referrals, prospects, 170; leads database, 250–total 708.

Year One key objectives:

- FCSI/CFP.
- $50 million under administration.
- 1 half-time marketing assistant.
- Attend two or three conferences.
- Launch updated web site in April.

Three-year target–$100 million under administration.

Five-year target–$150 million under administration.

Long-term targets–$500 million under administration; 500 clients/average account $800,000 to $1 million; 2 additional full-time financial planners.

6. Technology Strategies
- Minimize the paperwork by working in an electronic environment.
- Improve client reporting.
- Educational and marketing web site.
- Improve web site to allow exchange of information, education, and links with life insurance companies, investment partners, mutual fund companies, and term deposit providers.
- Implement electronic processing, whenever possible, of all investments, term deposits, and life insurance products.
- Client-centered contact management systems.
- Database mining contact management systems for prospects.

7. Support Staff

Philosophy: Treat support staff the same as our best clients.
- Year 1–Hire a half-time marketing and database person.
- Year 4–Hire an additional financial planner and additional support staff.

8. Professional Development
- 1-year plan
  - Attend two educational conferences.
  - Collect 30 educational credits.
  - Complete two additional courses to achieve FCSI designation.
- 3-year plan
  - Complete CFP and CIM professional designations.
  - Attend one national conference and one international conference.
- 5-year plan
  - Take advanced estate and tax planning courses.
  - Work with estate planning and inheritance planning educators.
- 10-year plan
  - Hire an accountant and lawyer to help clients.

9. Business-building Ideas to Review

Keep a file of ideas you come across that you may implement into your business. Each month plan to spend some time reviewing the ideas and how they may help your business.

10. Measuring Success

Assess at monthly meetings and review with Board of Directors quarterly and at brainstorming meetings annually.

See Strategy 3 on Successful Franchise-like Production Systems.

Early to bed early to rise, work like heck and advertise.

-Ted Turner

STRATEGY 2

Build a Marketing Plan Guaranteed to Increase Your Business

Concept:

To have an annual marketing plan and annual marketing calendar. This is to go along with your written business plan for success.

Objective:

There is nothing better in marketing than surpassing your targets and growing your business as you planned. On the flipside, there is nothing worse than finishing a slow month and starting a new month with few prospects and little potential business other than a desk full of cold calls to make. We all have financial goals and targets. Now we need a blueprint to start making those goals a reality. As an advisor, I know ups and downs happen. But I also know that with a consistent marketing guerrilla attack program, you will smooth out your production and be more consistent in your approach.

Strategy:

How do you sit down and write a marketing plan? Budget at least half a day to one full day. Grab a pad of paper and a pen and start writing. Sounds simple—well it is, so make it simple. Unless you're running the marketing of Proctor and Gamble, why do you need an exhaustive written plan? You don't! Try these simple steps:

First, write down all of the marketing you are doing now, the frequency, and the annual and monthly costs. You can use the Monthly Marketing Calendar worksheet at the end of this strategy to help you.

Second, write down all of the marketing ideas that you were thinking of pursuing in the next year. Write or collect a list of ideas. Don't discard anything until you have examined it further. At this point write it down. If you are looking for ideas, check out our web sites listed at the back of the book. Ask you manager or marketing wholesalers for ideas. Use this book as a guide to some of the best ideas. Just write them down.

Third, write down who is your competition and what your competition is doing for marketing.

Fourth, write down what your peer group or the top advisors you aspire to emulate are doing in terms of marketing and their costs.

Fifth, create an annual and monthly budget. Excluding the cost of personnel and assistants, the marketing budget should be between 10 and 20% of your gross income. *Remember marketing is an investment in your business, not an expense.* The second part of budgeting is time. Your time or a staff person's time, or both, must be allocated. How much time will you devote to developing your marketing? How much time during the day do you spend on marketing? Now, how much time should you spend on marketing during the day? (I always schedule a half-day per month to work on my marketing and client communications strategies. This scheduled time is very productive time in my practice.) If you don't have time now, how will you have time in the future to grow your business?

Sixth, we will identify your ideal client profile in a later chapter, but for now write down what you think is your ideal client profile.

Seventh, decide what marketing mix will work for you. What will and what won't work depend on your commitment. This is where you make decisions based on projections of growth that you want to achieve. For example, if you want to increase revenue from $100,000 to $150,000 per year, your marketing budget is $2,000, and you have no major plans for marketing, how are you going to achieve that growth? Although some advisors say their business grows by referrals only, what do they do to generate those referrals? Do they provide exceptional service? This costs money and may be defined as an excellent communication program. Well, guess what, their dynamic communication program is part of their marketing strategy. We will discuss internal (existing clients) and external (new clients) marketing in a later chapter. What is your ideal marketing mix?

Eighth, once you have decided on what you are going to do in the next year, break it down into a monthly marketing calendar. Decide which months you are going to do what.

Ninth, decide on costs and put annual and monthly costs down on paper. At this point make sure that you can afford your program. If you cannot, consider the consequences of borrowing to invest into your business. That is solely your decision. I remember once when I first started in the business, I borrowed money on a credit card to attend a conference. I couldn't afford to go; however after I returned I realized I couldn't have afforded not to. I learned that I was investing in myself and not just spending money on my business.

Finally, put the plan into a working document. Share it with your peer group or manager and your staff. Then commit to completing it, revisiting it on a monthly basis, and measuring the results.

Grant's Tip:

The simpler your marketing plan, the easier it will be to complete successfully. The marketing plan should be simple to execute once you have put enough thought and effort into it. The most challenging part of your marketing plan may be time and timing. I know several advisors who started working on a marketing plan only to stop after a few months because they were too busy. The plan depends on a constant time commitment to complete. If you plan your seminars a year in advance and book the rooms, speakers, and invitations, you are committed. Instead, advisors have a speaker coming to town and spend a lot of time hoping one event will pay off big for them. Don't put your marketing eggs into one basket. Have multiple marketing ideas working for you.

Each quarter I take one day to review the success of the marketing plan, look at future ideas that I may implement into my plan, and set a course for the quarter. I write a mini-marketing plan for the quarter. That way I can review it with my team and advance-plan the marketing events and ideas.

Another key element is looking backward and forward. First, look back on what marketing worked for you and what didn't. Then project a vision of how you want to position yourself in your marketing messages. For instance, I manage retirement assets, so my title is "Retirement Planning Specialist", not "Financial Planner". Positioning means determining exactly what niche you're intending to fill. I live in a retirement community, so it is natural to work in that niche.

Finally, if you're happy with and expect average service, you are probably giving average service. But if you expect world-class service, then bring that element to your practice. The *Ritz-Carlton* motto is "We are ladies and gentlemen serving ladies and gentlemen." Look to first-class organizations with a high degree of service and attention to detail, and implement that type of philosophy into your business. This will help your marketing efforts when thinking of attracting new clients.

The first thing we should do is define this word, "marketing." Marketing for financial advisors means communicating with clients and prospects on an ongoing basis to help them achieve their financial goals. To some marketing means cold calling. It is all of your business efforts to communicate with people. Substitute the words "Guerrilla Communication" for "Guerrilla

Marketing"–it has a completely different meaning, yet it is the same thing. A good friend of mine and a successful realtor on Vancouver Island, taught me the importance of marketing and money-making activities. He said that if he is not selling or listing real estate, he should go and do something else in his life. His support people take care of everything else. That is his job, period; and he understands it clearer than any other realtor, which makes him successful. Start by examining your desk. How much paper and files are on your desk? How much time and energy do you need to spend on getting rid of that paper? Now take that energy and put it into your marketing.

Now what is your job? You know that working harder is not as efficient as working smarter. Let's start by delegating paper and clearing off your desk. Now let's examine your business. What percentage of time do you spend per day or per week on marketing? Remember that communicating with clients and prospects is part of marketing, not interviews or discussing financial plans. Write it down here: ___% time marketing. Now, what percentage of your budget do you spend on marketing and client communication? Write it down here: ___% of money from gross revenues. Finally, what percentage of time do you spend on educating yourself about marketing using books, tapes, etc.? Write it down here: ___% education. Let's look back at your business plan and the percentage of growth you want in your business. Is it 20%? Are you spending 20% of your time/money and education on marketing? If not, do you see a problem here? You want growth yet you, like most advisors and wholesalers, spend less than 8% of your time on marketing. This is why I have written this book and why I speak to advisors today. If I can help you change your habits and your activities to increase your marketing time, will you be more successful? The answer is yes, because that is what the successful advisors do. They spend 20% or more of their time, money, education, and energy on marketing.

What other activities are key to your success? Key Action 1 is to allot the appropriate time, resources, education, and energy to marketing. Our job is calling and seeing clients and prospective clients. Key Action 2 is to see the people. In real estate the three keys are location, location, location. In financial advising it's see the right people, see the right people, and see the right people. Key Action 3 is to examine all of the activities that keep you from doing Key Actions 1 and 2. Write down a list of all of the things that keep you from doing what you need to do to be successful. Examine this list as you would your eight-hour day. A time-management technique is to keep track of a few week's worth of activities. Write in your *DayTimer* the time you spent on each activity; then at the end of a few weeks examine where your time is going. When I first did this, I was shocked at the time wasted–all of the activities I could have delegated and all of the trivial items that chewed into my valuable action time.

At the end of this strategy is a sample marketing plan. Start right now by examining your marketing plans. Remember, your marketing plan is also your communication plan. Look at all of your written marketing material and your web site and circle the number of times you say "we," "us," and "I." Change most of those to "you" and "your." In all of your marketing, remember it is about the clients and not you. Communicate the benefits from the client's position and not yours. Just like you would prepare a financial plan as if you were in their shoes, your marketing should be viewed from their shoes. If your target market is wealthy retired people, then as a wealthy retired person, to what marketing will you respond? How would you choose a financial advisor? Put yourself in the target market. Walk a day in their shoes and find out to what marketing and communication they respond. Do this as part of your marketing and communications plans. Do your homework. Be specific and dig deep for details.

My recommendation is to have marketing files. In these files are categories of marketing such as seminars, client communication, marketing ideas, and business development. As you attend numerous business-building workshops and seminars and read ideas in your monthly publications, add the ideas to the files. I know that as a financial advisor you don't have time to do it all; however, if you allow some time to develop these ideas on a regular basis, your business will continue to grow and improve year by year as I have experienced.

Jay's Comments:

What is the outcome you really want? Be specific. A true guerrilla knows that the clearer the goal in the mind and on paper, the richer the rewards of your marketing efforts. Maybe it's to develop 100 new leads in the next month. Or to generate 1,000 web hits a day. Or cultivate ten new clients in the next 3 months. Send 100 newsletters targeted to the most influential people.

To build with success in the future, here are some tips to help you get the most out of your marketing. Forget the past. Changes in service, technology and competitive marketing savvy are taking place now. Read current publications on marketing, not the old way to do things. Expand your niche by offering what your competitors don't do well. If you're competing against a large organization, find out where they fall down and you pick up. Become your client. What do you expect as a level of service will dictate what they might expect. Do more fusion marketing. When your business is flat and you are not aware of how to change, team up with new collaborative marketing partners to help spread the marketing word for you, by benefiting both of you.

Your mission is clear.

Your task: Make prospects confident in you.

Your secret weapon: Commitment to your plan.

Your personality: Patient.

Your marketing: An assortment of great marketing ideas enclosed in this book.

Your format: The spirit of consistency.

Your finances: Some wisely invested in marketing.

Your energy: Most apparent prior to and subsequent to attracting a new client.

Your operation: The essence of convenience.

Your creative message: It always amazes readers.

Your ultra-profitable chore: Measurement of your marketing success.

There are your ten most important marketing secrets. You now have a head start on your competition. Completing your marketing plan will help you discover how to leapfrog ahead of the competition. In a few short years they will wonder why you passed them, and at such a great speed. Keep it simple and follow through. The results come with time.

Examples:
See Sample Marketing Plan and worksheets.

Action Summary:

To add to my marketing plans: Yes _____   No _____

Additional information required: Yes _____   No _____

I could use a hundred people who don't know there is such a word as impossible.

-Henry Ford

Sample Marketing Plan

1. Benefits to Clients
2. Target Market your Ideal Client
3. Competitive Advantages
4. Marketing Strategies–1-year Plan
5. Budget
6. Monthly Marketing Calendar and Review
7. Client Appreciation
8. Fund Companies
9. Marketing Ideas to Develop
10. Sponsorships and Community Involvement

1. Benefits to Clients
- You're a retiree with special retirement goals. Our business depends on listening to your plans and committed to helping individuals like you achieve your goals.
- You require trustworthy advice. We maintain high educational qualifications and ensure we are using the latest insights from the fields of tax, estate, law, and finance to keep you on the right path.
- You feel comfortable being in control of your retirement plans. Together we build a worry-free plan so you can financially enjoy your retirement.
- We'll provide you with a clear retirement plan that you can count on.
- It's simple to transfer your accounts to us. We look after all transfer fees and we discuss your switching costs up front, as well as any fees.
- Your money is important to you and your family. We find out about your values and what is important to you about money.

2. Target Market your Ideal Client
- Semi-retired or retired.
- Ages 50 through 70.
- Family income above $60,000.
- Net worth 1 million+.
- Assets to invest $400,000+.
- Wants a financial advisor for retirement planning.
- Wants a financial plan and an estate plan completed.
- Wants solid investment performance.
- Needs to minimize taxes.
- Wants control and simplicity.
- Wants appropriate products and strategies.
- Wants help in planning and maintaining a secure retirement.
- Needs guidance to avoid mistakes.

- Wants to invest conservatively.
- Knows money is love and need to plan for his/her family through the estate.
- Prefers money over material goods and wants financial security.

3.   Competitive Advantages
- Completing comprehensive written financial plans.
- Comprehensive written estate plans.
- Working with a team of professionals–see team list.
- Tax-efficient investment solutions–a tax-efficient investment focus.
- Excellent client communications.
- 90-day call program.
- Quarterly client reviews and comparisons to benchmarks.
- Monthly email programs–web site access.
- Client seminars focused on target market.
- One of the best follow-up communications systems in the industry for our clients.
- Client relationship building.
- Semi-annual client gifts for top clients.
- Listening and responding to their needs.
- Client portfolio binders.
- Gifts for referrals.
- Comprehensive client library.
- Excellent client service.
- Telephone rule–call back within 24 hours.
- Follow up including transfer follow-up and maturities.
- Available 9 to 5 Monday to Friday.
- Daily email follow-up.
- Monthly statements available.
- Consolidated statements available.
- Attention to detail and thank-you letters.
- New client introduction program–see Chapter 3.

4.   Marketing Strategies–1-year Plan
See Marketing Ideas to Develop and Monthly Marketing Calendar.

5.   Budget

• Seminars	$ 3,500
• Centers of influence	n/a
• Luncheons	$ 500
• Advertising	$ 4,000
• Web page	$ 500

• Brochure	$ 500
• Printing	$ 2,000
• Mail costs	$ 4,000
• Sponsorships	$ 500
• Client appreciation	$ 2,500
• Miscellaneous	$ 2,000
Total	$22,000

6. Monthly Marketing Calendar and Review
* Maturity list.
* 90-day call list–client reviews.
* Monthly statements.
* Outstanding transfers.
* Monthly email.
* Mailers.
* Centers of influence to see.
* Referral follow up and thank-yous.
* Web site updates.
* Monthly marketing calendar.

7. Client Appreciation
* Gifts to top 50 clients and centers of influence.
* Have an extra 10 gifts in my office for handouts to centers of influence/ new clients and referrals.
* To mail out before thanksgiving–thanks for being a client this thanksgiving.
* Thanksgiving gifts and spring gifts.

8. Fund Companies
* Working with wholesalers.
* Find better ways to work with the wholesalers.
* Discuss each quarter:
    * The fund managers–marketing products and material.
    * Education–products–book.

    * Marketing–industry trends to discuss–ideas.
    * How can they help my business.

9. Marketing Ideas to Develop
* Create list of potential advisors to buy out and purchase in the next year adding $xx million in assets under administration.

- Video conferencing with fund managers for top clients.
- Complete centers of influence team list.
- Update picture.

10. Sponsorships and Community Involvement
- Community and/or other foundation.
- Find a cause, charity, or organization in which to believe.

Monthly Marketing Calendar

The objective here is to get you thinking about your marketing each month. You can't just write a marketing plan for the year and not review it. Each month set aside half a day to work on your marketing plans to get you excited about your business!!!

Month _____

Activities Planned/Potential $ Cost/Dates Planned

1. Seminars   Completed _____.

2. Mailers:

   • Client monthly statements.   Completed _____.

   • Quarterly statements.   Completed _____.

   • Seminar invitations.   Completed _____.

   • Newsletters–due dates.   Completed _____.

   • Call-me letters.   Completed _____.

   • Other.   Completed _____.

3. Top investment opportunities–have a list of your best investment and financial planning ideas and review each month.   Completed _____.

4. Advertising:

   • Seminars.   Completed _____.

   • Announcements.   Completed _____.

5. Web site updating to do:

   • Top investment opportunities.   Completed _____.

   • Other updates.   Completed _____.

6. Newspaper articles:

   • Number of articles to submit _____.   Completed _____.

   • Submitted _____.   Completed _____.

7. Sponsorships.   Completed _____.

8. Emails–monthly. Completed _____.

9. Centers of influence:

   • Mailers/education. Completed _____.

   • Seminars. Completed _____.

   • Special seminars–centers of influence only. Completed _____.

10. Client appreciation. Completed _____.

11. Client reviews:

   • Centers of interest to meet with–one per week– Completed _____.
   educate with brochures in their office !

   • Ninety-Day Call Rotation Program Completed _____.

12. Referral thank-yous. Completed _____.

13. Potential other ideas to discuss and implement. Completed _____.

14. Maturity list. Completed _____.

15. Outstanding transfers. Completed _____.

16. Centers of influence to see. Completed _____.

17. Marketing Materials/printing/stationery/ Completed _____.
supplies.

18. Budgeting/costs. Completed _____.

Note: Review your annual marketing calendar and business plan each month–
Start a file called "Business Planning Ideas." When you go to seminars or
conferences, add ideas you obtained there to the folder. Then review and
implement at the end of each month.

Success comes to those who set goals and pursue them regardless of obstacles and disappointments.

-Napoleon Hill

STRATEGY 3

Successful Franchise-like Production Systems

Concept:

If you don't know where you are going, you will probably end up there. Consistency is the key to long-term success in this business. How many times have you started off with a great month and ended up slowing down because you're ahead of schedule, then suddenly finding yourself scrambling at the end of each month? If you are consistent week in and week out, you will find this business more enjoyable in the long run. This is one reason why so many advisors are transitioning to fee-based operations. They are establishing predictable cash flows for their business.

Objective:

A written inventory on tracking your progress from marketing and sales to focusing on referrals. Goal setting will make your success measurable and attainable.

Strategy:

Each month, set out the number of weeks you're going to work, the number of days, and your production target per week. Then plan your production target for the month. Keeping track with a daily log will also help you track month to date, year to date, and outstanding commissions. It can also be used to track different targets that you set such as new clients, specific product sales, and so on. You will find that you will also refer back to this sheet to keep track of transfers and information for your new and existing clients. Another key to planning your business is to decide whether fee-based is the way to go. If you have made that decision, you cant just expect to change overnight. Setting monthly goals on the transition to a fee-based operation becomes a critical step in your planning. How you are going to accomplish this on a monthly basis and tracking your results will give you comfort knowing you have a structured plan for the transition and tracking it monthly.

With your family, you can make a game of it by putting a target on the fridge at home, such as a sales thermometer, to give the family incentive for encouraging you and helping you reach your goals and the family's goals. You can have rewards for hitting the targets and for certain targets hit and surpassed.

Most successful sales organizations also use sales production reports to report increases or decreases of sales over the same period of time each year. This will help you keep track of your growth rate. For example, target your growth at 1% increase per month and you will see a 12% increase in sales each year.

Grant's Tip:

At the end of this strategy are sample worksheets. Use these sheets and track commissions and/or fees each month as well as completed transfers and client follow-up. Use the monthly reports to track year to date, targets, and comparison with previous months and years. You can easily customize this to track your growth.

This tracking system can be used for client anniversary dates from the time they started working with you. I recommend creating a separate follow-up file for work in progress and, at the end of the month, putting in a copy of the monthly production sheet and confirming all transactions in progress or completed. It should also be used to track referrals from clients, centers of influence, and others. This way it is a reminder to thank them for the referral in a special way.

At the end of each month, you should go over the numbers in these categories:
• Number of new clients.
• New assets in dollar amount.
• Total assets under administration in dollars.
• Commissions and/or fees in dollars.
• Number of referrals given out.
• Number of referrals received (see Referral Tracking Review Worksheet).
• Number of clients.

Planning for next month:
•Your database system should have follow-up reminders and produce a list of people to contact. (A great idea is have your assistant call for appointments; it will show your professionalism in how organized you are.)
•Any investment maturities for the upcoming month (calling for appointments).
•List of calls that need to be made for the month.
•Your monthly review of numbers. (I track the securities and funds that clients own as well as market indexes and print the numbers each month as part of my month-end review.)

Measuring your marketing monthly:

•As part of a monthly habit I started a long time ago, I measure the monthly marketing that we are doing as a firm and plan for the next month. I want to try to measure the effectiveness of our marketing methods (see Monthly Marketing Calendar in Strategy 2).

•As you can see, part of the habit pattern I created is keeping on top of everything in the business. Measuring and planning are parts of what I call my month-end.

•Each month, we have to account for receipts as a business, but do we plan our business once a year and try to follow a plan in our minds? I know I am inspired by marketing ideas and plans that come across my desk all the time, and it is easy to get off track, go in another direction, and completely change the business. That is why I developed month-end worksheets to reflect on the past and plan for the future as a process or habit and not once a year.

One last idea on your monthly marketing review. Each month I read and receive hundreds of great business-building and marketing ideas that I would love to implement. I collect them in a folder and, at month-end, review what I can implement in the next month or so, thus improving a little bit each month. If you put one new idea into your business each month and make it a habit as well as part of your business, in one year you will have twelve new ideas working for you. You can watch your business continue to grow each month and in three years you will find a half a dozen ideas that will make your business as successful as you want it to be and more!

Jay's Comments:

Measure the success of your marketing on a monthly basis. Track where your efforts are being demanded and the source of new and current business. Tracking and following your marketing will make it results-oriented. As a small business you can not afford to spend a fortune on image advertising or brand recognition without getting results. For example, if you did radio or newspaper ads based on your name and what you do and after six months to a year you did not have one new piece of business as a result of those ads or referrals because of your image then you are wasting your money.

Assume you're going to do what it takes to be a successful guerrilla marketer—be sure to know how to deal with success. Most people lack the skill. A good rule of thumb is to engage in no expansion until you have eliminated all of the mistakes in your current operation; otherwise, your mistakes will be magnified and multiplied. When you begin to hit new profits month after month, you'll be tempted to go for the gold and grow. Make sure you take some time each month for self-discovery and examining what is working and what is not working. Plan to schedule an uninterrupted afternoon to complete your month-end review and plan your next month. Schedule the time in advance. If you use a success coach, consider reviewing the results and discussing your plans for the following month. As a successful athlete, Tiger Woods examined his game right after he won the US Open with a record margin. He then decided to fire his caddy and change his game after reflecting on what he wanted his swing to be like. Tiger is an example of CANI—constant and never-ending improvement. You think, after doing that well, why would you want to improve on it? Tiger is an example of what Grant and I are talking about. Each month refine, refine, and refine your business.

Examples:

1. Monthly production worksheet.
2. Guerrilla Marketing Action Planning Worksheet on page 271-278.
3. Referral Tracking Review Worksheet.

Action Summary:

To add to my marketing plans: Yes _____   No _____

Additional information required: Yes _____   No _____

We are or become those things which we repeatedly do. Therefore, excellence can become not just an event but a habit.

-Albert Einstein

Monthly Production Worksheet

Monthly production review–Review the completed month and the next month. Month of _____.

Goals for Month		Actual Results
_____	Weeks/days in this month	_____
$ _____	New assets	$ _____
$ _____	Commissions/fees	$ _____
_____	Referrals given	_____
_____	Referrals received	_____
_____	New clients	_____
$ _____	Total assets under administration	$ _____
$ _____	Assets administration this time last year.	
% _____	Increase/decrease over last year.	
$ _____	Increase/decrease over last year.	

Referral Tracking Review Worksheet

Each month you will see where you are giving and receiving referrals. Set up a planned strategy to receive so many referrals each year from different sources; this will allow you to remember to focus each month on giving and receiving referrals by tracking them. Then, in your annual planning next year, you will know that you can count on so many referrals each year from various sources and map out the source of new clients each year. Wouldn't it be great to plan 50 referrals this year from your top sources so that you aren't wondering how you will build your business? Track them each month.

	Month	Referral Given	Referrals Reeived	YTD Totals

- Name of referral given:
- Referral received:
- Accountant A:
- Accountant B:
- Accountant C:
- Lawyer A:
- Lawyer B:
- Lawyer C:
- Top Client A:
- Top Client B:
- Top Client C:
- Top Client other:
- Center of Influence A:
- Center of Influence B:
- Referral–other:

- Target for month:
- Actual for month:
- Target for year:
- Year to date:

You can't build a reputation on what you are going to do.

-Henry Ford

STRATEGY 4

A Secret to Rapid Growth

Concept:

One way to build a business is to start from scratch. The second way is to buy one. I cannot think of a better way to be seriously "in" the business. This is the quickest way to be in front of several new clients and to help them continue to achieve their financial goals after taking over from another advisor. You could spend thousands on marketing plans or you could purchase a relatively predictable income stream from another advisor. Caution: Some firms will not allow this practice; however, there may be retiring representatives of that company who will allow you to service their existing clients. If you want fifty, one hundred, two hundred new clients, consider buying a book of business.

Objective:

As with any business owner, selling your book eventually should be your goal. When thinking of building your business, I recommend giving the business your name (such as Hicks Financial). This will allow more goodwill, since your name would carry goodwill at a high rate, just like Charles Schwab, J.P. Morgan, or Dean Witter. So how do you go about buying a book of business? The biggest question is valuation and price. This is all over the map; but just like stocks, sometimes they're undervalued and sometimes they're overvalued. I have helped several people buy and sell their books and I have personally done it. I can't think of a better way to grow your business and think like a business owner than buying a book of business.

Strategy:

If you are planning to buy a book of business and have identified potential sellers, use the "Buying a Book of Business" evaluation sheet at the end of this section to find out what the business is worth. Performing due diligence is more than price. Once you have decided to purchase the business, the critical step is the transition period. Every day we see companies merge; some are successful while other mergers cause both companies to suffer. It has to be a win-win-win. The client comes first.

When you are planning the transition, think in terms of dating. You first get acquainted. The former advisor should attend the first meeting. Then you want to present your value proposition to your new client. In the few months following you MUST restate your value proposition and personally learn about your client, bringing up what you have learned to show you are paying attention to him (or her). An example would be to learn about a family member. At the next meeting, ask about that family member. People don't care how much you know until they know how much you care. An additional strategy in your transition would be to bring one key thing to the table. You may bring several additional things to the table but find one key area, such as advanced estate planning, and demonstrate that additional benefit to the client. The client will want all the benefits he was receiving but not a lot more. Adding just one additional benefit and displaying it to him will show that you're adding value. From there you can build value because he have your trust and confidence. You said what you would do, and you did it.

The steps to a smooth transition are as follows:
• A letter from the retiring representative introducing the new advisor. The letter should include a brief bio on the new advisor but should be kept simple and should state that you will call to set up a joint appointment with the retiring representative and the new advisor. State the purpose of the meeting to be an introduction and brief discussion of the file (see the sample letter at the end of this section).
• Appointments made for all clients to meet with both advisors–both advisors review and discuss the files prior to the meeting. I recommend you make personal notes in each file to remember each individual. Build key points and information into a database. If you take more than a hundred clients, a few months from now it may be difficult to remember them all. Build memory triggers to help you remember each personally.
• A commitment letter sent out by the new advisor after the meeting, repeating the commitment discussed.
• Shortly after the introduction meeting, a review meeting with the clients to review their situations and update their overall financial planning.

Grant's Tip:
Plant the seeds with agents so they know, when they leave the business or retire, that you would like first right of refusal on buying their books of business. Finding a book of business suitable to buy can be a difficult task. Putting ads in your association publications may not be enough. You may have to do some digging.

If I moved to a new city and didn't know anyone, one of the first things I would do is look into buying a book of business. I would talk to all of the companies marketing wholesalers in the area and dig up leads from them. Then I would advertise in the local trade publications. I would attend the industry meetings and meet local representatives, look for older representatives, and ask that they contact me when they are considering retiring.

There may be buying and selling consulting services available in your area. As more and more representatives approach retirement, more opportunities will be available. Finally, if you find a book of business, consult with a qualified accountant and lawyer to structure the deal. Discuss with other representatives who have bought or sold before you finalize the terms of the agreement.

Jay's Comments:

One idea is to team up with a partner who will back your business until you want to retire or sell. Why not put a formula in place now and market it to a company that will help you when you want to sell or retire? For example, approach your company and see if they have a program in place to help you market it to another advisor. Maybe you can get more on the open market. However, that may not be the best solution for your clients. Make sure that your transition is seamless for your clients, otherwise why do it?

A great deal of business never occurs because the financial advisor makes a strong business bond with his client and leaves it at that. The guerrilla is all for business bonds, but the strongest are braided with a human bond. When you are taking over new clients in an acquisition, first make the human bond and then the business bond. As the months and years pass and as you take over new clientele in a merger, both bonds are strengthened, enhanced, and made permanent. To add more power to your human bond while increasing a client's sense of identification with your new company, educate the client on how he or she can succeed financially. Even if there is no immediate gain for you, helping your client will eventually be worthwhile.

The whole concept of "eventually" takes on special meaning to advisors who know that most, but not all, people respond to determination. Show your new clients that you and your company are determined to demonstrate the benefits of continuing to deal with you will benefit them for years to come.

Additional Resources:

Talk with other advisors who have bought or sold books of business. Review your contract, or ask your company to review your contract, on the ability to buy or sell. One key area you should have in your contract is what would happen in the event of your death. Some companies have a retirement program, and you may be able to purchase a book of business from your company. Talk to your wholesaler or your company about opportunities. When I go to industry meetings or associations and meet local advisors, I always mention to them that I would be interested in first right of refusal on buying their books of business if they decide to sell. Amazingly, a few years later, I receive phone calls from these representatives.

Examples:

Buying a Book of Business evaluation sheet.
Advisor letter–an advisor with whom we completed a successful transition.

Action Summary:

To add to my marketing plans:	Yes _____	No _____
Additional information required:	Yes _____	No _____

Excellence is a habit, not an act. We are what we repeatedly do.

-Aristotle

Buying A Book Of Business–Areas To Review

1. Verification Of Clients
- June 30 and December 31 Fund Company Statements
- Client Statements from Software Data System

2. Income Verification
- Trailer Fee Revenue
- Earnings Tax Slips
- Income Tax Returns
- Trailer Fee Statements
- Commission Statements
- PACs and SWPs
- Contract with Company and Current Payout
- Cash Flow
- View Files and Statements

3. Marketing Plans
- Advertising/Promotion
- Client Service Standards
- Business Plan
- Goodwill
- Client Communications
- Client Files/Organization

4. Asset Mix
- FE, DSC, Money Market
- Fund Companies
- Average Account Size
- Number of Clients
- Length of DSC Left on Files Per Average Client
- Product Mix

5. Penetration
- Cross-sell Products/GICs/ CDs /Life/DI
- Full Financial Planning
- Asset Gathering/Other Statements

6. Other Assets
- Life/Group Renewals
- Hard Assets/Computer/Desk, etc.

7. Buyout Contract
- Noncompete
- Transition Planning
- Retention

- Contract Completion
- Payout Formulas
- Client Complaints/Outstanding Legal, Risks/ Client KYC and Disclosure
- Securities Problems–E+OE Coverage, Liabilities
- Tax Ramifications
- Corporation Tax and Accounting Concerns

Sample Letter

Dear Client:

One of the most pleasant tasks for a financial planner is to tell his client that all financial goals for a worry-free retirement are met, that all the years of saving and careful investing have finally paid off.

Over the past few months I have taken a hard look at my own situation. I really enjoy working with my clients, but I also long for more time to enjoy other interests. My financial resources are more than sufficient, so I have decided I will retire from financial planning at the end of August. I will continue my income tax preparation service working from my home.

I have chosen Grant Hicks, General Manager of AAI, to assume responsibility for the management of your investment account. Grant was responsible for a good part of the growth of AAI over the last few years and it was he who encouraged me to join AAI in 1996. I respect his good business sense, helpfulness, honesty, and commitment to his clients. Grant and I will sit down with you to do a complete review of your portfolio.

My RRSP and pension portfolios and much of my nonregistered portfolio is invested in mutual funds that will be placed under Grant's management. Of course, I will still maintain an active interest in the news of the markets and welcome your future calls and visits to chat, investor to investor. While we will have to endure some periods of substantial volatility over the next ten years, it is my belief that global equities will produce superior returns. The technology revolution is driving the consolidation of industries into efficient, profitable, and well-run global businesses. I believe this works to the benefit of not just the investor, but also working people throughout the world.

Enclosed is Grant's personal brochure explaining the commitment he has made to help you reach the level of financial security you desire. If you have any questions or concerns, please give me a call. We will speak to you shortly.

Sincerely,

Jim Advisor

Enclosure

Opportunity is missed by most people because it is dressed in overalls and looks like work.

-Thomas Edison

STRATEGY 5

Success Secrets to Leveraging Time

Concept:

You should look at utilizing software to cover these six needs:
- Contact management (which is covered in detail in Strategy 10).
- Portfolio management software for statements.
- Financial planning analysis software.
- Market/research management software.
- Nonmanaged assets tracking software.
- Handheld PC-time and data management technology.
- Web sites and services.

Objective:

The most successful financial advisors learned early in their careers that time management is vital to success. How many time-management courses have you taken? How many software presentations have you attended? If you are like me, you embrace what technology can do for your business, yet you lack the time to learn about all the technology that can help. I have a file of technology to review; yet I never seem to get to that file. When I started in the business in 1989, our office was still using rate books and rate cards for insurance. Can you imagine how productive you would be if this was the case today? Make your practice more efficient by leveraging the use of technology.

Imagine if you sold your practice today. Do you have systems in place for gathering data such as name and address lists, prospect and centers of influence lists, a ninety-day call rotation schedule for your clients, a review process, or a financial planning and research process? Or are you old-school and doing it on paper and by memory? Think of your business as a franchise. If I stepped in tomorrow, would I have technology systems in place to carry on and make it a productive and profitable practice? Or would I have to search in each file for information? Look at your existing software and see if you have all five components to make your practice an effective success.

Strategy:

1. Contact Management:

If you are into database marketing, you must read *The One to One Future: Building Relationships One Customer at a Time* by Don Peppers and Martha Rogers, PhD., (Doubleday, 1996). This idea will be covered in more detail in strategy #10 on page 78.

2. Portfolio Management:

Most firms have packaged software for financial planners but, because we are individual business people, we look for software that we know is useful to our practice. We don't want, however, to spend an enormous amount of time and energy learning software, because we know it keeps changing and we can waste valuable time constantly learning new systems. The strategy is clear. Find the best systems and technology for your practice. This means systems that will leverage time for us, not software that promises to do more than leverage our time. If a software vendor can't convey this benefit to me in five minutes or less, I simply discard it. I need cookie-cutter systems to run my franchise. Systems that we can learn and use as a team, not some specialty program that will take three weeks to learn and run. Portfolio management software systems that are fully compliant for their representatives. Make sure you and your team learn the best way to present information to your clients. So many systems have graphics capabilities, and color does sell. Color pie charts are excellent to illustrate simple concepts to clients. Our web site has some excellent examples of systems. Check out *www.financialadvisormarketing.com* under Software.

3. Financial Planning Analysis Software:

Your clients ask you (after they have been clients for years), "Do we have enough money to retire in two years?" You respond by saying yes, they indeed have enough to retire, without illustrating to them with a written financial plan. You may know that they have enough, but it is more important that they understand it. Depending on the type of practice you have, such as specialized estate planning or general financial planning, your needs for this software will vary. The basic requirement of the software should be simulations of real-life situations for retirement and estate planning. You should have asset allocation software for simple and advanced portfolio analysis that can also design investment policy statements for your clients. While there are thousands of variations of software to examine and hundreds of client financial planning situations, a good word processor and spreadsheet will also do a great job of a handcrafted financial plan.

4. Market/Research Management Software:

Years ago I had to pay thousands to have tax programs, research programs, and data available on a monthly basis. Now a lot of information is available free on some excellent web sites. I could write another book on the Internet and its uses for financial planners, but I will summarize by saying the Internet has three main uses–research, client services, and marketing communications. (See the strategy on email.) Although the majority of information is on the Web, there is still a need for professional programs to do additional research. If you sell mutual funds, mutual fund research software can be an invaluable tool for research and creating and simulating portfolios. Software can also help you research insurance, stocks, or other investment instruments.

5. Nonmanaged Assets Tracking

Have a way to keep track of your clients assets that you do not manage. See Strategy 27 on managing nonmanaged assets. How many times have you heard clients mention that they have assets elsewhere that are not working that hard for them and that eventually they will bring them to you? You may forget about them, but the client doesn't. Also at the back of the book is a demo of this type of software, which I have designed for my practice and which my clients find valuable as a service to keep track of their assets.

6. Pocket PC

Another piece of the puzzle is technology that replaces your pager, cell phone, *DAY-TIMER*, calculator, notepad, and business card index. The technology, which takes minutes to learn, is an invaluable tool for time management. The pocket PC cell phone/*Palm Pilot* system is by far the best piece of equipment since the cell phone. Have you ever driven to an appointment and forgotten the address or telephone number? Have you and your assistant ever booked you for separate appointments on the same day at the same time? This system can be an extremely effective tool for productivity. I had a top producer introduce the system to me and in less than three minutes, I was using it. It's a no-brainer to add this system to your practice. If you want less paper and more time in front of clients, invest in a pocket PC.

7. The Internet

Do you use the Internet on a daily basis? Do your clients? Do you use email on a regular basis? Do you have a web site? Do you have a web site strategy? These questions are explored throughout this book in additional strategies, but here are some ideas to help you. First, see where you are spending money on software and see if you can't get it for free on the Internet. Second, look at your web site. Can it be improved? Third, if you are looking for a book of business, send out an email to other representatives in your area who have web sites. Finally, check out *www.financialadvisormarketing.com* for links to the best marketing ideas and web sites for financial advisors.

Grant's Tip:

Make sure you don't spend too much time in front of your computer screen examining and learning software programs. Some advisors use the computer screen as a part of call reluctance. After all, you can spend countless hours on the Internet at home, why not at work? Take computer courses or have a computer trainer. Put that in your annual planning budget.

Consider the time it takes to complete a full financial plan. Consider hiring someone to prepare your financial plans. Then you would complete the plan and add your recommendations. Can you have certified financial planners prepare the plans for you and save time?

For your handheld PC device, make sure you inject one rule regarding your team or assistants setting your appointments. Synchronize your software twice a day, first thing in the morning and at the end of the day and don't set appointments in the system for the current day.

As always with all software and technology, make sure you have backup procedures in place and system maintenance. Find a technology person and hire this person on contract to maintain your systems.

Make sure that, as part of your business plan, you allocate enough resources to technology, since technology leverages your time and can make you a lot of money or save you a lot of time.

Ask the top planners what they use for software and ask to see samples of their financial planning documents.

Jay's Comments:

Do you have the world's best client list? Orient your marketing plan to capitalize upon the most valuable client list in existence—your very own. There's nothing more exciting than a great hot list of prospects who fit your target market right on the money. Your own client list has a lot on it beyond names and addresses if you think like a guerrilla. Harvey Mackay, author of "Swim with the Sharks Without Being Eaten Alive" (Fawcett Books, 1996) is also Chairman of Mackay Envelope Corporation. Over ten years ago, before we had sophisticated computer programs for tracking client information, he figured out the value of every customer and key prospect, and so his customer list is loaded with details 66 of them, which should give you an idea of what bound-for-glory customer list is all about.

Harvey and his salespeople know the education of the people on their list. They know about their customers' and key prospects' families. They're all filled in on the business background, even the office décor. Their salespeople have details about their customers' lifestyles with lots of details. Can you imagine taking the time to gather all that information? You'd better imagine taking that time! That's part of your dues you pay to be a practicing guerrilla marketer. If you don't want to pay them, be warned that even if you try to substitute media mega money for in depth research, the investment won't pay off as well.

Harvey's company pays its dues and gains its customer and prospect data by devoting time to personal contact. It obtains more data from other customers, suppliers, banks, newspapers, trade publications, receptionists and assistants. Information doesn't care where it comes from. As a financial advisor, you should be able to obtain a fantastic database of information and attributes on all of your clients and prospects and use this to begin your guerrilla marketing.

Additional Resources:

Customized Contact, Client, and Office Management for Financial Advisors: Frequent contact with customers, or "relationship management," is important in building a successful business. The payback is clear: Retaining current customers costs five to seven times less than finding new ones. Studies show that over a lifetime loyal customers purchase more, cost less to sell to, and will refer five other people to a business.

Investment professionals that use the widely acclaimed *ACT!* software know the power and advantages it brings to their financial practice. With over 3 million users worldwide and 10,000 corporate accounts, *ACT!* has proven itself by bringing ease of use and powerful features that even a novice can master in just a few minutes.

Act4Advisors is a custom *ACT!* database and layout template designed specifically for financial services professionals.

If you have a question about Act4Advisors or desire *ACT!* consulting services or customization, contact them via email to *sales@software4advisors.com* or call 800-831-7636. Visit their web site at *www.act4advisors.com*.

Learn how to turn your *Palm*™ computer into a competitive tool for conducting and managing your financial planning business–check out *www.emobilities.com*.

Examples:

The Web is an excellent resource. Check out my master marketing web site, *www.financialadvisormarketing.com*, for links to hundreds of software programs and vendors.

Note: Before using any software, make sure it is fully compliant with your firm.

(For Great Financial Tools, check out Quotemedia. QuoteMedia develops and markets unique, Web-based software components that deliver dynamic content to websites. They have developed a full range of financial data applications. You choose from full tool packages or individual components to add dynamic, real-time financial information, customized for your company websites. Check out *www.quotemedia.com*)

Action Summary:

To add to my marketing plans: Yes _____   No _____

Additional information required: Yes _____   No _____

The most important weapon on earth is the human soul on fire.

-Ferdinand Foch

Effective communication is 20% what you know and 80% how you feel about what you know.

-Jim Rohn

STRATEGY 6

Learning From the Best

Concept:

The mastermind concept has been around for centuries–bring together the greatest minds and solve the world's problems. Mastermind groups are formed in all areas of society–religion, politics, world economics, and business. So why is it that we don't practice this thousand-year-old philosophy? Do we, as successful financial advisors, know the answers and decide to stop growing?

Objective:

Develop a mentoring system or peer group to develop each other's business and create your own mastermind group.

Strategy:

Plan to spend one day each quarter, or four to five days per year, working with a peer group. For new advisors, a mentoring system is critical for the first four years. Write a list of top advisors with whom you can develop a peer group. They may be local or not. Teleconferencing makes it easy to develop a world-class network for sharing ideas, giving feedback, and building ideas.

To organize such a meeting takes time, I know. How about leveraging your time? Ask your favorite wholesaler to develop the meeting for you and structure it with top advisors they work with in their regions. They may be able to cover costs of the meeting, scheduling, and room costs. Most wholesalers to whom I have presented this idea have jumped at the chance to brainstorm with their top prospects and clients. Make sure it is a win-win for everyone attending. You want the members of the group to be very compatible and open and willing to share ideas. Keep the list to between six and ten people. For larger groups, you can break off into discussion groups but it is not as effective as a group of enthusiastic professionals brainstorming their ideas, education, and experiences. Have each meeting with a main topic or two and have an advisor prepare a presentation for the meeting. That way, over time, each advisor attending will learn to come to the meetings prepared and willing to share. Someone such as the wholesaler should control the agenda as well as take notes on items to follow up and circulate.

Grant's Tip:

Be the ringleader on this idea. It will pay the most dividends you have ever seen. Start the group, schedule the calls or meetings, and develop and control the agenda. Then watch all the answers you have been searching for in business suddenly appear. Not only will your production go up, but also your enjoyment of the business will go sky-high. Instead of listening to the negative attitudes of other advisors, get with a successful group.

If you are in the developmental phase of your business and learning everything seems a huge task, work with a mentor or group of mentors who are willing to share time and expertise helping you find your way. Success leaves clues, and finding successful advisors in your area or your company shouldn't be that difficult. Approach them on a mentoring or peer grouping basis and you will be sure to find they are also willing to learn and grow from the mastermind principle.

This strategy can be developed in a couple of ways. First, form a peer group amongst associates in the industry in different cities. Then have a scheduled conference call each quarter, focus on a couple of topics, and invite a speaker to coordinate the call. For example, wouldn't you like to know more about developing effective seminars? Organize a conference call and ask a popular speaker in the financial industry (call me, for example) to host a conference call dealing with seminars. If the geography or time permits, hold the meetings face to face and deal with the issues and topics of importance.

A second way to do peer grouping is also a marketing idea. How about holding a meeting for successful entrepreneurs on business issues and topics such as marketing? Invite several successful CEOs and business owners and develop a success forum where they can meet on a regular basis and share ideas. Some advisors have used this method successfully to attract top business owners as clients. You are seen as the catalyst for bringing insightful ideas while meeting other successful people to learn from.

Do your homework and research numbers; bring it to the table of your peer group.
• Select the marketing weapons you will use.
• Create a guerrilla marketing plan.
• Develop a guerrilla marketing white paper.
• Decide the priority order of launching your marketing.
• Decide in your firm who will be responsible.
• Develop the plan, execute, and measure.

This is your chance to do an incredible amount of research and brainstorm an effective plan. Ask yourself, doing this exercise, whether it will be worth it. Will you get great sales and feedback and avoid mistakes, gain experience? Absolutely. This is a major key to your plan so put this on the list of to-do's!

Your peer group will be able to guide your development and grow. You can gain excellence by assembling this group.

Call up your favorite wholesalers and have them establish a peer group with their top representatives. They have a chance to sit in and learn and at the same time gain valuable feedback to help their business. They may even gain some referrals by finding out who are the members of your peer group and networking with them. Also, each of the representatives invited gets a chance to possibly meet a new wholesaler and other top representatives from whom he or she can learn. Your wholesaler will be delighted to be part of the process!

Jay's Comments:

Let's start with the bad news. Much that you have learned in the past, although God's own truth at the time, has changed, leaving you misinformed or uninformed, so that a lot of what you know is wrong. In social situations, your lack of information is inconvenient, but in business, it's suicidal. You've got to realize that in business, just as in sports, people are constantly trying to become better than you, and some of them succeed. The ones that do have mastered the art of learning. To do that, you simply acknowledge to yourself that learning should never stop and is an endless process.

Seagulls fly in circles in the sky, constantly searching for prey. When they find that prey, they land and eat their fill. Then, they return to the sky, only to fly in circles once again. It is their most powerful instinct. Guerrilla marketers have one instinct that is equally strong—the need for constant learning. They gobble up data with an intellectual appetite that can never be sated.

But anybody can read books, listen to tapes, watch the tube, attend seminars and browse the Internet. How do guerrillas learn differently from other marketers? They learn with two-way brains. That means that in addition to merely learning, they act upon their new information. They do things to take advantage of their newfound wisdom. This action is the essence of guerrilla marketing.

Learning is different these days from when you were a kid. The key to succeeding in your own business is not learning all about something but learning one thing after another. The information changes and it pours in from all over the place. So you've got to be selective in your learning. Learning something will always be possible and learning everything impossible, which is why guerrillas learn with a filter in their brains.

Never before in history has so much information been available to so many people with such simplicity. In one hour in your own office today, you can learn more than you could a decade ago with a week in a library. You can learn theories and facts, up-to-the-minute information, and competitive intelligence galore. You can learn about your prospects, your customers, your industry, and your marketplace. Key information, every bit of it.

The information that is so available has never been as important as it is right now—in The Information Age. You can give it away for it is often far more precious than any hard goods. Brochures and newsletters are very much appreciated by people who can honestly benefit from the information imparted. Because information is the currency of the times, guerrillas do all they can to help their customers learn how to succeed. They do it by providing information.

Guerrillas also know well the immense power of repetition in learning and in teaching. They've seen its potency in marketing. They know, too, the joy of learning—for its own sake, and for the sake of propelling their businesses to the top. Non-stop learning—that describes their journey there.

Additional Resources:

Create a list of areas in which you want further help. For example, I always want to learn more about marketing. Create a list of ideas and areas that you want to learn more about, form a group, and discuss them. You will find amazing resources brought out by everyone.

Action Summary:

To add to my marketing plans: Yes _____   No _____

Additional information required: Yes _____   No _____

You have to think anyway, so why not think big?

-Donald Trump

When you believe in people, they do the impossible.

-Nancy Dorman

STRATEGY 7
Finding Marketing Team Builders

Concept:

Here are some hiring techniques for financial advisors. Hiring and training people is the most costly and time-consuming expense in a financial advisor's business. You want to hire people who are like your best clients and treat them that way.

Objective:

In developing your business plans, you will want to hire individuals who are client and team builders. They don't need an MBA in marketing; however, having a client-centered approach is critical in building your image. Have you ever left a professional's office frustrated by the way you were treated by the staff? Or have you been impressed by the way you were treated? The next time you visit a world-class franchise, see if you can recognize the top staff. They are all getting paid the same but one person can make or break your experience. Now think of your practice. Are you impressed by the appearance and professionalism of the staff? A story I once heard about guests at a *Disney* resort was how the staff cleaning the room paid attention to placing the children's toys each day as they cleaned the room. The guests felt like every detail was important. Now how much did *Disney* pay that employee? How much did it cost *Disney* to give that family that great experience? It was worth a thousand referrals to their resort.

Strategy:

How do you treat your best client? Really think this question through. Now, how do you treat your team member(s)? Treat your team members as well as you treat your best clients and you will develop throughout your organization the experience you are seeking.

Grant's Tip:

Make sure that you are never completing $10-per-hour tasks as a financial advisor. Your time may be worth $60 or more per hour. It is costing you whatever your time is worth per hour to do these $10 tasks. When you are hiring, think down the road. Do you need two people, one for marketing and client communications, and one for administration and processing? Break down the daily tasks these people will be completing and put a dollar amount on the type of task.

Sales Support: Producers in this industry tend to use the term "sales assistant." If I go to the car dealer and I want service, I don't go to the sales department but to the service department, which is usually clearly labeled. If your clients want service, do they go to the sales assistant? Why not go to the client service manager? That is the title given to my "sales assistant."

The function of your "communications manager" is to ensure you have plenty of appointments set up. Whether client reviews or new contacts, the communications manager should be the one in touch with the clients in your database.

Depending on your size here is what your team may consist of:
• Full-time registered client service manager.
• Full- or part-time communications manager.
• Client service assistant(s).
• Top wholesalers.
• Printing and graphic designer.
• Compliance officer to approve your marketing.

The most important concept in team building is to get the right person for each function and use the time gained to see new clients. If you can't afford staff at this time (although I highly recommend you hire anyway), consider hiring out on contract. After the first few years in the business, I couldn't afford to hire a full-time person, but I hired a marketing consultant on a contractual basis to do newsletters, mailers, and prospect communication. This cleared up valuable time for me to look for new clients.

Also on your list of marketing team builders are wholesalers. They can be an invaluable part of your team when it comes to marketing. Their marketing departments usually have successful marketing and communications people to work with. See Strategy 15 for more information.

A marketing, printing, or communications company should also be a part of your team. Finding a great graphic designer to do ads, seminars, business cards, etc., is important to the successful delivery of your messages. Ask the top marketing people in your area who they use for their printing and design.

Finally, your compliance and/or in-house marketing people. You may have all the resources you need inside your own company. Your compliance officer may or may not understand your marketing efforts, but it pays to have him or her help you get the approvals you need. Remember, all printing and design MUST be pre-approved by your compliance department.

Jay's Comments:

The Designated Guerrilla

Reality in running a financial advisory practice means knowing exactly what you've got to do but not having enough time to do it. If you understand how guerrilla marketing can propel you into hyper-profitability but can't take the steps to activate and maintain the process, your understanding is wasted.

Here's the deal: Marketing can succeed only if time and energy are devoted to it regularly. Insight and understanding, savvy and skill, are useless unless action is taken and somebody is paying close attention to the marketing process. Maybe that somebody will be you. But perhaps you're too busy attending to the details of operations, finance, production, sales or service. If that's the case, that somebody should be your designated guerrilla—an individual who has the expertise, interest, desire and time to mastermind your marketing.

Select that person from within your company or from the outside. There are lots of hired guns who will be delighted to eat, sleep, and obsess over your marketing. Just be sure you select somebody. Find someone who will approach the marketing function in true guerrilla fashion—with enthusiasm, confidence, high energy, and a killer instinct. If the person running your marketing show now doesn't have those attributes, get yourself another guerrilla.

Marketing, for all its sophistication, is just like a little baby in that it needs constant attention and thrives best when it is nurtured and guided. Unless you or your designated guerrilla provides this parenting, your company will begin to fade from your customers' and prospects' minds. The companies that get into trouble are often those that establish marketing momentum, then move on to other things. Those other things should always include more and better marketing—because marketing is a continuing connective process and not a series of disconnected events.

Your designated guerrilla should be a person who knows how many marketing weapons are available to you, how many you can create right in your own office, which ones are free, what your competition is up to, and what kind of new technology can help you. Perhaps your designated guerrilla will be your marketing director or director of sales. It might be a marketing consultant, the account supervisor at an ad agency. It might be you. Just be sure it's someone who shares your vision and absolutely loves every aspect of marketing.

If you don't have a good one, you're going to miss a lot of opportunities. You'll constantly be in a position where your marketing must react rather than act. And the spirit of your company will never come shining through. If the person you need to shepherd your marketing doesn't quite know how to plan, launch, maintain, and succeed with a guerrilla marketing attach, train him or her. The science, art, and business of marketing can be learned. You don't have to be a born guerrilla. There are books, seminars, lectures, courses, newsletters, Internet sites, and audiocassettes that can give a bright person more solid and realistic information about marketing than four years of study at a university that teaches Dark

Ages tactics for companies with billion-dollar budgets.

How much time should your designated guerrilla spend attending to the actions required by guerrilla marketing? The most time will be necessary at the outset, when the planning is done. Less time will be required during the launch phase, when the weapons are fired. And still less time, but constant time—must be devoted as you sustain the attack. That time will be devoted to three tasks: maintaining the attack, tracking your marketing efforts, and developing improved marketing. It is rare for time to be spent more valuably in your pursuit of profits and joy.

Of the many reasons for business failures, an inability to market aggressively and constantly ranks right near the top. When that happens, the finger of fault always points to the CEO—the person who is too busy with other business functions to give proper attention to marketing, too egotistical to delegate the function to someone else, or too ignorant of the power of marketing to realize the need for consistent nurturing. The role of the successful financial advisor is to find marketing team builders that can help grow your business.

Additional Resources:

Visit *www.financialadvisormarketing.com* for a full array of marketing and communications web site listings.

Action Summary:

To add to my marketing plans:	Yes _____	No _____
Additional information required:	Yes _____	No _____

If you have integrity nothing else matters. If you don't have integrity, nothing else matters.
-Unknown

There is only one boss: The customer. And he can fire everybody in the company, from the chairman on down, simply by spending his money somewhere else.

-Sam Walton, Founder, Wal-Mart

STRATEGY 8
Finding Your Ideal Client

Concept:

I Still Haven't Found What I'm Looking For. Does that famous song by the band U2 sound familiar? If you are looking for new clients, you need to know the following about them:

1. Marital status.
2. Age.
3. Income.
4. Occupation.
5. Net worth.
6. Hobbies.
7. Risk tolerance.
8. Rate of return objective.
9. Family status.
10. Investable assets or estate planning needs.

Target marketing is key to your business plan.

Objective:

Can I find a married retired couple with approximately $50,000 of income, a net worth of $800,000 to $1 million, who like to golf, spend time with their children and grandchildren, who don't mind some moderate level of risk and a conservative rate of return? Also they must have investable assets of $600,000 and estate planning needs. Well, guess what? That is an example of a target client. Now where do you find these clients? How do you market to them? What brings them together? These are the questions about the start of target marketing that you need to consider. We could write another book on target marketing, but as advisors what follows is what we need to do in our business plans.

We can also dissect each component of the profile. It is not necessary to have married people but they are easier to find. Their age can help you target easier. Income is not necessarily important if you are dealing with retirees or business owners, but net worth is essential in all segments regardless of income. Net worth needs to be determined. Hobbies help you find out how your target group networks. Risk tolerance helps you design your money management programs, since you may not want highly aggressive or speculative investors if that is not your model. This also goes for rate of return objective. If you are targeting retirees seeking a high rate of return and low risk, this may not be achievable. This helps target the education level of investors in the group. Family status is very important since you must find out from clients who they love. Simply put, money is love. If they don't love someone and they are driven by greed, this may not fit your personal beliefs and understanding of clients. Finally, if all of their net worth is tied up in real estate and they have no estate planning needs, then they may not need your help. All components help identify what your ideal client should look like.

Strategy:

Many financial advisors are running two distinct models. First, the advisor who only deals in the high-net-worth, high-touch type of practice. Second, the advisor who looks after all types of clients and delivers a baseline level of service to all and a premium level of service for top clients.

Both models have one critical element to building. The advisor is faced with declining time as the business grows. So how do you grow your business each year and provide an increasing demand for more service? The short answer here is to target larger clients each year. In three to five years your client base will be dramatically different and you will be forced to get more sophisticated. By changing your target upward each year, not only will you improve your services, but also you will earn more and have a higher asset base. For example, set a minimum client account size if you are in the money management business and a target premium if you're in the insurance business.

• Year 1–minimum $250,000 assets.
• Year 2–minimum $350,000 assets.
• Year 3–minimum $500,000 assets.
• Year 4–minimum $750,000 assets.
• Year 5–minimum $1,000,000 assets.

Most advisors have never increased their target client. So how do they expect to improve, challenge themselves, and make more money? Remember, one definition of insanity is doing the same thing over and over and expecting a different result. When is the last time that you increased your minimum account size?

Grant's Tip:

Profit margins are shrinking, and service demands and costs are increasing. Welcome to the world of a growing financial advisory practice. Advisors continue to take on unprofitable and time- or service-demanding clients. Why do we do this to ourselves, only to hope that they eventually leave? With ideal client profiling you also need to ask a few tough questions up front to make sure that you want this client.

For example: You say to Mr. and Mrs. Client, "Your money is important to you; however, I take four to six weeks' holidays a year. In that time my team can service your needs, but I will be unavailable during these times. Are you comfortable with that? If the answer is no, then you may have a couple demanding high maintenance; maybe you should open the door right now, give them a mint, and send them across the street to your competition.

You ask Mr. And Mrs. Client, "How often do you expect us to sit down face to face and review your portfolio or retirement plan?" If the answer is at least six times per year and you cannot deliver on that, give them your competition's business card.

You can create your own service questions to help you choose the right clients. An easy way to do this is think of your top three clients, the ones that you really enjoy working with. Then imagine if you had twenty more of them. Would you not have your best year ever if that happened?

The challenge of increasing your minimum account size is that you will have clients that you might have outgrown. There are two schools of thought on this one. Some say fire the bottom 10% of your book each year. Others say service them with your team or hire people to service them. Regardless, make sure that you segment them first. The way to segment clients are not into A, B, C clients (which is the old way) but to put them into a grid based on the following:
• Assets under administration.
• Client potential.
• Referrals generated/referability.
• Profitability.
• Servicing time.
• Nice people.
• Want your help and trust you.

The next thing you must think about is your time and your target number of clients. How many clients can you truly service in a sophisticated high-touch relationship? For example, if you feel you can service 150 clients at an average asset base of $500,000, then your book of business target is $75 million for yourself. Then your service team will pick up the rest–say $25 million. Your total book of business will be $100 million. Develop your targets around realistic numbers of clients you can personally handle. If you are working in a team the numbers may be different, but each person only has so much time.

Potential Results: Bigger fish = more fish per pound. Make sure they don't have too many bones with their last advisor.

Simple Rule: An advisor's income is in direct proportion to the income and assets of their clientele.

Jay's Comments:

Geoff Ayling, in his superb book, "Rapid Response Advertising," provides wannabe guerrillas with a full fifty reasons why people buy. There are really far more than fifty, but I have a feeling that these fifty will get your creative juices flowing. People make purchases for these, among many reasons:

1 To make more money–even though it can't buy happiness

2. To become more comfortable, even a bit more

3. To attract praise–because almost everybody loves it

4. To increase enjoyment–of life, of business, of virtually anything

5. To possess things of beauty–because they nourish the soul

6. To avoid criticism–which nobody wants

7. To make their work easier–a constant need to many people

8. To speed up their work–because people know that time is precious

9. To keep up with the Joneses–there are Joneses in everybody's lives

10. To feel opulent–a rare, but valid reason to make a purchase

11. To look younger–due to the reverence placed upon youthfulness

12. To become more efficient–because efficiency saves time

13. To buy friendship–I didn't know it's for sale, but it often is

14. To avoid effort–because nobody loves to work too hard

15. To escape or avoid pain–which is an easy path to making a sale

16. To protect their possessions–because they worked hard to get them

17. To be in style–because few people enjoy being out of style

18. To avoid trouble–because trouble is never a joy

19. To access opportunities–because they open the doors to good things

20. To express love–one of the noblest reasons to make any purchase

21. To be entertained–because entertainment is usually fun

22. To be organized–because order makes lives simpler

23. To feel safe–because security is a basic human need

24. To conserve energy–their own or their planets sources of energy

25. To be accepted–because that means security as well as love

26. To save time—because they know time is more valuable than money
27. To become more fit and healthy—seems to me that's an easy sale
28. To attract the opposite sex—never undermine the power of love
29. To protect their family—tapping into another basic human need
30. To emulate others—because the world is teeming with role models
31. To protect their reputation—because they worked hard to build it
32. To feel superior—which is why status symbols are sought after
33. To be trendy—because they know their friends will notice
34. To be excited—because people need excitement in a humdrum life
35. To communicate better—because they want to be understood
36. To preserve the environment—giving rise to cause-related marketing
37. To satisfy an impulse—a basic reason behind a multitude of purchases
38. To save money—the most important reason to 14% of the population
39. To be cleaner—because unclean often goes with unhealthy and unloved
40. To be popular—because inclusion beats exclusion every time
41. To gratify curiosity—it killed the cat but motivates the sale
42. To satisfy their appetite—because hunger is not a good thing
43. To be individual—because all of us are, and some of us need assurance
44. To escape stress—need I explain?
45. To gain convenience—because simplicity makes life easier
46. To be informed—because it's no joy to be perceived as ignorant
47. To give to others—another way you can nourish your soul
48. To feel younger—because that equates with vitality and energy
49. To pursue a hobby—because all work and no play etc. etc. etc.
50. To leave a legacy—because that's a way to live forever

I must add one more area about which you should be creative, one more reason that motivates people to make a purchase, and that area deals with pain. Thomas Jefferson said, "The art of life is the art of avoiding pain; and he is the best pilot, who steers clearest of the rocks and shoals with which it is beset." More recently, Sam Deep and Lyle Sussman, who wrote "Close The Deal," teach the importance of pain and the ways to learn where it resides. If you know exactly, you've got a heckuva great starting point for your creativity.

There. Now that you've got 51 ways to win the hearts and business of your prospects, I think you'll have an easier job of winning sales and profits.

Action Summary:

To add to my marketing plans: Yes _____   No _____

Additional information required: Yes _____   No _____

Never, never, never, never, never give up.

Sir Winston Churchill

The time to repair the roof is when the sun is shining.

-John F. Kenndy

STRATEGY 9
Secrets of Selecting Marketing Methods

Concept:

There are hundreds of marketing concepts to choose from (the subject of my next book). As you go through the various methods, you are faced with questions, "Which mix of marketing strategies do I choose in my business?" "How do I select the best ones?" "Which ones will work for me?" The answers are obvious. Read on.

Objective:

If you went out fishing for a day and tried a few different approaches and lures but were not successful, would you change your style? Tough question after only one day, but if you go out every day for a week, you know you need to change something. As a fisherman I know that once you find something that works, you stick with it. A very successful fisherman friend taught me that location and presentation are the keys to fishing. Presentation can mean the lure, the speed of the boat, the flasher, and other things in connection with presenting the bait to the fish. In other words, it's not just one thing. That was great advice from a great fisherman. In Dr. Thomas J. Stanley's *Marketing to the Affluent* (McGraw-Hill, 1988), he points out that successful financial advisors didn't just try one thing and it worked, they fished for strategies that would work and continued to improve the strategy until they were successful. There were not one or two things that worked well but usually a half a dozen things done together that made 80% of the difference between not catching any fish and catching the big fish they wanted. For your marketing to be successful, location and presentation are keys to your success. It becomes obvious to you which ones you should use once you cast your line several times. It is a unique combination of techniques that will work for you—not necessarily for the advisor next door, but for you—what works as you adjust for the best presentation and location.

For example, if I was to put ten top advisors from across the country in a room and asked, "What are your five keys to successful marketing?" I would find that some keys are similar but not all five keys are the same.

Strategy:

Repeating the questions asked at the outset, "Which mix of marketing strategies do I choose in my business?" "How do I select the best ones?" "Which ones will work for me?" The answer should be obvious–as many as you can do well.

Once you have selected the marketing strategies, be sure you use and implement them in a systematic way. Make all of your marketing a system and put it into an operating manual. Just like Ray Krok of *McDonald's*, record your marketing info systems and keep duplicating your success.

As we suggested earlier, write down all of the marketing strategies you have planned to use and are using now. Then, go through what will be your marketing mix. See if you can't mesh some of the strategies–such as your web site, brochure and mailings. Some of these have a common theme.

Every marketing method has its own particular strength. Radio is the most intimate of the media, allowing you to spend time one on one with the audience. Newspapers are great for disseminating news. Although most advisors find newspaper advertising to be useless, it is a great medium for delivering news, which can be done through advertising, specialty ads, or articles. Newspapers are for people who want news, not advertising. Magazines are where readers become more involved.

- TV is most comprehensive.
- Direct mail helps you take aim.
- Brochures are for great detail.
- Seminars–To sell yourself and your ideas.
- Internet–Useless for prospects unless it is advertised.
- Trade shows–To make contacts with purchase-minded people.
- Sponsorships–To build stronger relationships.
- Telephone Marketing–Most effective when used in another medium; e.g., Internet, CDRom, mailer, or other!

Grant's Tip:

Make sure you distinguish how you want to market yourself. The biggest hurdle here for most advisors is ego. You want to be seen as a true professional who deals only with the affluent and never needs to market. If you're that good, why are you reading this book? There is always the best of the best, and they may be at a stage where the business grows from within. But most advisors can handle more assets to manage, not necessarily more clients, but assets.

Try this exercise right now. Write down all of the marketing methods you use today. Beside each item on the list, write the approximate percentage of new business that comes directly from that source. Now combine three or four of those items and write down how they can work together. Now with these items together, add up the percentages again. You see the percentage can dramatically increase by combining your marketing strategies. For example, your web site linked to your newspaper ad linked to your articles linked to your seminars linked to referrals linked to word of mouth linked to inviting a friend. Linking your marketing into one linked method of marketing will increase the likelihood of each marketing method as a stand-alone item. $1 + 1 = 2$, but $1+1+1+1+1 = 5$, now you are 5 times more successful in your marketing.

So find your ideas mix and develop your plan and implementation schedule; revisit it and stick with it, improving it along the way.

Jay's Comments:

Succeeding with a guerrilla marketing attack is a very simple seven-step process. Take all seven steps and watch your profits rise and your competitors cringe. It's not as hard as you may think to succeed at a guerrilla marketing attack. And if you launch one properly, you'll find that succeeding at business is also not as hard as you may have thought. Don't even think of skipping any of the seven steps to success because all seven are necessary. We're not talking about playing with marketing. We're talking about succeeding with marketing.

1. The first step is to research everything you can. That means carefully investigating your market, your product or service, your competition, your industry, and your options in media. What media reach your target audience? What media make them respond and buy? Should you focus on advertising or direct marketing or a combination of the two? There are answers to these questions and guerrillas have the knack for coming up with the right answers. As a person who is already connected to the Internet, you've got a head start in the research department. There is loads of information on line that can propel you in the direction of success.

2. The second step is to write a benefits list. Have a meeting. Invite your key personnel and at least one customer—because customers are tuned in to benefits that you may not even consider to be benefits. For example, my wife patronizes a certain bookstore regularly, not because of their books, but because of the carrot cake they serve in their cafe. Once you have a list of your benefits, select your competitive advantage because that's where you'll hang your marketing hat. If you haven't got a competitive advantage, you'll have to create one because you'll need it. After all, anyone can come up with a benefits list. Figure out why people should patronize your business instead of that of a competitor.

3. Step number three is to select the weapons you'll use. I listed 100 weapons from which you may make your selection. My recommendation is to use as many weapons as you can. Fifty of the hundred weapons are free. Grant has over forty weapons in this book to add to your arsenal. After you've selected the weaponry, put the weapons into priority order. Next to each weapon, write the name of the person who is in charge of masterminding the use of the weapon plus the date it will be launched. Consider each date you write to be a promise you are making to yourself. Guerrillas do not kid themselves or lie to themselves, so be realistic. The idea of a guerrilla marketing attack is to select a lot of weapons, then launch them in slow motion—at a pace that feels comfortable financially and emotionally. My average client takes 18 months to launch an attack. Don't rush.

4. The fourth step, and this is a toughie, is to maintain the attack. The first three steps are extremely simple compared to this fourth step. Maintaining the attack means sticking with your plan and your weapons even though you don't get the instant gratification you want so much. Everyone wants success to come instantly, but it doesn't happen that way in real life. The Marlboro Man and Marlboro Country helped make Marlboro cigarettes the most successfully marketed brand in history. But after the first year of marketing, they didn't increase sales one bit for Marlboro. Maintaining the attack made it happen.

5. Step five is to keep track. Some of your weapons will hit bulls-eyes. Others will miss the target completely. How will you know which is which? By keeping track. By asking customers where they heard of you. By finding out what made them contact you. Keeping track is not easy, but it is necessary. If you aren't ready to keep track, you aren't ready to launch your attack in the first place.

6. Step six is to make a guerrilla marketing calendar, just as Grant outlined in Strategy 2, your marketing plan. This should be 52 rows long and five columns wide. The first column is called "Week," listing in which week of the 52 weeks you did what you did in marketing. The second column is called "Thrust," referring to the thrust of your marketing that week. What were you saying? Offering? The third column is called "Media," and it refers to which media you were using that week. The fourth column is called "Cost," and lets you project how much you'll be spending that week. The fifth column is called "Results," so you can give a letter grade to the week—you know, an A, B, C, D or F. After one year, you compare your calendar to your sales figures and eliminate all but the A's and B's. It takes about three years to get a calendar loaded with slam dunks. Once you have one you'll feel like the client who said, "It's a lot like going to heaven without the inconvenience of dying."

7. The seventh step is to create a guerrilla marketing plan. Seven steps to succeeding with a guerrilla marketing attack. If it sounds easy, reread this column. It works, but it's not easy.

Additional Resources:
See 100 Guerrilla Marketing Weapons in Chapter 9.

Action Summary:

To add to my marketing plans:	Yes _____	No _____
Additional information required:	Yes _____	No _____

Do, or do not. There is no "Try."

-Yoda (The Empire Strikes Back)

You can have everything in life you want if you help enough other people get what they want.

-Zig Ziglar

STRATEGY 10
What Sets You Apart from the Rest

Concept:

Unless you have new qualified people to talk to every day, why should you go to work? If you don't have a target database or network of people, get one. The key here is database and contact management systems.

Objective:

There are two parts to your objective here. The first part is a solid list of qualified prospects to contact every day. The number of qualified prospects on the list depends on your business plan. For example, if I want to deal with 200 people with an average of $500,000 investable assets and I only have 50 people who fit that profile, I will need at least 150 people on my list. However, I don't expect every one to do business with me; so I really need about 300 solid prospects on my database. The second part of the objective is your client communications standards. Be known for client communications. For example, what if you could say to a prospect, "We have one of the best client communications systems in the financial industry today. That is one reason people deal with us." Now imagine what's going through the prospect's mind. The number one reason why people leave their advisor is lack of contact. If you can say that your clients will never leave you because of lack of contact, you set yourself apart from the rest.

Strategy:

The old life insurance sales ratio was 10:3:1–For every 10 people you talk to, 3 people will come in, and 1 person will do business with you. What is your sales ratio? If you talk to 100 prospects from your database in the next year, how many of them might do business with you? Be honest with yourself here–this will help you improve dramatically over the next few years. It will also help you in becoming a better qualifier of prospects and to gather more and more information on prospects.

Grant's Tip:

Do you remember the movie *Wall Street*, with Michael Douglas? He said in one part of the movie "What I need is information." How can you gather more information? Harvey Mackay said the single most important word in the English language is not in the dictionary. It's *"Rolodex."* Harvey wrote about database management in his book, *Swim with the Sharks Without Being Eaten Alive* (Fawcett Books, 1996). He talks about having more than 50 different categories of information on prospects and clients. Another book on contact management is *The One-to-one Future: Building Business Relationships One Customer at a Time,* by Don Peppers and Martha Rogers (Doubleday, 1996).

While I think that there are great ideas in both books and that you will be more successful the larger your database of information, I have a simple solution for financial advisors when it comes to gathering information.

We are information gatherers. We gather tons of information from people on everything from taxes and investing to families and estates. But how can we use all of this in marketing? Besides the system of collecting important information (such as dates of birth, risk tolerance, time horizon, etc.) on the know-your-client forms that we fill out and update every day, develop a simple system that will help your memory as well as your database. Create three categories. Call them "hot buttons," "excitement buttons" and "the WOW factor."

The first, the hot buttons, are what the client values towards money. Some clients want to minimize taxes as much as possible, so any communication or discussion on minimizing taxes will get their attention.

The second are the excitement buttons. My excitement buttons are hockey and fishing. If you were to talk to me about hockey or fishing we could have a conversation for hours. It puts me in a positive frame of mind and allows me to tell stories about myself. If your communication includes anything about my excitement buttons, you WILL get my attention.

The third button is the WOW factor (which we will discuss in more detail in Chapter 5–Wowing Clients). It's something that will make you and/or your client say "Wow!" about something you or your team did. It can include client appreciation, extraordinary service, or something close to the client's heart.

On our fact finder we have the three button categories. When we get new clients, I sometimes sit with my assistant and we brainstorm on how can we WOW them? What gets them excited? What are their hot buttons? These three attributes will also be easy to remember and call up from your database.

How do you make your practice more valuable? Have a large database of qualified targeted prospects. If you have the best prospect list, with tons of qualified clients waiting to hear from you, would you be excited? How do you develop this list? Chapter 2–Getting New Clients from Outside Sources has several strategies for finding prospects and putting them on your list. Just buying lists and marketing to them is the old way of doing business.

Along with the ideas in Chapter 2, here are some ways successful guerrilla marketers and guerrilla financial advisors develop their own custom-made lists:

•Create lists from classified ads posted by people selling businesses.

•Create lists from real estate ads posted by people selling large homes or vacation property.

•Create lists from ads selling expensive items such as cars, boats, etc.

•Seek to acquire lists from *Welcome Wagon*.

•Seek to acquire lists from companies with which you work–orphan accounts.

•Create lists of target market prospects–target successful engineers in your area through their association or trade magazines.

•Team up with a company–some companies let you set up office in general insurance agency premises.

•Team up for expertise–insurance and investment professionals sharing their lists and cross-selling services (an instant qualified list).

•Talk to a successful financial professional who want to starts taking time off– he or she developed a huge list of prospects and now is not going after them.

•Talk to a financial advisor who is a great prospector but not necessarily a great manager of clients.

•Talk to a key influential client or person in a group club or association and has a common network; for example, recreational associations such as golf or tennis clubs.

•Seek lists from business clubs/associations.

•Seek lists from trade associations and publications.

While I won't reveal all of the secrets to creating a great prospecting list in this chapter, most successful financial advisors know that a combination of marketing strategies consistently applied continues to put qualified prospects on the list every day.

Jay's Comments:

You work like crazy trying to attract attention and business, operating from a marketing calendar, committing to your strategy and doing everything right, resulting in an influx of clients–but you lose them. They never come back. You did your marketing so well and marketed so wisely that you're almost in a state of shock at how your customers ignore you.

You treated them well while you were making your business transactions. You gave them your best advice. You assured them service is your middle name. You smiled and used their names when you said good-bye, thanking them for the business. And then, after all that caring attention on your part, they completely ignored you, never set foot in your business again.

Do you want to know why they ignored you, why it was so easy for them to put you out of their minds? It's because you ignored them.

It's because you made the sale and then made the grave but all-too-common error of thinking that your marketing job was over. That was a terrible error. But at least you've got a lot of company making the same terrible error. Nearly 70 percent of business lost is lost due to apathy after the sale. Apathy is the deadliest enemy of marketing. A "love 'em and leave 'em" attitude is usually fatal to profitability.

The opposite of apathy is follow-up. Guerrillas have a "love 'em and love 'em" attitude, marketing to prospects like crazy till the sale is made, then continuing to market like crazy to them after the sale. Apathy never sets in. Customers never feel ignored. Guerrillas do all in their power to intensify the relationship with caring follow-up and loving attention. They know that once they have established a relationship, their product or service is no longer thought of as a commodity. Businesses that offer commodities often lose customers due to competitors offering lower prices. Businesses that form warm relationships transcend being thought of as a commodity and maintain their customer relationships with service and constant contact.

No wonder they don't lose business so readily. People want relationships, want the businesses they patronize to stay in contact, want to feel cared for and not ignored. All guerrillas know that their customer relationships are their most precious assets. They know that if customers purchased from them one time and had an enjoyable purchase experience, they are very likely to buy from them again. And again and again. And to provide many referrals over time.

To nourish these kinds of lasting relationships, guerrilla financial advisors create constant communication systems. They send thank-you notes after the sale—within 48 hours. They contact customers within a month of the sale to make certain they are satisfied and have no questions. They get in touch with customers once again three months after the sale, this time suggesting new items that may tie in with the original purchase. And three months after that, they make another contact. This kind of guerrilla follow-up not only prevents dreaded apathy from setting in, but also increases business anywhere from 20% to 300%. That's because customers, in their hearts, silently hope for recognition, acknowledgment, information, advance opportunities to purchase, and new calls to action.

Instead of the kind of apathy that loses customers forever, constant attention and follow-up results in healthy back-end sales. This means repeat sales, ancillary sales, and referral sales. And this means big profits to you—because it costs six times more to sell something to a new prospect than to sell that same thing to an existing customer.

These days, all the true marketing experts ask you to calculate the lifetime value of a customer. If you don't understand the damaging effects of apathy after the sale, that lifetime value is pretty small, probably a few hundred dollars, if that. If you do all in your power to prevent apathy from ever setting it, the lifetime value of each customer may be measured in hundreds of thousands of dollars, maybe even more. You'll profit from the initial sale, from the repeat sales, from the referral sales, and from the long, mutually beneficial relationship. It happens only when you defeat the most deadly enemy of marketing. And now you know how to do that.

Action Summary:

To add to my marketing plans: Yes _____   No_____

Additional information required: Yes _____   No_____

Strong reasons make strong actions.

-William Shakespeare

Chapter 2

Getting New Clients
from
Outside Sources

You need to be persistent to be successful in calling people.

-Grant W. Hicks

STRATEGY 11
The Five-touch System

Concept:

If I asked you the name of a great financial advisor and you said a name I have never heard of, I might not feel comfortable going to see that person. But If I had heard the name before, seen ads or marketing and/or received a mailing, seminar invitation, or phone call, I would feel more comfortable in seeing them.

Objective:

Use the law of familiarity to your favor. Successful financial advisors know that through their constant marketing programs, people want to know you before they see you. How do they get to know you first?

Strategy:

The law of prospecting states that you are 80% more successful after the fifth contact. Seven contacts with a prospect is the ideal number. Here are the numbers:

• 70 - 80% of all new files are opened after the fifth contact.
• 50% of advisors will call once and never again.
• 20 - 30% of advisors will contact a prospect the second time and follow up.
• 10 - 15% of advisors will contact them three times.
• 5% of advisors will contact or "touch" people five times or more before doing business with them and open 80% of the accounts.

When was the last time a prospect gave you a big account on the first meeting? The strategy is to have as many touches as possible.

Here's an example of five touches. I send out a seminar invitation. The client doesn't know me but soon notices I have an ad in the local paper (which ad has been running weekly for years). The ad has my web site address. Interest in the seminar is piqued so they check me out on my web site. Then our office calls and invites the client to the seminar. The prospect declines and forgets about us. One month later he or she receives another seminar invitation and a phone call. They now know and remember who we are. The prospect decides that the issues in the seminar are interesting and knows this is an issue that needs to be dealt with (such as tax planning or retirement income planning).

Then I call and invite the prospect to have a coffee and talk on a one-to-one basis about items discussed in the seminar. The appointment is set because the client has heard of/from us five times or more and is familiar with who we are. Eventually we help another client solve financial problems—all because we are persistent and have a marketing program that is based on five touches, not just mailing and calling.

Most of the marketing was done already. All the advisor did was make one phone call and set up an appointment.

The old way of just one marketing method is less effective. Examples of combinations of touches:

• Ad in paper.
• Seminar ad in paper.
• Article in paper.
• Mailing.
• Seminar invitation.
• Flyer.
• Email.
• Web site.
• Word of mouth.
• Phone call.

If you can blend these marketing methods into your target market, you will dramatically increase your marketing and double or even triple your response rate and number of potential clients.

Grant's Tip:

Did you know that a typical ad that runs every week is not usually seen by your prospects after it has run for eight months? A guerrilla ad can be seen much more quickly (see Strategy 18). Most advisors give up after the fourth contact and wonder why they are not successful. They're 80% of the way there and all they have to realize is that people will not do business with them until they are familiar with them and comfortable. They fail to realize that they need to constantly market to their prospects in different ways to make them familiar. Ask some of the top advisors and they will tell you their top clients came after months or even years of follow-up. In one seminar I gave, an advisor asked when he should give up on them. The answer is simple—when they are no longer qualified. If you believe that you have answers to their problems and you can solve their problems better than anybody else on the planet, then why wouldn't you want to continue to try to help them? Believe in yourself through your marketing. You have the power to help them.

Consistency is key in gaining five touches.

Another strategy to gain a touch with a prospect is adding them to your email database. While this can be a waste of time if you never send anything, or if you send tons of junk, actually sending something specific to them and targeting their financial hot buttons makes effective use of email. Always try to obtain prospect and client email addresses. See Strategy 38 for more information.

One of the greatest marketing pieces I sent out to prospects and clients was a postcard. A handwritten postcard about a great idea will get people's attention, more so than any letter or marketing piece. The postcard is something personal; the ones I used had a calming scene on the front like a resort or golf or vacation or travel destination. On the back, write out their address and a handwritten note that says something like, "Hope you're having a great summer; here is a great investment idea and opportunity that I thought I would share with you. If you have time to discuss this, please give me a call." The phone calls I received were from investors asking how much was the minimum or how much they should put in? They already had my trust and confidence, and they knew that I invest my own money in these opportunities, so the questions weren't about the investment, but how much. Try it. Send some postcards to clients and selected prospects. One request we always hear from clients is to let them know when opportunities arise. Make sure it is reviewed by compliance, then be prepared to be surprised by the results.

Jay's Comments:

Direct response marketing is a lot different from indirect response marketing, although guerrillas like it best when the two are teamed up. The first is geared to obtain orders right here and right now. The second is geared to obtain orders eventually. Although a fair amount of standard, indirect marketing often is necessary to set the stage, to make prospects ready to buy, and to separate your company from strangers, it's when you initiate direct marketing that you first taste blood.

As you well know, we are living in the Age of Information, most of it very easy to obtain. But information is hardly enough for a guerrilla. And information is not insight. It's the combination of information and thought that leads to insight and it's insight thats going to make you a stand-out in the direct response arena.

The first insight for you to absorb is that direct response marketing either works immediately or not at all. Unlike standard marketing that changes attitudes slowly and ultimately leads to a sale if you go about things right, guerrilla direct response marketing changes minds and attitudes instantly and leads to a sale instantly if you go about things right.

When it works, you know it. You don't have to sit around and wonder. You don't have to wait months and months for your message to penetrate the mind of your prospect. Your time-

dated direct marketing offer either results in a sale right now—or it doesn't.

To succeed with direct marketing in any medium, remember always:

1. Your offer is omnipotent. The best presentation in the world has a major uphill battle if you make a weak or ordinary offer.

2. The market to whom you direct your message can make or break your campaign. Saying the right thing to the wrong people results in no sale.

3. What you say and how you say it is easily as important as to whom you say it. Talk in terms of your prospects and how your offer benefits them.

4. Carefully planning every cent of your campaign for maximum profits requires as much creativity as your message. Guerrillas excel at this.

5. The more that people have been exposed to your other marketing, the more readily they'll accept what you offer with your direct marketing.

Some principles of indirect marketing apply to direct marketing. You must still talk of the prospect, not yourself, and you must make a clear and cogent offer. But from that point on, direct marketing is a whole new ball game. And its one that you can win with the insights of the guerrilla.

Stupid mistakes in horrid abundance have been made by otherwise bright companies when testing the direct response waters. Fortunately, guerrillas can learn from these blunders, making those waters a bit safer.

Listing them would take an endless series of columns, but it's worth your time if I make a start by providing insight into ten of the most notable:

• Failure to attract attention at the outset dooms many brilliant campaigns before they have a chance to shine. Envelopes, opening lines, email subject lines, and first impressions are the gates to your offer. Open them wide.

• Not facing the reality of a direct marketing explosion relegates your attempt to the ordinary, which means the ignored. Guerrillas say things to rise above the din, to be noticed and desired in a sea of marketers.

• Focusing your message on yourself instead of your prospect will usually send your effort to oblivion. Prospects care far more about themselves than they care about you. So talk to them about themselves.

• Not knowing precisely who your market is will send you into the wrong direction. Research into pinpointing that market will be some of the most valuable time you devote to your direct marketing campaign.

• Mailing or telephoning to other than honest prospects wastes your time and money. If you make your offer to people who don't really have a need for your offering, they'll be an incredibly tough sale.

• Initiating direct response marketing without specific objectives gives you too hazy a target for bull's-eyes. Begin by creating the response method for your prospects so you'll know what your message should say.

• *Featuring your price before you stress your benefit will be telling people what they don't want to know yet. First, your job is to make them want what you are offering, then you can tell them the price.*

• *Concentrating on your price before your offer is wasting a powerful selling point. Even if your price is the lowest, people care more about how they'll gain from purchasing. Give your low price at the right time.*

• *Failing to test all that can be tested is a goof-off of the highest order. Test your price points, opening lines, subject lines, envelope teaser lines, benefits to stress, contact times. and mailing lists to know the real winners.*

• *Setting the wrong price means you've failed in your testing and your research. Guerrillas are sensitive to their market and their competition, testing prices and constantly subjecting them to the litmus test of profits.*

As direct response vehicles become more sophisticated and prolific, guerrillas have the insight to zero in on the exact people to contact, so as not to waste time or money on strangers. Successful mailings to strangers net as high as two percent response rates. Successful mailings to customers and qualified prospects net up to ten percent. Precision leads to profits. The direct mail route is only one of five avenues you should have in your guerrilla marketing attack.

Action Summary:

To add to my marketing plans: Yes _____   No _____

Additional information required: Yes _____   No _____

Discipline is remembering what you want.

-David Campbell

You miss 100 percent of the shots you never take.

-Wayne Gretzky

STRATEGY 12

Who You Need to Call Now!

Concept:

Each day you have to make the calls to your clients and prospects, no matter how big a clientele you have. With so many calls to make and so important to your commitment to keep constant client communications, how do you organize your time effectively?

Objective:

Develop an organized approach to your calls. Organize in three ways—types of calls, call times, and callback times. If you have assistants or a team, develop the team approach and delegate low-priority calls or routine calls, such as calls to set up review appointments. You have three main categories of calls daily—first, to new prospects and centers of influence; second, to clients; and third, other calls such as client service callbacks, marketing with wholesalers or head office, etc. Which take priority? How much time does calling take? This is the most underestimated part of daily planning for most financial professionals. I have taken several excellent time-management courses, and most underestimate the time our industry spends daily on the phone. Our job is seeing clients and prospects face to face or talking to them on the phone. That is 80% of our day.

Strategy:

We know each day we have to make calls. For your clients, develop a client service communications call rotation schedule. For example, develop a ninety-day call rotation schedule if you call all clients quarterly. Or you can develop a schedule, depending on the type of client, on how frequently you wish to contact the client. Several contact management software programs can help you with an alarm or callback dates. Get the software, plug in the dates, and work the system. This will help you with your client communications system. How about your centers of influence? You can also put them on a schedule to keep a system.

The next important group is the referrals and prospects you receive. Develop a contact log in a binder and keep it by your phone. List the calls that you need to make each week. Keep excellent notes in your contact log, and use this to keep in touch with them. Top advisors tell me that some of their top clients took two years to become clients. They can also tell me how many meetings and phone calls it took. It is obvious they have a contact log to which they can refer.

As an advisor, I challenge you to try this. Every morning for the next month, take two hours to call top prospects. Make those calls each and every morning. This idea came from the most successful financial advisors ever. This one strategy alone can catapult your business to the next level. As an advisor I found I had to stop calling because I couldn't keep up with the business. I'm sure after one month your next call will be to thank me for the idea. Set up the discipline and watch your results soar.

Grant's Tip:

Have a call list. Have a prewritten and tested script. Just like when an actor or actress takes the stage in a live performance, any flaw can be noticed and the performance suffers. Be prepared. If you do not take the time to organize your calls and your approach, you might as well not even pick up the phone.

Have you ever been called by a top-notch marketer? He or she asked you "yes" questions? This type of marketer does not ask if you are interested in anything, but rather asks a few simple questions to which you will say yes. Then, once you have said yes two or three times, he or she asks the question that is important to securing a meeting or follow-up conversation. If the answer is no, a good marketer goes back and asks one or two yes questions and then an important question.

Have you ever played telephone tag? Sometimes it can take weeks to communicate with someone. If you're trying to reach clients or prospects, there is nothing worse than telephone tag to try your patience. We want instant Internet trades, yet your client cannot get hold of you. Add to your frustration that you have several callbacks to do and no time to call new clients or prospects. The single most important idea for maximum results is to have a scheduled time to complete your calls. For example, I tell my assistant not to make appointments most days until 11 a.m. From the time I arrive in the office until 11, I make calls. I call clients and prospects and I make my service calls and other calls then. I also schedule the time between 5 and 5:30 p.m. to return calls. I have a sundown telephone rule. Return all calls before sundown or return them first thing the next morning. My schedule allows me to do it. The first few hours each morning, I have schedules on the phone. Initially it can be only an hour since you may have a smaller client base; but as your clientele grows you also need that hour to call new clients, because if you don't schedule it, when will you have the time?

For centers of influence, I try to have a breakfast or lunch meeting once per week and discuss cases and ideas and build relationships with them.

Daily Schedule:
- 8 to 9 a.m.–client prep/meet with assistant.
- 9 to 11 a.m.–calls to new prospective clients.
- 11 a.m.–first appointment.
- 12 noon–lunch or lunch appointment.
- 1 p.m.–second appointment.
- 2 p.m.–third appointment.
- 3 p.m.–fourth appointment.
- 4 p.m.–fifth appointment.
- 4:30 p.m.–return calls/prepare files/meet with assistant.

Client Calls: Each quarter you can call your top clients to touch base and work on their life goals, not just monetary goals. For example, in the fall, call your top clients and ask, "How was your summer?" If they answer, "Not bad, what's going on with the markets?" you need to work on the relationship more. If they talk for half an hour about the great time they had boating this summer, send them a subscription to a boating magazine. In the spring you can ask, "Any plans this summer for you or your family?" Take a personal interest in them and use it a point of contact three to four times per year.

Jay's Comments:

One of the least understood secrets of successful marketing is the ease with which new business may be won. As powerful as you may be with that knowledge, your power increases when you comprehend the importance of gaining that new business in the first place.

Although it now costs you six times more to sell something to a new customer than to an existing customer–which is why guerrillas market so caringly and consistently to their customers–there is a constant need to increase your customer base. Therefore, you're got to be willing to turn cartwheels in order to get a human being converted into a real live paying customer. Break even or even lose money in the quest for a new customer because your investment in securing these precious souls will be returned manyfold.

Once your prospects become customers, they're a source of profits for life–because guerrillas know the crucial importance of non-stop follow-up. The follow-up increases your profits while decreasing your cost or marketing. Remember, it's only one-sixth the cost of marketing to non-customers. But let's get back to those non-customers and consider a potent guerrilla tactic to win their business and transfer them from the twilight zone to your customer list, where they belong.

The tactic begins with a phrase: A powerful guerrilla phrase to emblazon amidst your memory cells is "pilot project." It is often difficult to get a company or a person to agree to do business with you. It is much simpler to get them to agree to a mere pilot project. Even if companies or individuals are unhappy with their current advisor, they may be reluctant to sever the relationship and sign up with you—just in case you turn out to be flaky. But you defuse that reluctance when you assure them that you don't want to get married—and get all their business. You only want to become engaged—and get a simple pilot project. That's certainly not asking for much.

Pilot projects are very tempting to companies and to individuals because they allow these good people to see if you're as good as you say you are, without going too far out on a limb. Even if the project is a bust, it was only a pilot project. No big deal. But if the project is a success—well then, that certainly indicates that a larger project should be undertaken, then a larger one still, and eventually, all the business. Moral? It's tough to get an okay for all the new business. It is far less tough to get an okay for a pilot project.

The concept of aiming for pilot projects may be applied as easily to a service business as a product business. If you perform services, offer to perform them for only part of the customer's needs, not all of them. Offer to perform them for a test period only, something like six weeks or so. Maybe even less if you feel that less time will be enough for you to prove your worth. A simple phone call or call it a pilot project will tell.

Pilot projects are rarely profit producers all by themselves. But they open the door to a world where profits abound, a world where relationships are lasting. That's why savvy companies and individuals say "yes" to offers of pilot projects. These projects are inexpensive learning and high potential earning opportunities. Hey! Why not do a pilot project on pilot projects? Take the word phone call every morning as Grant suggests and call it pilot project calls for prospects.

Telephone sales, or telemarketing, is an effective system for introducing a company to a prospect and setting up appointments. After a sales call, a telephone follow-up may set up a prospect interview. Some stockbrokers have become masters at telemarketing and increased their business on this one marketing factor alone.

Guerrillas know that the modern telemarketer has to cut through more "communication clutter" than ever before. Not only are you competing with other telemarketers, but also with direct mail, print, and broadcast advertising. You can't hide behind glossy brochures. Prospects can't see the car you're driving or the snazzy new suit you're wearing. You have only your words and your tone of voice to convey your message.

Of course, telemarketing is not your entire sales strategy, but it is an essential weapon in your sales arsenal. And success in closing sales over the telephone is contingent on finding qualified prospects to call. There are distinct benefits and disadvantages to selling by telephone. We've outlined a few of them below.

Advantages of Telemarketing

• *Increased efficiency since you can reach many more prospects by phone than you can with in-person sales calls.*
• *Quick and personal response to prospect's questions and concerns during the sales process.*
• *Improved relationship marketing. The phone is a great tool for maintaining contact with existing customers and introducing new products to them.*

Disadvantages of Telemarketing:

• *Overcoming the bad image that telemarketing has due to unscrupulous salespeople.*
• *Mailing lists of prospective customers are costly and often contain a number of unqualified prospects.*
• *You may expend a lot of time and energy just getting through to busy prospects.*

Telemarketing Tips

Be prepared. Because you have just a few seconds to capture the prospect's interest over the phone, you should be well prepared. Since you are using your voice to convey your honesty, sincerity, and professionalism, be focused and relaxed. Even if you get a rude response, remain courteous and professional. If you are dressed professionally and have an orderly workspace, you will sound more organized and competent to the prospect.

Practice. Some salespeople practice their sales routines on low-probability prospects. This is disrespectful and could backfire. It's better to role-play with a friend or coworker, or just have an imaginary conversation to warm up. A script is a great way to maintain focus. Write the script using your own words and phrasing. If you improvise, you'll appear more natural.

Follow up. Always send introductory or follow-up letters, product brochures, or other marketing materials. Be sure to offer product information sheets by fax or email. End calls quickly, but politely, when it is obvious that a prospect is either not qualified for your product or is not going to buy. Your time on the phone is precious. Spend it selling!

Find other successful brokers or financial advisors who have used telemarketing successfully. Grant and I could write another book on this topic alone (maybe we will). At the very least, make a list of your daily, weekly, and monthly calls to prospects and clients in an organized fashion.

Telemarketing works wonders, but only if you do it right. Guerrillas know exactly how to do it right, and when you read this, you will, too. Five crucial points have been discovered and followed by guerrillas. These are the five simple things you should do to match them:
1. Find out who are your top three telemarketers.
2. Make an audiocassette of those top three people.
3. Create a script, using the words, phrases, and voice inflections of the top three. In that script, underline the phrases stressed by these top producers.
4. Distribute copies of the three cassettes plus three scripts to go with them. Give a set to each

of your other telemarketers.

5. Ask those other telemarketers to memorize the script and get it down so pat that it sounds as though it's delivered straight from the heart.

It's okay for the telemarketers to eliminate any words that seem uncomfortable to them, substituting another word. But they should not get rid of any words and phrases that all three top producers are using.

Okay, now you've got your script. How do you make it work wonders? First, recognize that you must deliver the words on that script to the right audience. That's a full 40% of your success equation. It comes ahead of everything else. Since the people calling you have responded to your ad, there's a good chance they are the right audience when they call. This gives you a lot of momentum.

The right offer is the second 40% of your equation. It tells about the benefits you offer, your company, your product or service, and includes how you present your offering.

The right creative approach to a telemarketing script includes the actual words and phrases that will be used. It's the last 20% of your success equation. The right audience and the right offer are considerably more important than the right words. Still, the script you use can make the difference between mild success and wild success. What about that script?

Start by realizing that it has three parts. The introduction is where you introduce yourself by name and begin to establish rapport. The body is where you present the logical (for the left-brained callers) and the emotional (for the right-brained callers) reasons that they should buy right now. The close is where you ask the person to respond positively to your offer. Be sure, when creating your script, that you know:

* *What the caller should do after hearing the message.*
* *Whether the caller should make an appointment.*
* *Whether the caller should send for your brochure.*

People are more powerfully motivated by security needs than almost anything else. In direct marketing, you give that security by offering a guarantee or a trial offer. Are these really necessary? Yes, they're crucial.

Your introduction is the most important part of your script, even though it's the second impression that you will make. The ad was the first. Remember that the introduction is the headline of your message and that the headline is the real name of the game. The close should be written next because it's your final goal. The body should be created last—so that it leads right into the close. Edit it mercilessly, making sure every word and phrase adds to the effectiveness of your introduction. If not, scrap them.

Yes, you should ask questions. Yes, you should respond to the answers. Yes, you should read over your opening line and see if it would excite you as a caller. Questions you might ask at the close include:

- *Are these the results you want for yourself or your company?*
- *Shall we get started?*
- *May I set up an appointment?*

I know that it's tough to operate from a script if you're a free spirit. But I also know that free spirits fail dismally at telemarketing. I've witnessed several tests of scripts versus outlines and the scripts win every time. The winning combination for guerrillas is a potent ad, followed by a potent script. What they win is sales, relationships, customers' hearts, and profits.

Action Summary:

To add to my marketing plans:	Yes _____	No _____
Additional information required:	Yes _____	No _____

The only way to fail at prospecting is to avoid it.

-Unknown

The biggest mistake people make in life is not trying to make a living at doing what they most enjoy.

-Malcolm Forbes

STRATEGY 13
Building a Dynamic Referral Team

Concept:

Having a team of professionals behind you makes you look increasingly valuable to a client with large investment, estate, or tax problems. Build a network of professionals to help your client's overall financial plan. Have a list handy to give to clients, and market your services and education to these professionals.

Objective:

• To help your clients' overall financial planning needs and gain referrals by referring your clients to your external team of professionals.
• To gain years of valuable advice and knowledge by building a team of professionals.
• To make yourself more referable.

Strategy:

Set up a team of professionals who are currently not working with several other financial planners so that they can refer business to you and so that you can build trust together. Look for the best people; strive to find the best and tell them you only want the best for your clients. Build the relationship by doing seminars and educational sessions for them (see Strategy 14–Center of Influence Seminars). Ask for their permission to publish a list of your team (see the Guerrilla Marketing Action Planning Worksheet at the end of this book) and add their email and web site links to your web site under your professional team.

Grant's Tip:

How do you find the best? If you don't get a copy of the client's tax return and will, then at least have the name of the client's accountant and lawyer on your database. If you don't have this information, get it. Ask your clients if they're happy with their accountants, lawyers, mortgage persons, realtors, etc. If they are, get the names and let them know that you will contact those professionals because you are always looking for great professionals on your team. Then you have an opportunity to meet new professionals through your clients. The accountants will want to meet with you because they will not want to upset their satisfied clients. If your clients say they're not happy with them, then you have a fantastic opportunity to refer a professional on your team. Either way it's win-win.

You can also send questionnaires to your clients to let them know you are looking out for their best interests in building a great resource team to help them. If a client has a great accountant or lawyer, etc., you want to hear about them and possibly add them to your list. Eventually other professionals will hear about your team list and will want to get on the list, especially if you print it and send it to your clients as a resource.

Most advisors deal with a few professionals, but are sometimes frustrated by the lack of referrals returned to them. So they either get discouraged at sending out referrals or try to find a few more centers of influence. I have found that a lot of advisors are either intimidated or frustrated with this process. Those advisors usually have less than five people to whom they can refer business. Why not have a team of 10, 20, 30 people and have them complete with the referrals you give out. Make it a rule of thumb that you try to give out one referral per day. That can add up to a lot of referrals in one year! Only giving them to five people might not be enough unless you have a partnership arrangement that is fully disclosed to the client. Some top advisors pay for top clients tax returns as part of their services and use an accountant who will give a bulk rate on tax returns.

Look for marketers. Some accountants and centers of influence may like marketing as much as you and you might find synergies in your marketing. You will be more likely to get referrals back from a firm that understands marketing and referrals. You can usually tell if they understand marketing by their Yellow Pages ad or other materials such as brochures.

Make sure you don't give your business card to the centers of influence. This leads them to think they will sit back and hand out your business card and tell the client, "Call this guy because he is a great financial advisor." The client rarely calls. Instead, tell the centers of influence to call you if they have referrals and to let the referrals know you will be calling them. I have heard accountants say to me, "I handed out a lot of your business cards, did any of them call?" In those cases I cross them off my list—they must call me with the information. Sometimes they will also call two financial advisors to make sure they are unbiased in their referrals. Remember to teach them how to refer business to you.

Consider having a certificate program. Hand your clients or prospects printed certificates that qualify them for 10 to 15% off the services of a professional you refer, such as an accountant or lawyer. That way they are more likely to use the referrals and receive discounts in the process. You can go to any stationery store to buy the certificates.

Jay's Comments:

The key to successful guerrilla marketing is in embracing not the concept of competition, but the beauty and advantage of cooperation. Their marketing exposure has just been expanded. Their marketing costs have just been reduced. List your fusion marketing partners below and track your follow-up contacts in the boxes.

Partners

1	
2	
3	
4	
5	
6	
7	
8	
9	
10	

1
2

3

4

5

6

7

8

9

10

Examples:

See the following Client Questionnaire, Team of Professionals document, and Letter to Professionals.

Action Summary:

To add to my marketing plans: Yes _____   No _____

Additional information required: Yes _____   No _____

I have always wanted to be somebody, but I see now I should have been more specific.

-Lily Tomlin

Client Questionnaire for Professional Advice

I want to build the best financial planning team possible. I need your help.

If you are impressed with your professionals, I would like to meet them and possibly add them to my list of professionals.

If you are seeking one of these professionals, I would be happy to refer you to one or more of the areas professionals on my team.

I am looking for the best people that can help my clients.
- Accountant
- Lawyer
- Estate planner
- Insurance professional
- Realtor
- Banker/mortgage lending expert
- Other

Please complete and return in confidence to:

Grant W. Hicks

Example of Your Team of Professionals Document

JOE LAWYER, BA, LLB: Joe Lawyer and Co.–Estate Planning
Mr. Lawyer has been practicing tax law for more than 15 years. He specializes in family trusts, professional incorporations, estate planning, corporate reorganizations, aboriginal taxation, immigration to and emigration from Canada, and investment in Canada by nonresidents.

JOHN Q. SMITH, CA Smith Tax.–Tax Planning
Mr. Smith has a special interest in tax-effective structuring of corporate reorganizations. Prior to joining Smith Tax., Mr. Smith was involved in drafting income tax legislation in a number of areas, including international taxation and corporate reorganization, while at the Department of Finance.

ALVIN JONES, BA, CA, CBV, XYZ and Co.–Mortgage/Lending/Financing Specialist
Mr. Jones' areas of expertise include business valuations arising from shareholder/partnership/matrimonial disputes, purchase/sale, and financing requirements. Additionally, he provides business advisory services to growth-oriented small- and medium-sized clients in a variety of industries.

D.A. BROWN, B.Comm., CA, CBV, ABC Benefits–Group Benefits
Mr. Brown has been in public practice for 26 years, 18 years with ABC Benefits. His areas of expertise include: Group Insurance and Employee Benefits Consulting.

Note: We are not affiliated with these firms and are not paid any fees as a result of your choice to work with any firm mentioned. Make sure you check with your compliance department.

Letter to Professionals:

I hope you're having a great summer. It's hard to concentrate on work when the weather is so nice. Looking to the fall when things get busy, I always look forward to helping my clients and enhancing their overall financial plans. This is where I need your help.

I have developed a list of professionals who I consider to be members of my team to help my clients. I would like to add your name to this list and use it as a handout and add it to my web site, *www.ghicks.com*. Your email address and web site address will also be added, if applicable, so that clients can go to you directly if they choose.

If you have a moment, please call or email Carol or me and let us know if this is acceptable. I look forward to hearing from you soon.

Sincerely,

Grant

PS: Have a great summer.

Success comes to those who set goals and pursue them regardless of obstacles and disappointments.

-Napoleon Hill

STRATEGY 14
Center of Influence Seminars

Concept:

Hold a luncheon seminar with accountants, lawyers, and other centers of influence such as mortgage brokers, realtors, and business associates. The purpose is to share ideas on tax-advantaged investing, estate planning, and other topics of mutual interest to help clients with estate planning, tax minimization, etc., or to help business owners with wealth transfer issues.

Objective:

The primary objective is to gain valuable referrals from a network of accountants, lawyers, and other centers of influence. The secondary objective is to build a team network of professionals to support clients in all areas of financial planning. You always want to build relationships with a team of professionals in order to educate other professionals about valuable client planning ideas.

In turn they will be able to share these ideas with their clients. Set the agenda to use real client examples and case studies to create true-life scenarios in order to apply ideas in informative and practical ways. This communication and work with a team of professionals will further enhance your clients overall tax, estate, and financial plans.

Strategy:

Bring in a guest speaker such as a mutual fund wholesaler or insurance expert to share different tax and estate planning ideas. Topics include insurance planning, estate planning, retirement planning, tax, or your area of expertise.

You can do special seminars just for accountants or lawyers. You could have a trust officer come out and speak about estate planning experiences and advanced techniques to organize affairs through trusts, estate freezes, and other planning vehicles.

Another theme: Set up an educational series and have a schedule to send to your centers of influence along with a survey about topics they might be interested in hearing about. Another variation is hosting a dinner. A dinner may be a more formal way to build the relationship. A breakfast is also very convenient for most professionals.

Grant's Tip:

When you do these types of seminars, plan for one hour and buy lunch for the participants. All invitations should be followed up by phone and confirmed the day before the seminar. Try to target eight in total, which may include accountants, lawyers, realtors, mortgage brokers, insurance brokers, or other members of your professional team or network. Show these professionals that you have tremendous resources within your company and industry and that they can tap into these resources as a member of your team.

The key is your presentations. Make sure your presentations are in a case study format where you take an example of work you have done to help someone and illustrate the kinds of problems you face and can solve. It will also show that you need their help in completing the case and that the next case may be a referral to them. Another case study you can do is an example of a client who is an accountant. You may end up with some accountants in the room as clients. That isn't the objective, but you identified with their own situations and became their problem-solver too.

The uniqueness of the center of influence meeting idea is that the investment or insurance company can share the company's view on tax reduction and what they try to do for the investor in developing products for the marketplace. For example, you can use company materials to explain what they are doing about taxation; and you can demonstrate how they help clients solve problems through case study examples using their products.

The attendees now have a better understanding of the company's position on taxation. Ask people to stay after the presentation to ask the wholesaler specific questions on taxation and estate issues that can be addressed in further meetings. The participants usually agree that they now have a clearer understanding of the mutual funds company's position towards tax and estate planning.

Potential Results: Ongoing relationships with and future referrals from these professionals position the financial advisor to be known for ideas and education. Referrals from other professionals will be triggered by case study examples of how they can help their clients and enhance their professionalism. A secondary benefit is to get the professionals as clients as well. These professionals may also be referring additional business to each other as a result of this meeting. The keys to making it successful are follow-up, feedback, additional seminars, and referrals.

Additional Tips: Don't call it a seminar; call it a case study meeting or peer group case study meeting. Plan to do this on a regular basis and set up a regular time that is flexible for all attendees. Print a schedule of meetings. Let them participate and be future presenters. Have them design future topics of interest to keep them coming out. Ask them to bring their clients to the meetings to learn more and enhance their relationships with top clients. Have some of your clients attend the meetings to show them you have a powerful networking group to help them. You may be able to use cooperative marketing dollars from companies with which you work. Check with your compliance department for more information.

Cost: The cost for lunch for 10 people is $100 to $200, including 8 centers of influence, yourself, and the wholesaler. The cost for the meeting room and invitations will total $100 to $300.

Jay's Comments:

The key to successful guerrilla marketing is in embracing not the concept of competition, but the beauty and advantage of cooperation. Fuse for fun and profit.

One of the most rewarding, inexpensive, underused, and effective methods of marketing is to tie in your marketing efforts with the efforts of others. In the U.S. this used to be known as "tie-ins." A recent Business Week cover article referred to it as "Collaborative Marketing," In Japan and by guerrillas worldwide, this make-everybody-wealthy marketing tactic is called "fusion marketing."

Fusion marketing is the guerrilla saying, "Hey Sara, if you enclose my brochure in your next mailing, I'll enclose your brochure in mine." "Randy, put up a sign for my store in your business; I'll put up a sign for your business in my store."

Sara and Randy immediately see the wisdom in the guerrilla's offer. Their marketing exposure has just been expanded. Their marketing costs have just been reduced. Hey, this is a good idea! Of course it is! Why do you think you're watching all those McDonald's commercials which turn into Coca-Cola commercials and end up as Lucasfilm commercials? Why do you think so many members of frequent flier clubs have learned that their airlines have fused with hotel chains, auto rental companies, even cruise lines? Because there's a whole lot of fusing going on.

It's happening very visibly among the large businesses, but it's happening more frequently among small businesses. The gas station fuses with the video store. The restaurant fuses with the clothing store. The sporting goods store fuses with the ski area AND the tennis club AND the golf course. It's happening all over!

Many organizations that have leads know that other organizations, marketing different things, have the SAME kinds of leads. So what go guerrilla organizations do? They form Leads Clubs. At the end of each month, they trade leads. Who wins? EVERYONE.

Who loses? Nobody. That's why fusion marketing is such a HAPPENING guerrilla marketing tactic. And that's why you'll love it so doggone much.

The purpose of a fusion marketing arrangement: Mutual profitability. Glad we're clear on that one. Realize that almost everyone in your community is a potential fusion marketing partner, that almost all of them will see the wisdom in your suggestion of a tie-in together. So why aren't they doing it yet, wise guy? Because YOU haven't suggested it to them.

Once you do, you'll see the utter simplicity of SPREADING your marketing wings while REDUCING your marketing costs. Okay, go out there and FUSE!

Additional Information:
• Read Strategies 13, 15, and 16.
• Ask your centers of influence and/or peer group about doing the seminar and find mutual topics of interest.
• Ask your regional wholesalers or company marketing directors about available speakers and topics of interest. They will have libraries of topics of interest, including case studies.

Action Summary:

To add to my marketing plans: Yes _____   No _____

Additional information required: Yes _____   No _____

I knew I was going to take the wrong train, so I left early.

-Yogi Berra

Our greatest glory consists not in never failing, but in rising every time we fall.

-Ralph Waldo Emerson

STRATEGY 15

Finding Great Partners–Working With Marketing Wholesalers Part 1

Concept:

There are fantastic resources at your fingertips. Find companies to work with that will support your business and help you and your clients.

Objective:

You cannot do it alone. Investment companies spend millions each year trying to market their services. One of the best routes is through their wholesalers and marketers of products. Find wholesalers or insurance marketers who will help you grow your business, not just your product or technical knowledge.

Strategy:

I was taught by Denis Rochon, a great veteran of the business, to develop relationships with wholesalers. They can help your business grow in more ways than you could imagine. Find business builders who love to do marketing instead of talking about technical knowledge or products all day.

Develop a win-win approach with wholesalers by asking them these questions:
• What are top representatives doing for marketing and building their business?
• Are there any representatives in your area I can talk to about marketing and your business-building ideas?
• Do you have any samples of marketing ideas that you have helped implement and/or have seen work?
• Does your company have a catalog of marketing ideas or materials?
• What is your commitment to helping build my business?
• What amount of time do you spend with top advisors on marketing each year? (Ask them for their time commitment.)
• Do you have any good books on marketing ideas? (Like this one!)
• Does your company sponsor marketing events or have any affiliation or recommendations to top marketing people?
• Does your company have an intranet to access on your web site for marketing ideas and materials?
• Do you sponsor marketing materials such as newsletters?

• What are your cooperative policies and procedures? Do you have a system or manual?

• How can you help me with ideas and cooperate for client appreciation?

Grant's Tip:

Some of the best ideas I have used have come from one-on-one business-building meetings with wholesalers. Ask your top wholesalers to be on your board of directors and ask for half a day twice a year to go over your business plans, marketing plans, and upcoming ideas. This is in addition to your regular quarterly meetings and updates. Ask for feedback on your plans. Give them a copy in confidence and make yourself accountable to the wholesalers by reviewing your results and plans with them. Sometimes feedback can be invaluable. You don't want to climb the ladder of success and find out that the ladder is leaning against the wrong wall.

Make sure that you get a commitment from over the course of one year of not only their ideas, but their time and feedback. In your peer group, ask other top producers how they work with their wholesalers and the ideas and support that they bring to the table.

An easy way to find a great wholesaler is to look for one that has a written business and marketing plan that covers more than one year. Most wholesalers don't have ten-year business plans, which they should; but the ones that have their commitment on paper and can share that commitment with you are worth their weight in gold.

A number of years ago I was interviewed by a few mutual fund companies for a wholesaling position. I was asked what makes a great wholesaler. My candid answer was listening and marketing. If you asked me the same question today, the answer would be listening, marketing, and relationship building. I didn't say anything about product. That is a given, that you should know your product. More importantly, wholesalers can help top advisors by listening to advisors and asking better questions. Secondly, wholesalers should know a lot about marketing. I typically ask if wholesalers have read certain marketing books for financial advisors. If they haven't read them, how can they help me? They are not on the same page. Wholesalers should have a broad knowledge of marketing in order to be supporters of financial advisors and their marketing. Too many companies pay marketing people big bucks to spend huge marketing budgets, only to see their efforts make a marginal difference. If they spent time educating their sales force on marketing instead of product, do you think sales would increase? The final part of hiring successful marketers is the relationship. As I mentioned in previous chapters about hot buttons, excitement buttons, and the WOW factor, these simple database keys to relationship-building will exist a hundred years from now. You can't build a relationship by email. You can't build trust by head-office marketing experts and their mailings. It takes people, who know how to build trust and relationships, to educate, coach, and inspire top financial advisors on marketing and to listen and ask key questions in helping financial advisors succeed. It is client success that leads to advisor success that leads to wholesaler success that leads to company success. That will not change for a hundred years. Maybe there are companies out there willing to interview me again?

Jay's Comments:

Save money by accessing co-op funds. It not only saves money for advisors but it lends credibility to your offerings by mentioning the name of a nationally known company. Some companies that offer co-op funds insist they be the only company mentioned. Others may just want their logo along with other company logo's mentioned. A smart advisor interested in saving lots of money will include the names of several co-op companies, thereby saving a large percentage of the marketing cost.

1. Line up your marketing calendar for the year.

2. Line up your estimated costs.

3. Check with the companies that you want to do business with and obtain copies of co-op marketing policies, sample manuals.

4. Remember, co-op means more than just advertising. It can include newsletters, e-mail programs, web sites, seminars, mailers, specialty items such as pens, sponsorships, charities, etc. Always check with your compliance officer first. Obtain securities com. copy of co-op policies, your company's policy and the sponsoring companies policies to make sure they all jive. Review all company marketing material–ideas and policies.

5. Develop your co-op marketing strategies and the companies you will use them with.

6. Sit down with the wholesalers and finalize the plans for the year. Obtain co-op agreement.

7. Complete the necessary forms and paperwork in line with compliance.

8. Depending on the co-op request, ad approvals, or other marketing approvals from the companies and your compliance must be met and signed off before proceeding. Note: I learned a valuable lesson by having the newspaper push me on releasing ad copy without sign off. Make sure it is right or don't do it.

9. Once you have successfully completed marketing a request for reimbursement, see each company's rules and policies, etc.

10. Have wholesaler/company and you do follow up on success of the program and measure results and plans to improve.

Additional Resources:

Murray, Nick. *The Excellent Investment Advisor.* The Nick Murray Company, Inc., 1996.

(Your list of top Wholesalers to work with)

Action Summary:

To add to my marketing plans: Yes _____   No _____

Additional information required: Yes _____   No _____

A great wholesaler can help your business grow faster than you can ever imagine.

Grant W. Hicks

Be the change you want to see in the world.

-Ghandi

STRATEGY 16
Meetings/Seminars with your Partners–Working with Wholesalers Part II

Concept:
To educate clients and prospects, and to encourage investment in funds and companies promoted in the discussion.

Objective:
This is a strategic seminar for clients and prospects to attend and ask questions of the specific companies in which they are investing or considering. Invite two or three speakers to do a presentation; then have a discussion at the end with you, as the moderator, handling and asking questions of the speakers.

Strategy:
A panel-discussion-type seminar offers a chance to communicate with clients and to show prospects the advantages of investing with you and the expertise that you bring to your clients. Instead of completing client reviews, schedule those specific clients and/or prospects to attend an afternoon or evening session to discuss a timely and relevant financial planning topic, investment idea, or market review. It may also give your clients an opportunity to talk directly with a wholesaler or money manager and ask questions to give them an opportunity to gather more information and make them better educated investors.

Hold a small seminar (for 20 to 30 people). Invite your clients and prospects. You can also select a target group or audience such as dentists or doctors to invite. You can utilize the media to promote your educational approach by advertising in the paper, on TV, or on the radio. You can invite all clients, prospects, and your centers of influence.

Grant's Tip:
I would complete this seminar once or twice a year. I would keep it small and informal because more questions are asked in a smaller group.

Depending on your money managers and the companies, utilize your top investment carriers and find dynamic speakers, not product sellers, for these presentations. You can make this an annual event for clients, invite them well in advance, and let them know they are welcome to bring a friend to the event.

This is a great opportunity to be in front of your top 20 clients and add value to their investments by inviting them to listen to you and your recommended investment companies or managers.

Several different variations on this concept:

• Hold a conference call with a fund manager for your clients and prospects. They can attend in person or dial in to the conference call.

• Offer to do the seminar or meeting to various groups in your community. Besides offering your speaking services, offer services of listening to world-class money managers or other experts to groups who are looking for interesting speakers.

• Have conference calls with speakers provided by fund or insurance companies as part of your client communications commitment. Talk to your wholesaler about speakers or have your wholesaler do the speaking.

• Have your panel discussion include several speakers lined up at the front of the room with you moderating a question and answer period. Give ample time to each speaker.

• Target hot buttons for your clients such as tax risk management and other areas.

See Strategy 22–Successful Seminar Strategies. Remember to invite top clients, prospects, and centers of influence.

Costs: Usually $500 to $1,000 depending on the meeting room, refreshments, and advertising and mailing costs. I recommend theatre-style seating with tables if possible. The meeting room should be the best available in your area.

Jay's Comments:

When guerrilla marketers think of economizing, they don't necessarily think of trying to save money. What they do think of is getting the absolute most from any money they've invested in marketing. They realize there are two kinds of marketing—expensive and inexpensive—and they know that expensive marketing is the kind that doesn't cover the investment they've made in it, while inexpensive marketing pays rich rewards for their investment. Guerrillas have the insight to know that economizing has nothing to do with cost; it has everything to do with results.

To be sure, guerrillas adopt a philosophy of frugality and thrift. They know well the difference between investing in something disposable such as paper and accounting services—and investing in something that's truly an investment, such as a telephone system or customer-tracking software—items they'd use on a daily basis. There's a big difference in these two expenses, so you won't be surprised to learn that guerrillas rarely waste their time and effort on relatively low-cost disposable purchases, but are willing to expend the time and energy to enjoy a large savings on a an expense that's really an investment in disguise.

A key to economizing is to think not in terms of purchasing, but in terms of acquiring. That means you open your mind to bartering, sharing, renting, modifying an existing item or borrowing it. It means possibly learning a few skills so that you can do rather than hire. Desktop publishing software enables you to save a ton of money usually paid to pros.

Guerrillas are also keenly aware of when it makes sense to hire a pro, knowing that amateur-looking marketing is an invitation to disaster. They might hire a highly-paid professional designer to give their marketing items a powerful visual format, then use their own staff members or themselves to continue generating marketing materials that follow this same format. They learn from any consultant they hire.

By understanding that economizing does not mean saving money, but investing it wisely, guerrillas test their investments on a small scale before plunging headlong into any kind of marketing. They have no fear of failure, providing the failures are small ones and knowing that even one success in ten tries means discovering a path to wealth and profitability.

They know in their hearts that money is not the key to happiness or success, but that enough of it enables them to have a key made. Real frugality is more about priorities and results than just saving money.

Guerrillas can economize with wholesalers and investment company marketers. First they usually have terrific web sites with marketing materials. Second, their professionally produced investment materials are valuable in the hands of clients and prospects. Finally, their co-op dollars and marketing support.

Of all the methods of wasting money and not economizing, the number one leader in marketing is failure to commit to a plan. Untold millions have been invested in marketing campaigns that had everything right about them except commitment on the part of the marketer. Guerrillas know that it takes time for an investment to pay off and instant results are rarely part of the deal. Abandoning a marketing campaign before it has a chance to flourish squanders money in three ways. First, it means all prior investing in the campaign has been for naught. Second, it means new investing will be necessary to generate the share of mind that precedes a share of market. Third, it means creating new marketing materials all over again. Small business owners have other ways to waste money as well. Many of them invest in research instead of doing it themselves. Others dare to commit to a campaign they haven't tested. Still others create marketing materials that must be updated regularly, rather than creating timeless marketing materials. When you say in a brochure that you've been in business five years, you must update that brochure next year. When you say you've been in business since 1995, that's always going to be the truth.

Action Summary:

To add to my marketing plans: Yes _____   No _____

Additional information required: Yes _____   No _____

The greatest discovery of my generation is that a human being can alter his life by altering his attitude of mind.

-William James

If you can dream it, you can do it.

-Walt Disney

STRATEGY 17
Your Media Advantage Part I–Radio And TV

Concept:

Do you have the substantial time and resources to develop an effective radio commercial campaign? The radio station would love to sell you an expensive marketing campaign. Is this the best alternative for developing new clients? How about developing your own radio or TV show?

Objective:

Develop a dynamic personality and name through your own radio show. A very successful advisor I met at a conference built his business around his radio show. The keys were to develop his personality and name recognition, build credibility, and be known for ideas, not just offer a news-market summary.

Strategy:

Why not have your own radio or TV program or call-in show. In our area I always hear that people tune into a regular financial personality on Saturday mornings and always enjoy his show. Several successful advisors have their own shows and use it as a springboard to successful name recognition. People think that if you're in the media you're an expert, and they trust what you have to say.

When I looked into developing a radio program, we needed to do some homework and research such as target audience, time slots, and impact. This is easy to research since most radio stations have preformatted sales facts and figures and media packages to develop your show. Define the selected audience you wish to target and ask the radio station sales representative for detailed information on how effectively the station reaches your targeted group. If the station doesn't want a show, don't consider advertising unless your voice is heard by the public. Several stations offer program sponsorships such as newscasts, sports traffic, and weather. Also remember to consider cooperative advertising sponsorship such as "brought to you by Best Mutual Funds and Grant Hicks, your local financial advisor." Plan the length of your campaign and consider negotiating with the station for volume discounts. Radio "air time" is usually in 30- or 60-second spots for commercials. Be sure to read the contractual agreement and ask for it in advance to see the cancellation clauses, terms, and conditions. Also inquire the cost per thousand, the cost incurred to deliver the message to 1,000 people, and the CUME or total number of hours.

Grant's Tip:

Some stations have a strong focus on financial news and are looking for someone to help them out. Smaller or community broadcasting networks may also be seeking creative programming ideas. Local community TV guides can also be looking for show developers or advertisers. When you develop your show, focus on developing your personality. Include your name in the title of the show and get creative to make an impact. When I developed a radio show, we called it *Grant Hicks, the Money Man.* I did interviews and commentary for a half-hour in the morning once a week. There were several advertising spots that I purchased to promote the show. I integrated the show with newspaper advertising showing a photograph of me in the radio booth. We also sent out flyers and newsletters to our clients letting them know about the show. The impact of putting it all together worked better than if I just did a radio show. The results were instant credibility, recognition, and awareness. For certain special-topic shows, I would send out a special invitation for clients to listen in. I would then have ten recorded copies of the show on cassette or CDRom to send out to clients and/or prospects. Marketing the show and prospecting. It all ties together. Now when I approach potential clients I may mention the radio show; and even though they may not listen to radio, they may have seen my ad in the local newspaper.

We had call-in shows, to give feedback opportunities. I frequently had guests such as money managers and wholesalers, lawyers and accountants, to help promote my expertise in certain areas of retirement planning (estate planning, investing for income, and insurance). The guests appreciated the coverage as well as a chance to promote their companies and ideas.

The show's format was laid out for months in advance. Make sure you don't let the radio station do your show or have a strong radio personality run your show. You will only get lost in the development. We scheduled guests, completed cooperative marketing requests, and had a standard discussion format prepared for the show. The guest coming on knew how much time they had, what we were going to discuss and/or promote, and how to get the message across. With today's technology, you can have radio guests live on the air from anywhere across the country.

Always, always do your own scripts and read them out for the radio spots. Remember, you are developing your personality. When writing your commercials, keep in mind that you have three seconds to catch and hold the attention of the listener.

Costs: This depends on your format, news or shows, and length. Contact your local media radio and TV stations, ask their sales directors for media kits, and discuss possible ideas for a show; possibly they're seeking an expert who can do news for free!!

How about saving on your advertising costs? The radio station we worked with helped us develop an advertising reselling opportunity. During the radio show we had a certain number of advertising spots. If we sold all of those spots to people who would want to advertise during my show, then the radio station would do our radio spots free. We basically were selling radio spots for our show. We could then approach sponsor companies, suppliers, or other businesses we knew in the area to work with us in developing the time slot. The radio station was getting a fully paid time slot and promotion as well as a completed radio show. A lot of their work was done. It saves thousands of your marketing dollars in airtime also. At the very least, call the news director of the radio stations in your area and mention to them that if they need a comment on any financial news story you would be happy to supply a comment or opinion to help. You eventually can become an authority on financial news items.

Potential Results: This can be measured after one or two years of working with the media. Ask your top clients or board of directors, friends, and neighbors for feedback. Make sure you track your radio or TV show or advertising responses to measure the success. Once in a while, ask your clients if they tuned in. Make sure your mom and dad are not the only ones listening. Use the radio station's resources and people to help make it a success.

Jay's Comments:

Television time is more inexpensive than ever. It can also be more effective than ever if you understand it.

Just as radio didn't disappear when TV entered our lives, TV won't disappear now that being on line is rapidly becoming part of our lives. Yes, it's true that people are spending more time with their PCs and less time with their TVs and it's also true that the lines between them are blurring. But television deserves a place in the arsenal of financial advisors now more than ever.

The main reasons why this is true are:
• Television now allows you to target your audience more precisely than you could in the past. It lets you single out specific groups of people, such as business people, and it enables you to home in on selected neighborhoods in your community. These phenomena are due to the growth of cable TV.

• *Television is now more affordable than it ever has been, in many cases lower in cost than radio. Direct response companies by the carload are discovering this and also discovering there is a 24-hour viewing audience out there with even lower rates and there are program-length infomercials that cost what regular one-minute spots used to cost. Again, we tip our hats to the cable industry for putting TV within everybody's reach.*
• *Guerrillas rarely expect reward before Day Ninety.*

Is it really possible to learn about television in one section of this book? It is not only possible to do that but also possible to unlearn many fantasies you may have believing about television commercials. Like the joke that it's supposed to entertain and amuse, make people laugh, be a work of art. Guerrillas don't fall for this joke. They know selling when they see selling. They know that marketing is a pretty fancy word that means selling and that selling has very little to do with entertaining and laughing.

Of the myriad of things you should know about television, I've limited my list here to only ten. There are one thousand ten things to know but these ten are the most important and every guerrilla knows them:

1. Television is inexpensive. The cost to run commercials is no more than $2,000 during prime time in most markets in the United States. The cost to produce a commercial, although $197,000 in 2001, should run you no more than $1,000. You don't need Michael or Tiger or Dennis endorsing what you have to offer. And you're after sales, not Emmies.

2. Television is a visual medium. Don't think of it as a radio spot with pictures. Think of it as a visual story with a beginning, a middle and an end. Because over 70 percent of us mute the commercials with our remote zappers, if you're not telling your story and saying your name visually, you're not telling your story or saying your name at all.

3. Television is powered by an idea. Forget the special effects, music, staging, and lighting. First think of the idea. That's what makes a commercial successful—a strong offer, a visual expression of a good idea. Once you have the idea, everything else will fall into place. Without the idea, your commercial has hardly any chance of success.

4. Television is made fascinating by special effects. Many people get carried away at their opportunities to be like Steven Spielberg and fall prey to gizmos and gimmicks. Use special effects to highlight your idea, to focus on your idea, to further your idea and then you'll see why they're so special. Otherwise, they act like vampires, sucking attention away from your offer with their dazzle.

5. Television doesn't cost as little as you think. Here I am telling you right off the bat that TV is inexpensive and here I am one minute later telling you that it's not so inexpensive. The spots are inexpensive. The production can be inexpensive. But you've got to run several spots every day, several days a week, three weeks out of four, and for a minimum of three months—unless you're making a direct response offer—before you see any glimmerings that TV is about to do the job for you. If you're looking for instant gratification, look somewhere other than the tube.

6. Television is made better if you operate from a script. You need not waste your precious money having somebody produce a storyboard for you because you don't need one. But you do need a script that tells the exact visuals and the exact sounds that will go on for 30 seconds.

7. Television production costs are lower if you pre-produce with care. The way guerrillas cut $196,000 ugly dollars from their TV production costs is by having pre-production meetings where all production details are handled. These are followed by rehearsals for the talent and the technicians. There should be zero surprises on the day of the TV shooting.

8. Television production costs are lowered still if you produce your sound track first. After you've got it, you can shoot footage to match the amount of time the words and music take. Shooting sound and picture at the same time means that if a plane flies overhead or a truck drives by, you've got to re-shoot. Do your sound first, using professionals, then shoot the visuals.

9. Television's greatest strength is its ability to demonstrate. As newspapers give the news and magazines involve readers, as radio provides intimacy and direct response adds urgency, television's power is the way it can demonstrate. It can show before and after, with a shot of the product in use during the middle. It can hit left and right-brained people. It can combine all the art forms into a masterful blending of show and sell.

10. Television is still the undisputed heavyweight champion of marketing. I love on-line marketing so much that I'm nearly bursting with enthusiasm for it. I know it's gonna make every other medium stronger and more effective. And I know it's not a matter of if, but a matter of when you go on line. Until then and after then, you'll find that television can talk directly to your specific target audience, that it will cost you much less than you figured, and that if you've got the patience to commit to a TV campaign, you're going to be delighted at how it rewards your patience.

A final word: Just as being on line doesn't mean beans unless it's part of a well-crafted marketing program, being on television is also no guarantee of profitability unless it is part of a program and supported with other media. Never forget that somebody once defined a TV commercial as "a dream interrupter." I look forward to your commercials interrupting my dreams.

Examples:
See The Money Man ad on the following page and radio format ideas under "Strategyy" above.

Additional Resources:
Your local radio and television stations—call them and ask for their media kits.

Action Summary:

To add to my marketing plans: Yes _____   No_____

Additional information required: Yes _____   No_____

In order to succeed we must first believe that we can.

-Michael Korda

Every Wednesday morning from 9:05 am to 9:30 am on CKCI 1350 it's,
The Money Man Show

Grant Hicks,
General Manager
of AAI Financial
Group is the
"Money Man"
your retirement
specialist."

Grant Hicks,
AAI *FINANCIAL GROUP*
"Call the Money Man
Wednesday mornings with your
questions about
financial planning."

Parksville • Qualicum Beach
CKCI 1350
am
Great Music • Great Memories

Use with permission from Courtesy Island Broadcasting

When all think alike there is no thinking.

-Limpa

STRATEGY 18
Your Media Advantage Part II–Prospects Calling You

Concept:

Have you ever wanted more information on something in which you're interested? How about a brochure on a new car or boat you're thinking of buying? You might go to the Internet for more information, but if I offered you a free report on new cars to buy, would you call me for the free report? Bingo, you not only have someone who is interested in new cars, but contact information to keep them interested.

Objective:

Most advertising is targeted to get your attention in five seconds or less. To learn more, people need a source of information. Searching the Web only gives half of the information and doesn't give sources with whom one can personally speak. If you offer a free booklet, packed with information, enough information to rouse people to doing something, they have you as the source to call and discuss. In writing it's called "the book and the hook." Several of the most successful advisors built their entire businesses around this cornerstone of marketing. They do it consistently for years and have their target prospects calling them each week. The success of this approach lies in the fact that the target audience responds to this type of marketing. Key headline ads can bring in thousands of dollars of new business.

The four main ingredients you want to find in a prospect are motivation, interest, willingness to take action, and qualification. By advertising to elicit a direct response you are finding three out of the four prerequisites. You have found someone who is motivated, interested, and willing to take action but who may not qualify as one of your ideal clients. What better way can you find people? How many hours have you wasted with people who were not motivated? Or not interested? Or not willing to take action? This process eliminates these up front and brings the right people to your door.

Strategy:

Through advertising, offer free books or booklets on topics of interest to potential clients. Put yourself in the clients' shoes and uncover some of the problems they face. For example, if you're retired, you would want to know how to maximize your income with little risk; so you need to find the right income solutions. Where do you start? Think of all the places you would go to find your information—a library or bookstore, the Web, friends or colleagues who are in similar situations. If you have an advisor you will ask him or her. But what if you learn something that not everyone is telling you?

How about an ad with the following pitch? "The ten pitfalls to avoid in your retirement planning. Income options you need to know. Call now for a free 20-page booklet you don't want to miss reading. The obvious choice in retirement options may not be your best choice." Make sure you have headlines and sayings in your ad that accomplish two things:
• Catches the readers' attention to read further.
• Rouses them to action.

Grant's Tip:

We have all seen pre-approach letters. I have hundreds of examples. Most of them are passed up by advisors because they fail to get their attention.

Want great headlines? Go to the newsstand and look at the tabloids and the magazines that sell the most. Read the headlines at the grocery checkout that grab your attention. Once you learn this skill, you will train your mind to find good headlines for your marketing. I usually look for the longest line at the checkout, not the shortest, so I can read headlines.

Offering a booklet in a pre-approach letter can be done instead of advertising but is far less effective. Your audience is very narrow; however, you can target a wealthy or affluent neighborhood in which to practice target marketing your headlines and do market research. Then you can target your audience even more. Or you can combine an ad with a pre-approach letter. You may even want to send the letter to existing clients that may have assets elsewhere. Then you can announce on your web site that interested parties can call for the free booklet, and you're using multiple sources to get new people.

This program, however, works well with one-shot advertising and not with continuous advertising. If I saw the same ad for several weeks, what is my sense of urgency to call? You must create a sense of urgency by only doing one ad or letter and stating that it is new and/or revealing information and that it is for a limited time. You can advertise to offer different booklets at different times of the year. For example, if you want retirement business you might advertise on how to increase retirement income without increasing risk. You might advertise year-end tax planning booklets in November.

Choose the topic or topics on which you want to focus. If you're in the retirement market like me, topics may be long-term care, retirement income options, estate planning, and so on.

The Ad: The ad or pre-approach letter should look like a small article with a big headline. Just like a column in a newspaper, it's about grabbing your attention. If you're retired and seeking income options, the headline will grab you. Just like when you buy a new red car, suddenly there appear to be more red cars like yours on the road.

The Booklet: Now that you have this great idea, where do you get the information? Your investment or insurance company spends millions on great booklets each year. Look for something fresh or find something that has worked. You can create your own, if you have the time. Look in the newspapers and trade magazines and you'll find some companies are using this technique. Why not call for their free booklets or packages and see how they do theirs? Make sure the information is accurate and available to send out. Always check with your compliance office before proceeding.

Your booklet should be packaged in a folder with information mainly about you. You are selling yourself at this point. Include your business card and a call to action by providing a letter thanking them for their interest and offering them a teaser to get them to come in. For example, in the letter , offer them a free follow-up book or booklet dealing with more details. "Call me to discuss and we can go over it in more detail and provide you with answers to common questions." This follow-up booklet is invaluable.

You now have an interested person for a target subject and one with whom you can book an appointment to discuss and offer more free valuable information.

A key tip for your ad is to use a calling service to collect the information for you. For example, at the end of the ad it says, "Call 1-888-xxxx toll-free 24 hours to receive your free booklet." Then set up the calling service to send you the information they gather (instead of having the calling service direct them to call your office—they likely won't call).

The Follow-up: Your receptionist should be aware that people may call in for the booklet. The booklets should be packaged up and mailed out the day they are requested. Make sure you track all this information and put the list of potential people in a database along with which booklet/information they requested. Then you can start your follow-up and offer more detail to the problems and solutions presented in the booklet.

Jay's Comments:

These days, there seem to be two kinds of businesses: givers and takers. Giver businesses are quick to give freebies to customers and prospects. The freebies may be gifts, but more likely come in the form of information. The right information is worth more than a gift and often even worth far more than money.

In fact I've added a new personality trait to my list of characteristics possessed by successful guerrillas. I've always known they were blessed with infinite patience and fertile imaginations. I've written in awe of their acute sensitivity and their admirable ego strength. I've raved about their aggressiveness in marketing and their penchant for constant learning.

Now, I'm impressed, but not surprised, at their generosity. They are, every single one of them, generous souls who seem to gain joy by giving things away, by taking their customers and prospects beyond satisfaction and into true bliss. They learn what those people want and need and then they try to give them what they want and need absolutely free.

The result? Delighted prospects who become customers and delighted customers who become repeat and referral customers.

What kind of things do guerrilla financial advisors give away for free? Let's start with a list and your mind will be primed to dream up more:

• They give printed brochures to anybody who requests one. Customized brochures, as Grant describes, that will help them solve their financial problems.

• They give electronic brochures, on audio and video, once again to people who ask for them. And they are quick to offer their free brochures in their other marketing.

• They give money to worthy causes and let their prospects and customers know that they support a noble cause, enabling these people to support the same endeavor.

• They give free consultations and never make them seem like sales presentations. They truly try to help their prospects.

• They give free seminars and clinics because they realize that if their information is worthwhile, it will attract the right kind of people to them.

• They give invaluable information on their web sites, realizing that such data will bring their customers and prospects back for more, thereby intensifying their relationships.

In addition to these ten, guerrillas are highly creative in dreaming up what they might give for free. Of course, many advertising specialties such as calendars and scratchpads, mouse pads and ball-point pens are emblazoned with their names and theme lines, but they seem to exercise extra creativity as well.

Case in point: When an apartment building went up, signs proudly proclaimed that you get "Free Auto Grooming" when you sign a lease. Soon, the occupancy rate was 100 percent. The salary they paid the guy who washed the tenants' cars once a week was easily covered by the difference between 100 percent occupancy and 71 percent occupancy, the usual occupancy rate in that neighborhood.

That means your task is clear: Think of what might attract prospects and make clients happy. Be creative. Be generous. Then, be prepared for a reputation embracing generosity, customer service, and sincere caring. Today's customers are attracted to giver companies and repelled by taker companies. What kind of company is yours?

Examples:
See the ad following this section.

Additional resources:
Look for advertisers trying the same thing. Ask wholesalers if they have useful advertising or pre-approach letters and booklets. Target your audience by your booklet.

Action Summary:

To add to my marketing plans: Yes _____   No _____

Additional information required: Yes _____   No _____

If you could give your son or daughter only one gift, let it be enthusiasm.

-Unknown

Reprinted with permission from the *Parksville Qualicum News*

640K ought to be enough for anybody.

-Bill Gates

STRATEGY 19
Build Money on the Net–Your Web Site Strategy

Concept:
While the Web has many uses, the majority of your clients and prospects are using it for financial education and information.

Objective:
Your web site's primary purpose is to educate and service your existing clients, and the secondary purpose is to develop exposure and new clients. Since the technology boom started in the late 1990s, more and more people are disappointed with on-line results for marketing and advertising.

Strategy:
Your web site accomplishes two main strategies. First is client services and communication. Second is prospecting and advertising. How many times in the last year has a client called in for an updated statement? If your firm allows Internet access to accounts, put the link on your web site and drive Internet traffic through your web site instead of through your company web site. This will accomplish two things. First, you are adding value by helping clients get set up with personal identification numbers (PIN) and passwords, rather than having your head office technology department (which doesn't know your clients) do it; second, you are promoting investment ideas and educational information. You may also have seminar opportunities and can let your clients know of all the areas that you cover, such as estate planning and insurance.

Grant's Tip:
Set up your web site in a very simple manner to start. Don't waste lots of time on it, but improve it over time. Make sure you put your web site address on all your correspondence, emails, business cards, etc. Your web site can show the benefits to clients and if you can add testimonials, it will greatly enhance your appeal. I can't stress how important it is to focus on what the client wants and is seeking through your web site instead of listing all the products and services. An excellent example of this is *www.schwab.com*. The *Schwab* web site clearly demonstrates why clients should do business with them. They have testimonials stressing the benefits of *Schwab*, which is one step better than coming from *Schwab*.

Another key is to put as much as you can on the first page. Large corporate web designers know that if you have to search and dig for information or get lost in a web site, you will not come back. Everything should be on the home page.

Consider viral marketing in your community. Find good community web sites or businesses you may want to contact and ask for a link exchange. In other words, have a link to your web sites on the web sites of the businesses you work with or are targeting. Now imagine if your web site was linked on hundreds of businesses in your community? Would you possibly have traffic from prospects doing business with these firms? You can also link it to chambers of commerce or related business directories. Design an email and send it out to all the businesses with which you want to exchange links. Then on your web site you can build a link directory of businesses that can be a resourceful guide for your clients and prospects. Let the concept of viral marketing work for you. You will be amazed someday by receiving an email from a stranger, who came across your link on some other site, who wants to talk to you about financial advice–all because you sent a bunch of emails. You can have your marketing team do this in a matter of days and watch it grow and compound. Also make sure your web site provider can keep accurate statistics of where your web site traffic is coming from. If you find out that a lot of business is coming through a certain company's web site, you should contact and thank that company. Who knows, maybe they will also want to become clients, when you thank them. A great marketing opportunity evolves through your web site.

For marketing, consider hosting a lecture or a computer lab training session on web sites and learning financial education and research. I know that several on-line financial firms offer these courses to their clients free of charge.

Using the Internet enhances your marketing; for example, a direct mail campaign with a giveaway for people who respond via your web site email. You can list seminars on your web site and people can sign up on line.

Costs: These can vary greatly depending on how you want your web site developed. You can get one started for a few hundred bucks or it can cost thousands. Typically there is an annual maintenance fee and, depending on your host, this can be a few hundred to a thousand each year.

Jay's Comments:

Once you have even the spark of a notion to market on line, let that spark ignite thoughts of how you'll promote your site. Have the insight to know this means thinking imaginatively about two worlds.

The first is the on-line world, where you'll think in terms of multiple links to other sites, banners leading to your site, search engines directing browsers to your site, postings on forums alerting on-liners to your site, chat conferences heralding your site, recommendations of your site by Internet powers, emailing to parties demonstrably interested in learning about the topics covered on your site, writing articles for other sites in return for links back to your site, mentioning your site in your email signature, advertising on line to entice people to your site, preparing an on-line version of your press kit to publicize your site on line, and connecting with as many other on-line entities as possible, all in a quest to make your site part of the on-line community, an Internet landmark to your prospects, a not-be-missed feature of the Web.

The second world in which your imagination should run rampant in a mission to achieve top-of-the-mind awareness of your site is the offline world. Most of the population of the real world still resides there. That's where they continue to get most of their information—for now.

And that's where you've got to let them know of your on-line site teeming with information that can shower them with benefits—for their business or their lives or both.

Tout your site in your ads, on stationery, on your business cards, on signs, on brochures, fliers, Yellow Pages ads, advertising specialties, packages, business forms, gift certificates, reprints of PR articles, in your catalog, newsletter, and classified ads. Mention it in your radio spots, on television.

More than one company now has a jingle centered on their web site. Never neglect to direct folks to your site in direct mail letters and postcards, in all your faxes, almost anywhere your name appears. If the world begins to think that your last name is dotcom, you're going about your offline promotional activities in the right way.

Some companies think that by including their site in tiny letters at the bottom of their ad or by flashing it at the end of their TV commercial, they're taking care of offline promotion. They're not. All they're doing is going through the motions. Talk about your web site the same way you'd talk about your kid—with pride, enthusiasm and joy. Make people excited about your site because they can see your pride.

Will local or industry newspapers write about your on-line site? Of course they will if you make it fascinating enough for their readers.

That's your job. Promotion will get them to your site. Killer content will get them to make return trips.

The insight about content for a web site is it should be the information your prospects and customers want to know the most. It's not necessarily the content you want to put forth and boast about. Instead, it's data about how your company can have a positive impact on visitors to your site.

To create the best content, work backwards–beginning with the goals you wish to achieve with your site. Put into writing the specific goals you wish your web site to obtain for you. The more specific you are, the more like you are to hit those goals.

Next, put into writing the obstacles that may stand in the way of your company attaining its goals. Usually, these obstacles center around a lack of information by your target audience. When you're clear on that information, become a bridge-builder. Build a bridge between your goals and your target audience. Construct it of valuable information.

Guerrillas know well that their sites will succeed or fail based on how much overlap there is between their content and the needs of their target audiences. They realize that exquisite design and spectacular promotion are meaningless if their content doesn't fill the needs of their market.

To develop that kind of content, answer these questions, for your specific answers will provide your content:
• What is the immediate, short-term goal of your web site?
• What specific action do you want visitors to take?
• What are your specific objectives for the long term?
• Who do you want to visit your site?
• What solutions or benefits can you offer to these visitors?
• What data should your site provide to achieve your primary goal?
• What information can you provide to encourage them to act right now?
• What questions do you get asked the most on the telephone?
• What questions and comments do you hear most at trade shows?
• What data should your site provide to achieve your secondary goal?
• Where does your target audience look for information?
• How often do you want visitors to return to your web site?
• What may be the reasons you don't sell as much as you'd like to?
• Who is your most astute competition?
• Does your competition have a web site?
• What are ways you can distinguish yourself from your competitors?
• How important is price to your target audience?

Your answers point the way to what competitive advantages to stress, what to show, what to say, what to feature. Serve up your content in bite-sized pieces, all valuable–for it's clear current content that leads to success on the Web. If it's a winner for your guests, it will be a winner for you.

Eight Golden Rules For Your Web Site:
1. Planning. That means you must know ahead of time exactly what you wish to accomplish with your web site.

2. *Content*. That's what's going to attract visitors to your site, then keep them coming back for more visits on a regular basis.

3. *Design*. There's a "hang or click" moment when people first see your site. Should they hang around or click away? Design influences their decision.

4. *Involvement*. Guerrillas take advantage of the Net's interactivity by involving visitors rather than just requiring that they read.

5. *Production*. This refers to putting your first four elements on line. Easy-to-use software now can do this job for you.

6. *Follow-up*. People visit your site, email you, ask or answer some questions. Guerrillas respond to their email, stay in touch.

7. *Promotion*. You must promote your site on line by registering with search engines and linking with other sites, while promoting it offline in mass media, mailings, wherever your name appears.

8. *Maintenance*. Unlike other marketing, a web site requires constant changing, updating, freshening, renewing. Like a baby.

Additional resources:

• A great book to read is *Multiple Streams of Internet Income* by Robert G. Allen (John Wiley & Sons, 2001.)

• I can list several thousand web sites to look at but you can start by going to the best web site on marketing for financial advisors, with loads of information, *www.financialadvisormarketing.com*. Consider adding great financial tools to your website. Check out *www.quotemedia.com*

Action Summary:

To add to my marketing plans:	Yes _____	No _____
Additional information required:	Yes _____	No _____

If you see a fork in the road, take it.

-Yogi Berra

If one advances confidently in the direction of his dreams, and endeavors to live the life he has imagined, he will meet with a success unexpected in common hours.

-Henry David Thoreau

STRATEGY 20
Ultimate Public Relations-Part I–Newspapers

Concept:

Using newspapers to build your image, name recognition and prospecting.

Objective:

Using newspaper advertising on a constant basis to build your image is a waste of time and money for most guerrilla marketers. Your objective is to get people calling you through strategic advertising or to build your image through newspaper articles.

Strategy:

As discussed in Strategy 18, use newspapers to target interested prospects. No one is going to call as a result of an ad that lists your name, your qualifications, and what you do. Unless you live in a small town, don't plan on advertising your services. People are interested in what they want, not who you are or what you do. The strategy you should be thinking about is obtaining a newspaper column or "advertorial." At the very least, call the news director at your local paper and send them your credentials. Ask him or her to call you the next time the paper needs backup on a financial news story. Next thing you know, you might be quoted in the news about certain financial events. Your credibility will shoot up and you can reprint the story to use as a prospecting piece in your communications material or to resend to clients as a mailer or email.

Grant's Tip:

A better way to use newspapers is to write financial articles for your local newspapers. It is a great way for you to put out your best ideas and share case study articles for interested investors. Certain well-worded articles can have a tremendous response rate. Writing generic articles on simple financial topics will not garner any calls. If you decide to take up the challenge to write articles, learn what hot buttons your audience may have and trigger calls through your articles. Use the articles in your prospecting and marketing materials by reprinting them in a glossy format and cite on them, "Reprinted from XYZ Newspaper." It adds credibility for prospects who may not know you write for the paper or read the articles.

Use the articles you write as a communications strategy. Resend copies of them to prospects and clients who may then be triggered to call you on a certain topic. You can also resend them through email as a client piece. If you can't obtain a regular column, ask the paper whether you can submit one column in order that you can get reprints for your marketing. They will usually request you to place it in a paid advertorial column–also a great way to establish your marketing materials.

I have tried every type of newspaper advertising to get a response. I set up weekly financial tips ads called "Hicks Financial Tips." I have done full-page ads on why you should do business with me. Nothing works as well as the call-for-booklet response advertising discussed in Strategy 18.

One experience your clients can share with you is what marketing attracted them to you.

For example, I am retired and my investments don't mature for another six months. I don't worry about my finances, yet I see Grant's ad weekly on investment options or articles for retirees. All of a sudden I receive an unexpected inheritance and my investment maturity is coming up in weeks. I need to do something. For the past six months I have seen Grant's ads and articles, so I go to his web site. I then ask some friends about Grant. I have to do something, so I go to my bank for information. They give me some information, but I now need a plan. The bank gives me a plan, but because it is a substantial amount of money, I decide to get a second opinion. I decide to call Grant for a plan. I have been thinking about it for a while, so the advertising and articles worked over time.

The prospect decided to contact me when it was important to him. That is how today's marketing can work if you're consistent and patient.

Get published. How? Make a list of all of the financial publications, associations, and newspapers in your area. Then make a list of all of the editors or business editors. Call them and take them out for breakfast and lunch. Build relationships with them and offer your help once they get to know you. Offer your help by asking that they call you for a comment or quote the next time there is an important financial news story. Then once the article is published, make up glossy reprints and send it to clients and prospects. Put it in your newsletter and marketing items. You are now seen as a valuable resource and you build credibility. You can also help their web sites department by providing articles, comments, and quotes. The cost is your time and maybe breakfast or lunch. Make a list of publications, contact people, build your own public relations list, and make the calls. Watch your credibility soar. The mutual fund companies are masters at sending financial advisors reprints of news articles and stories from their managers. You can use the same strategy for the Internet, television, and radio.

Take a reality check to determine how clearly you understand what your prospects are thinking each time they look at your advertisement.

The owner of a small business takes a leap of faith and contracts to run a weekly ad in the local newspaper with a frequency of once a week for a full year. After five weeks, the results displease him so much that he cancels his contract.

Five ads in five weeks seems like a lot of frequency in marketing. Five exposures do, indeed, establish some momentum. But they don't even come close to creating enough desire to motivate a sale. To truly comprehend how much frequency is enough to spark that sale, you've got to know just what your prospects think from each exposure. Here is exactly what each one thinks as he or she looks at the ad you've run:

The first time a man looks at an advertisement, he does not see it.

The second time, he does not notice it.

The third time, he is conscious of its existence.

The fourth time, he faintly remembers having seen it before.

The fifth time, he reads it.

The sixth time, he turns up his nose at it.

The seventh time, he reads it through and says, "Oh brother!"

The eighth time, he says, "Here's that confounded thing again!"

The ninth time, he wonders if it amounts to anything.

The tenth time, he asks his neighbor if he has tried it.

The eleventh time, he wonders how the advertiser makes it pay.

The twelfth time, he thinks it must be a good thing.

The thirteenth time, he thinks perhaps it might be worth something.

The fourteenth time, he remembers wanting such a thing.

The fifteenth time, he is tantalized because he cannot afford to buy it.

The sixteenth time, he thinks he will buy it some day.

The seventeenth time, he makes a memorandum to buy it.

The eighteenth time, he swears at his poverty.

The nineteenth time, he counts his money carefully.

The twentieth time he sees the ad, he buys what it is offering.

The list you've just read was written by Thomas Smith of London in 1885.

How much of that list is valid right now, today? The answer is all of it.

Guerrillas know that the single most important element of superb marketing is commitment to a focused plan. Do you think commitment is easy to maintain after an ad has run nineteen times and nobody is buying? It's not easy. But marketing guerrillas have the coolness to hang in there because they know how to get into a prospect's unconsciousness, where most purchase decisions are made. They know it takes repetition. This knowledge fuels their commitment. Anyhow, they never thought it was going to be easy.

As real estate is location, location, location, marketing is frequency, frequency, frequency.

Jay's Comments:

Headlines are used in ads, commercials, telemarketing calls, direct mail letters, web sites, sales presentations and more. Can you write great ones?

Every guerrilla destined for marketing victories knows very well that if you have ten hours to spend creating a marketing weapon, you should spend nine of them creating the headline. It's the first impression you make, often the only impression, and the rest of your marketing weapon will live or die by the quality of that headline.

Don't think that just because you don't run print ads your headline is not important. Another way of thinking about a headline to think of it as the first thing you say to prospects. Wise marketing people have said that you should picture yourself knocking on someone's door, which is then opened by a very busy person. You can say one thing before that person slams the door in your face or opens it widely and invites you in. You have the opportunity tell your whole story in one line or to say something so intriguing that the prospect will want to hear more.

You'll have this opportunity in print ads to be sure, but also with first lines of TV spots and radio commercials, with opening lines of letters and postcards, with first statements made by sales reps or telemarketers, in brochures and on web sites, in yellow pages ads and sales videos, in classified ads and infomercials, at trade shows and catalogs. People will decide to read or hear your message or to ignore you completely. It all depends on your headline. If your headline is a loser, you have three strikes against you when you step up to the plate. Lotsa luck!

All guerrillas on earth are delighted that technology now makes marketing easier than ever, that web sites enable them to market with even more fervor, that new software lets them create dynamite marketing materials right in their own offices—but they never lose sight of the fundamentals and headlines are the cornerstone. It's the headline that dictates your positioning in your prospects' minds and it's the headline that will attract either attention or apathy. Nothing you say to a prospect is more important.

In print, you have one line to get that attention. On radio or TV, you have three seconds, and you have those same three seconds with any sales presentations or telemarketing calls. Win attention and interest during that brief period or you won't win it later. There will be no later. Now that I've alerted you as to the importance of headlines, here are 20 hints to help you create winning ones:

1. Know that your headline must either convey an idea or intrigue the reader or listener into wanting to learn more.

2. Speak directly to the reader or listener, one at a time, even if 20 million people will be exposed to your message.

3. Write your headline in newsy style.

4. Use words that have the feeling of an important "announcement."

5. Test headlines that start with the word "announcing."

6. Test headlines that use the word "new."

7. Put a date in your headline.

8. Feature your price, if you're proud of it, in your headline.

9. Feature your very easy payment plan.

10. Announce a free offer and use the word "free."

11. Offer information of value right in your headline.

12. Start to tell a fascinating story; guerrillas know that marketing really is the truth made fascinating.

13. Begin your headline with the words, "How to."

14. Begin your headline with "why," "which," "you," "this" or "advice."

15. Use a testimonial style headline.

16. Offer the reader a test.

17. Use a huge one-word headline.

18. Warn the reader not to delay buying.

19. Address your headline to a specific person; every day there are specific individuals who want exactly what you are offering.

20. Set your headline in the largest type on the page and start your verbal presentations right with the headline.

If the reader or listener isn't stopped by your headline, they'll move onto something else that does stop them. After all, they're looking to be stopped by something and if it's not your message it will be someone else's. Headlines and opening lines are your initial bonds to your prospects. And never forget for one second that what you say is the manner in which you say it. Bend over backwards to be believed. Boring and indirect headlines sabotage thoughtful *copy and brilliant graphics every day of the year, including Christmas.*

Stupendous offers are not accepted by a ready public because the headline or opening line fell down on the job. There are far more terrible headlines than great ones in every edition of every newspaper and magazines. In such an atmosphere, guerrillas thrive. They love when others run headlines that are cutsie-pie and off the point. They are enthralled when competitors run ads that draw attention away from the prime offering because a copywriter wanted to make a pun or get a laugh.

But you can be sure their own headlines always get noticed, generate readership, attract responses, and result in profits. Although a company cannot achieve greatness solely based upon their headlines and opening lines, without solid first impressions, its growth will be seriously impeded. Your job may be to create headlines or to judge them. It is one of your most important tasks.

Examples:

See the newspaper ad on the next page.

Action Summary:

To add to my marketing plans: Yes _____   No _____

Additional information required: Yes _____   No _____

We are all faced with a series of great opportunities brilliantly disguised as unsolvable problems.

-John W. Gardner

finances

More money & few taxes: Part I

How come some retirees have more income and less tax. Over the next few weeks, I will share with you some actual client examples.

Today we have Norma, a 75-year-old retiree in Qualicum Beach. She inherited $200,000 and was looking for income and less tax. She also didn't want to take a lot of risk.

We decided to invest half into GIC's and half into an annuity. While she wanted income she thought she would want access to some capital but not all. Here is what Norma ended up with.

The annuity for $100,000 provided her with $774 per month guaranteed as long as she lives. That's $9,288 per year on $100,000 which will always be there for her. We also put in a 10 year guarantee to her children for 10 years' worth of payments. That means the payments

Where it counts
GRANT HICKS

> We decided to invest the GICs with insurance companies so that we can name a beneficiary and avoid probate costs when Norma dies.

will continue until 2013 if she dies.

The second portion we invested into a one-year and a five-year GIC. The average return on those funds was four per cent combined. We suggested investing into GIC's using the barbell technique, half short term and half long term. Because we don't know what interest rates may do we take the averages, which in this case is four per cent (3.4 per cent one year and 4.6 per cent for five years)

Norma's payout will be $4,000 from the GIC's which gives her a combined income of $13,288 per year on $200,000 or 6.64 per cent approximately.

Now comes the tax.

Since the GICs are fully taxable, she has $4,000 of interest income. We decided to invest the GICs with insurance companies so that we can name a beneficiary on the plan. So when Norma dies, there is no probate costs. The taxable portion on the annuity is

only $2,494 per year, since we used a prescribed annuity for tax efficiency.

Although Norma received income of $13,288 per year she has taxable income of only $6,494 per year. Now Norma doesn't have to worry about market risk or a higher tax bill. She has a steady income and less tax.

When Norma dies, all of the funds and or income will go directly to her children which are her beneficiaries, free of any probate fees.

❏ *Prepared by: Grant W. Hicks, CIM, Retirement Planning Specialist with Partners In Planning Financial Services, Parksville. Information provided is not a solicitation.*

Although obtained from sources considered reliable, it is not guarantee. Comments or questions – Grant can be reached at 248-2824 or email ghicks@pipfs.com. www.ghicks.com

Courtesy of Parksville Qualicum news *www.pqbnews.com*

Throw your heart over the fence and the rest will follow.

-Norman Vincent Peale

STRATEGY 21
Ultimate Public Relations–Part II– Your Marketing Statements

Concept:

What type of messages are you sending to the public every day? Building your image, building your brand, and branding you–whatever you want to call it, it's your marketing statement.

Objective:

To illustrate the necessity for a marketing statement, examine what your prospects are all about. They fit your client profile, they have money to invest, and they are willing to make a purchase or a plan. They are precisely the kind of people you'd love to add to your client list, but they have no intention of buying or investing with you. They just plain don't need what you're offering, and they're very happy investing with their existing advisor (your competition). They're not hostile toward your company or your offering–just indifferent. So the big question is: What would have to happen to move them to be receptive about your product? Here are the answers:

Get inside your prospect's head and connect with him (or her). This is not easy, but I never said creating marketing statements was easy. In Jay's comments accompanying Strategy 8, he discusses fifty reasons why people buy. In the financial services business there is one key way to connect; show the prospect how to avoid pain. You must make that connection. Where to find that connection?

View your offering from the standpoint of a prospect. When you create a shift in perception, you can create a shift in attitude, which can create a shift in behavior–and that's the goal of your marketing statement.

Your marketing statement should be a definition of what your prospect's problems are. This should be evident in all communications, from newsletters to business cards.

Strategy:

Define your focus of what you want a slogan to say about you. Is it service, is it the type of management or planning, is it a feeling, or is it defining your services? Whatever the focus, have fun reviewing other company slogans and look at developing one for yourself. To help you out, here are some of the top slogans of the twentieth century.

"Diamonds are forever"–*DeBeers*.
"Just do it!"–*Nike*.
"The pause that refreshes"–*Coca-Cola*.
"Tastes great, less filling"–*Miller Lite*.
"We Try Harder"–*Avis*.
"Good to the last drop"–*Maxwell House*.
"Breakfast of champions"–*Wheaties*.
"Does she...or doesn't she?"–*Clairol*.
"When it rains it pours"–*Morton Salt*.
"Where's the beef?"–*Wendy's*.

Here are some examples from the financial industry:

"What are you doing after work?"–*AGF Mutual Funds*.
"Gain from our perspective"–*Franklin Templeton Investments*.
"Invest with confidence"–*T. Row Price*.
"A firm committed to your evolving needs"–*Charles Schwab*.
"Invest with discipline"–*AIM Mutual Funds*.

Grant's Tip:

At the very least, use one slogan in your marketing. Some advisors work under two names and therefore can use two slogans. Use the slogan on business cards, letterhead, envelopes, newsletters, and other correspondence. In marketing, this is also known as a USP, or unique selling proposition. If I meet you at a cocktail party and ask you what you do, saying "I'm a financial advisor" doesn't tell me anything unique about you. Changing your title may help. For example I have "Retirement Planning Specialist" as my title. But if you ask me what I do, my answer is "I help successful retirees maximize their income and save income tax to enjoy a fulfilling retirement." Now does that pique your curiosity and motivate you to ask me more questions? Your marketing statement or unique selling proposition should do just that. It should be short and enticing, not a paragraph explaining what you do.

Some advisors have taken on a strategy that deals with their clients' hot buttons, such as focusing on tax and estate planning. They are known as the advisors who will save you money and create a large estate. I know some advisors who can help you save tax money through specialized tax structures. Do you have a focus for your clients?

Look at all of the companies that you deal with or read about, and you will start to see different themes for different companies. The slogan can sometimes define a company or give you a sense of their purpose. It can also create a sense of perception about a company. It is a way to brand you.

You can influence them with how you market yourself.

To market yourself properly, answer these three big questions:
1. Who are you now? If friends described you, what would they say? Be honest rather than complimentary.
2. What do you want out of life? Be specific.
3. How will you know when you've reached your goals?

If you can't answer these questions, you're doomed to accidental marketing, spending your life reacting instead of responding; and the odds are against you reaching your goals.

How do you send messages and market yourself right now? With your appearance, to be sure. You also market with your eye contact and body language, your habits, and your speech patterns. You market yourself in print with your letters, email, web site, notes, faxes, brochures, and other printed material. You also market yourself with your attitude–big time. You market yourself with your ethics.

How people judge you: You may not be aware of it, but people are constantly judging and assessing you by noticing many things about you. You must be sure the messages of your marketing don't fight your dreams. What are people using to base their opinions, to make their decisions about you?

• Clothing	• Teeth	• Home
• Hair	• Smile	• Nervous habits
• Weight	• What you carry	• Handshake
• Height	• Eye contact	• Stationery
• Jewelry	• Gait	• Availability
• Facial hair	• Posture	• Writing ability
• Makeup	• Handwriting	• Phone use
• Business card	• Spelling	• Enthusiasm
• Laugh	• Hat	• Energy level
• Glasses	• Thoughtfulness	• Comfort on line
• Neatness	• Car	
• Smell	• Office	

You're fully aware of your intentional marketing and possibly even invest time, energy and imagination into it, not to mention money.

But you may be undermining that investment if you're not paying attention to things that matter to others even more than what you say: Keeping promises, punctuality, honesty, demeanor, respect, gratitude, sincerity, feedback, initiative, reliability. They also notice passion—or the absence of it. They notice how well you listen to them.

What to Do Now: Now that you know these things, what should you do? Although Ben Franklin himself said three of the hardest things in the world are diamonds, steel, and knowing yourself, here's a three-step plan to get you started on the road to self-awareness and self-marketing acumen:

1. Write a positioning statement about yourself. Identify just who you are and the positive things that stand out most about you.
2. Identify your goals. Put into writing the three things you'd most like to achieve during the next three months, three years, five years, and ten years.
3. State your measuring stick. Write the details of how you will know when you've achieved your goals. Be brief and specific.

To guerrilla market yourself, simply be aware of and in control of the messages you send. Do that and your goals will be a lot easier to attain. Are you a financial advisor? Or are you a retirement planning specialist or counselor? Because some states and provinces regulate our titles, a description or slogan stating what you do will define you and/or your services. Make sure you check with compliance first before using your title. I have seen titles such as "Mutual Funds Advisor." How does that help me if I am a prospect? Do I need to buy mutual funds, or do I need to ensure that I invest for a secure retirement and future? Remember one thing. You help people achieve financial goals. Be passionate and enthusiastic about what you do. It will make your marketing a lot easier.

So, in your marketing statement make sure you identify what's important to your client or prospect that you're passionate about helping them with. If I was a client of yours and I was getting ready to retire, what would I want from you? I would want a comprehensive retirement plan, a conservative investment style, and an approach that minimizes taxes. These are some of the features that I would want but what are the true benefits I want? I want peace of mind, security and safety. I want less worry. The real emotional benefits are what I am after, not just financial benefits. Most advisors compete on features and not benefits. Focus your marketing on the benefits such as, "Helping you achieve financial security and peace of mind through retirement strategies for you and your family proven for years and decades."

Make your title exciting. I meet financial advisors and before they know me I ask them, "What do you do?" The typical response is, "I'm a financial planner." Have you ever had someone say back to you, "Wow, how exciting, Tell me more"? Now how about giving an interesting or exciting spin on your business card title. If you met me on a golf course and asked me what I did, my reply would be " I help retirees maximize their income and have less worry in retirement." The typical response is, "How do you do that?" or "Are you an accountant or tax professional?" It conveys an exciting message and describes what I do instead of developing a script and repeating a paragraph of marketing messages. Try it next time you meet someone new. Email us the results.

Jay's Comments:

The prehistoric man, Uba, spent all day in the rain trying to catch a fish because his family was very hungry and in dire need of food. But he was unable to grab a fish from the stream even though he occasionally got his hands on one. Frustrated and weak from hunger, he just couldn't grab any fish firmly enough because it would slither from his hands and return to the stream. Worse yet, the light rain turned to a heavy rain and Uba was forced to seek shelter in a nearby cave.

Entering it, when his eyes became accustomed to the dark, he noticed a series of paintings in the cave. One depicted a deer. Another represented a godlike figure. But it was the third that captured his attention.

There on the cave wall, was a simple drawing—a stick figure of a man holding a long stick. At the end of the stick, a fish was impaled. Suddenly, Uba got the idea! Within an hour, he returned to his family carrying five fish, all of which he had caught with a stick that had one end sharpened.

Uba's family was saved by a meme. A meme is a self-explanatory symbol, using words, action, sounds, or in this case, pictures, that communicate an entire idea. Uba may have discovered the first meme in history.

Since Uba's time, there have been many more memes. In fact, as much as you used to see the word "Internet," during the nineties, that's about as many times as you'll see the word "memes" during the aughts.

Memes in marketing are a whole new idea. Some have existed, but those were created long before the concept of memes was known. The word meme, though coined in 1976 by Oxford biologist Richard Dawkins in his book, "The Selfish Gene," has been the architect of human behavior since the beginning of time. The wheel was a major improvement in transportation and conveyance, and was also a meme because it was a self-explanatory symbol representing a complete idea.

There are three things you should know about memes:
1. It's the lowest common denominator of an idea, a basic unit of communication.

2. It has the ability to alter human behavior.
3. It is energized with emotion.

In guerrilla marketing, a meme's purpose is profiting, selling, motivating, and communicating instantly how your product or service improves lives. It can do this with words (Lean Cuisine), pictures (Marlboro cowboy), sounds (from the valley of the Jolly, ho ho ho, Green Giant), actions (Clydesdales pulling Budweiser wagon), or imagery (Burger-King's flame-broiled image).

For guerrillas, a meme is a concept that has been so simplified that anybody can understand it instantly and easily. Within two seconds you must convey who you are, why someone should buy from you instead of a competitor, trigger an emotional response and generate a desire.

To put you even more on my wavelength, consider many of the other memes we have learned to know and possibly even love:

Healthy Choice
Be Direct–Dell
Intel inside
Got milk?
Capitalist Tool–Forbes
Panasonic–just slightly ahead of our time
Where do you want to go today?
America Online
Drivers wanted–VW
I'm going to Disneyland!
UPS–moving at the speed of business
M&Ms melt in your mouth, not in your hands
Be all that you can be
SlimFast
Weight Watchers
NBC–must-see TV
A diamond is forever
Toys R Us
Staples–yeah, we've got what you want
Foot Joy
V for victory
Gatorade poured on winning coach
Things go better with Coke
7-Up–The Uncola
I want my MTV!
The Mall of America
Snap, Crackle, and Pop

Keep in mind that in marketing, a meme is an idea or concept that has been refined, distilled, stripped downs to its bare essentials, then super-simplified in such a way that anybody can grasp its meaning instantly and effortlessly.

Try to imagine a motorist speeding down a highway, just entering a curve. All of a sudden, a billboard comes into view. It shows a mutilated child, an ambulance, paramedics, flashing lights, weeping parents and a grim police officer. The billboard copy: Speed kills.

The combined effect of the photo and copy constitutes a meme that instantly, effortlessly and lucidly transmits an entire complex message into a human mind in a single involuntary glance. If you saw it while driving, there is little doubt that you would cut your speed without even thinking about it on a rational level.

From Geoff Ayling's Rapid Response Advertising (Business and Professional Publishing, 1998, Warriewood, Australia, info@woodslane.com.cu) we learn that memes have an enormous impact on our lives. They invade our minds without either our knowledge or our permission, and initiate a chain reaction. They create an involuntary shift in perception, which in turn creates a shift in attitude, which creates a shift in behavior—and that is the ultimate goal of all marketing.

With so much marketing and advertising, both on line and off line, assailing our senses, it's more important now than ever to create a meme for your own company. I didn't say it was easy, but I am saying it is mandatory if you're to stand out in an ever-competitive crowd—a crowd that relishes its time more than ever. Don't be like Uba and wait till you've all wet and hungry.

A good friend of mine wrote a great book entitled *Life After Wealth, When is Enought Engough?* - By Franco Lombardo - Roper House Publishing. Check out *www.lifeafterwealth.com*, take the quiz, then order the book. It is a MUST read for Financial Professionals.

Action Summary:

To add to my marketing plans: Yes _____   No _____

Additional information required: Yes _____   No _____

To attain knowledge, add things everyday, to attain wisdom, remove things everyday.
                                                                -Lao-Tse in Tao Te Ching

I shall either find a way or make one.

-Eleanor Roosevelt

STRATEGY 22

Successful Seminar Strategies

Concept:

Seminars are a very popular way to attract and retain clients. Call them workshops, luncheons, meetings, or whatever; seminars can be very profitable for both new and existing clients.

Objective:

I can write a book on this one idea alone. The objectives are to educate existing clients and generate more business and referrals, generate new clients, or both. You may have different objectives such as educating clients or prospects, introducing new ideas, or other. But the bottom line is: How do you generate more business from seminars? Seminars should be a way to attract more clients or assets–period. No matter how you slice it, you want more business.

Strategy:

Who is your target audience? In what is your target audience interested? What is the desired result? For example, if you do a seminar on tax planning, do the clients feel motivated to take any action during or after the seminar, or are they just going to file the information away and see their accountant later? If you're giving a tax seminar, mention a case study where a client (similar to your target audience) saved thousands on taxes using several different investment strategies recommended by the advisor. It is a sample of solutions that fit your target audience.

Here are some tips for successful seminars:
- Plan your overall objectives.
- Plan the marketing mix of your seminar.
- Plan your invitations and approach.
- Plan your target group.
- Plan your target list of attendees.
- Plan your date and location.
- Plan your type of seminar–large or small.
- Plan your speakers and topics.
- Plan your venue and details.
- Plan your staff time and resources.

- Plan your budget.
- Plan your handouts and questionnaires.
- Plan your equipment.
- Plan your talk and time.
- Review all details over and over.
- Plan your follow up.
- Repeat and improve.

Grant's Tip:

The great debate. Some advisors say seminars and meetings don't work anymore. Clients and prospects see it as a sales push. These are the same advisors who are experts at seminars after holding two or three and finding out they didn't work for them. They are the same people that held public seminars. Today's advisor needs to hold targeted seminars. Let me give you an example. What if you sent out a wedding-style invitation to people of a certain community and invited them to the local club to a seminar on a topic that was important to them? Mail an exclusive invitation for residents of any affluent neighborhood in North America (get the mailing information through post offices or directories) to discuss a topic specific to their community needs or concerns such as estate tax rates lowered via estate trusts. Include lunch or dinner and hold it at the local club. The club should help you with the meeting because it can possibly attract new members as well. This is an example of targeted seminars and not just public seminars. How many exclusive communities are there in your area?

Barry Freedman's four keys to making your seminar work (courtesy of *Deena Katz's Tools and Templates for Your Practice: For Financial Advisors, Planners, and Wealth Managers*, Bloomberg Pr, 2001) are:
- *Don't give the seminar to educate; give it to disturb.*
- *Don't give it to inform; define problems.*
- *Don't give the seminar to offer solutions; provide just a foretaste of solutions.*
- *Don't do it to sell products; do it to sell YOU and your style.*

Ask your board of directors or top clients what type of seminars or information they might be interested in. Find top advisors who have completed successful seminars.

You need to practice, practice, practice and copy from the best to make seminars work. I have done several and, after doing a dozen or so, I found a formula that works. Have daytime seminars in a top-notch venue with a targeted list of clients, and follow up with them until you get them into a seminar or two.

Some of the top representatives in the country have been doing the same seminar every month for ten years. They have their seminars so finely tuned that they never worry how they will grow their businesses from one year to the next.

A couple of ideas that work: First are client workshops, where you ask your clients to invite a friend. Birds of a feather flock together. You can mix your audience with clients and prospects, so that if a prospect asks one of your clients about you after the meeting and you receive a strong endorsement, the offer you presented seems much more inviting.

Second are conference calls. You can do a luncheon conference call with top managers for clients or prospects. Discuss, after the conference call, why the investment should take place now. Make sure there is a sense of urgency created during the seminar and a recommended implementation schedule.

You can get creative with topics and speakers. Remember two things people remember–pictures and stories. Paint the picture for them by telling them a great story.

One successful idea I learned is to time your seminar. Retirees are less receptive to lunch, afternoon, or evening presentations. The best time is breakfast. An early morning presentation that includes breakfast and coffee is best. Another tip I learned is to co-market with the facility in which you are holding your meetings. First, ask what other meetings are scheduled for that date so there is no conflict. I once held a seminar at a hotel the same day one of our major political leaders was holding a meeting. Some people ended up going to the political meeting instead of mine. Then ask whether there are coupons or special invitations that could be printed up to bring these people back to their restaurant or to recommend the facilities. The meeting coordinator is usually delighted to make something up and it's another free giveaway that you get to offer.

If you want prequalified prospects at your seminars, display the minimum account size or minimum investable assets in your advertising, such as "$250,000 or more investable assets." That way you can offer a free financial consultation for attending. You want to be able to spend time with investors that are at or above your minimum target.

Jay's Comments:

Free Seminars

You can attract a fair number of hot prospects if you offer free seminars or clinics on your topic of expertise. Don't expect the crowd to be standing room only, but do expect the people who show up to be seriously interested in what you have to say. As with free consultations, you're not allowed to give a sales presentation—at least not at first. But you are encouraged to give a lot of valuable information of worth and value, information that proves your authority. I recommend that your free seminar or clinic be one hour in length. You should use the first 45 minutes to fill the heads of your attendees with solid and usable data. You can use the final 15 minutes to sell your offering. People won't resent the sales pitch because you've given them a lot of meaty information before you tried to sell.

If you do a superb job at providing worthwhile information during the first 45 minutes, the 15 minutes at the end should be a breeze—because you've already established trust with your audience. Some of my clients report that 33% of attendees end up becoming customers. And it will happen not because you invested money in marketing, but because you invested your time, energy, imagination, and expertise.

Some business owners improve upon that one-third closing ratio by doing one of three additional things:
• They have a different person take the stage during the final 15 minutes, someone with a knack for motivating groups of people.
• They have salespeople in the doorways exiting the venue, thanking people as they depart, and selling to them at the same time.
• They make a very special offer that's available that day only.

Hold your free seminar at your own place of business, if possible. Market your seminars in on-line newsgroups and forums, in chat rooms, and in emailings. You might post signs in appropriate locations and announce your session at community groups or in community newsletters. Since you won't be charging for it, perhaps you can enlist the aid of the media.

Experiment by offering the seminar at two different times—something like twelve noon and seven in the evening. Experiment by offering it on Saturdays or weekdays. You can determine the best times and days based upon the attendance.

Additional Resources:
• Contact your peer group for ideas.
• Contact your top wholesaler for ideas, topics, and speakers.
• Contact your top clients to discuss topics of interest.
• Create a list of target clients and/or prospects.
• Check out my web site under seminars and marketing for more ideas.

Examples:
See the following Tips for a Successful Seminar and sample invitations.

Action Summary:

To add to my marketing plans: Yes _____   No _____

Additional information required: Yes _____   No _____

If I have been able to see farther than others, it is because I have stood on the shoulders of giants.

-Sir Isaac Newton

Tips for a Successful Seminar

Two months prior:
• Decide on the venue, speakers, topics, agenda, and refreshments; plan a budget and target clients or revenue.
• Develop attendee database.
• Arrange advertising, invitations, and/or mailer with local newspapers. Arrange for professional-looking invitations. A variation is to send out handwritten postcard invitations.
• Arrange the venue and refreshments and/or meals and, if you select to serve a meal, send out meal choices in RSVP envelopes just like a wedding invitation.
• Arrange for speakers to attend, requesting confirmation in writing.
• Look into cooperative marketing if possible.

One month prior:
• Ensure that advertising is carried out as requested.
• Ensure that all necessary tools/equipment will be available for speakers.

Two weeks prior:
• Call all clients, etc., to remind of seminar.
• Prepare sign-up sheets and questionnaires for seminar.
• Arrange for door prizes–possibly supplied by fund companies.
• Arrange for promotional materials from fund companies, some to be included in presentation folder given to attendees at the door and some to be placed on display in seminar room.
• Practice the presentation and opening and closing remarks.

On day of seminar:
• Ensure all materials are ready.
• Arrive at seminar location at least one hour prior to start to ensure seating properly arranged and all other requirements are in place.
• Set up a table near the entrance to the room and arrange for helpers to assist in registering attendees and handing out folders.

Post-seminar, within two weeks:
• Advise winners (if not present at time of drawing) of door prizes and arrange for pickup.
• Send out information requested on questionnaires.
• Send out thank-you cards to attendees and guest speakers.
• Call all attendees and no-shows to obtain feedback and set appointments. Do not send out follow-up letters; make the calls!

Sample Invitations:

As part of my continued commitment to being one of the best retirement planners on Vancouver Island and educating investors, I am delighted to present a conference call seminar with Eric Sample, Senior Vice-President of the XYZ Group of Funds.

Eric is the lead manager of the XYZ Dividend Fund. The objective of this fund is to generate a high level of dividend income and to preserve capital.

Please join us for lunch in the boardroom of our Partners in Planning Parksville office at 12 noon on February 14, 2002.

Please RSVP to Carol Hagel at 248-2824. As seating may be limited, please register promptly.

Sponsored in part by XYZ Funds.

An Invitation...From Grant Hicks

As part of my continued commitment to being one of the best retirement planners on Vancouver Island and educating investors, I am delighted to present the following breakfast seminar:

Monday, January 13, 2003, 9:30 to 10:30 a.m.

The Boardroom, Partners In Planning Office.

Speaker: Joe Wholesaler, Vice-President ZZ Top Financial.

Topic: Income options for conservative retirees–looking for more income.

Learn about:
• Today's options for retirement income.
• How to generate more income.
• How to minimize taxes with retirement income.
• Income portfolios.

Please join us for a light breakfast and feel free to invite a friend!

Please RSVP Carol Hagel at 248-2824 as soon as possible as seating in our Boardroom is limited to twelve persons only!

This seminar is sponsored in part by XYZ Asset Management.

Mutual Funds are not guaranteed; their values change frequently and past performance may not be repeated. Commissions, trailing commissions, management fees and expenses all may be associated with mutual fund investments. Please read the prospectus before investing.

Chapter 3

Getting New Clients from Internal Marketing

Being rich is having money, being wealthy is having time.

-Stephen Swid

STRATEGY 23
How to Double Your Business by Cloning Your Top Clients—The Secret Strategy of Getting Referrals

---

Concept:

Are you ready for the secret? There are two parts to it. First you have to ask. Second you have to ask often. That's it, you have to ask and make it part of your vocabulary. Just like when you learned your ABCs and 123s, this teacher says learn to ask for referrals early and often.

Objective:

Finding the best concepts for your business in developing referrals. While there are several concepts of developing referrals, finding one that fits your style and your business is unique.

Strategy:

Here is a list of great referral marketing ideas:
• Referral research method.
• Getting-married philosophy.
• Nonverbal referral communication.
• Up-front referral business.
• Competition-target method.
• Clone-your-best-clients method.
• Centers of influence referrals.

The first idea is to do research on selected referral targets. Show your clients or centers of influence the ideal client profile you are seeking or targeting. Let them know you are constantly trying to improve your business to help people achieve their financial goals. While clients are happy with the services they receive, you would like to interview potential prospects to conduct research on the marketing, communication, and advice that you help people with and the perceived value. Ask them for names of people that match your unique profile purely to do market research.

You want to let them know that it will greatly help identify and target your ideal prospect. Then call these referrals and you will be amazed at the amount of information you can gather about your target market. How they network, the clubs or associations to which they belong, the type of advisors they work with, and how they network. Along the way the people on whom you conduct research may provide referrals directly to you.

The next referral strategy is the getting-married philosophy. Think for a moment if you were to marry, who you would want to meet (who is associated with that person) to find out more about them. First you may meet their parents; you might want to meet their friends, colleagues at work, and possibly their neighbors.

We'll ask the client, "Now that you have become a client of ours, have you talked with anyone in your family, at work, or your friends about us?" Chances are if they just moved a large investment account to you, they at least told their best friends. In their center of people close to them they have the ability to send friends and family your way as referrals. Talking about it up front may make it easier to refer these people to you. You can ask if any of these people, family, friends, or work colleagues might need your help and say you will be more than happy to accommodate their needs. While they might not fit your ideal profile, usually birds of a feather flock together and their friends' profiles will be similar to theirs. Get married to your clients. At least help the people around them.

Nonverbal Messages:
• Newsletters. At the bottom of my newsletters, I write, "I would like to thank my clients for thinking of me and helping their families and friends by referring their names to me. Referrals are always welcome and greatly appreciated." Another idea for your newsletter is have a draw for a dinner gift certificate for clients who referred business to you, announcing the winners there, too.
• Message visible on your desk or business cards. On my desk, my business card holder carries the message, "The best compliment you can give is a referral."
• Letters to clients. Why not select a few clients to start with and send them a letter asking for referrals. Then follow up with a phone call, not to directly ask for referrals, but to see if they received the letter and ask if they would like join you for coffee so you can share an investment idea. You can ask for referrals once you see how they feel about referrals.
• Client surveys. Positive or negative, everyone needs feedback. Surveys are a great way to ask for referrals if your clients are happy with you. Only survey clients from whom you are comfortable soliciting referrals.
• Seminars and seminar invitations. You can see the strategy on seminars, but you don't want to miss these ideas. First, in your invitations, always state that your clients are free to bring a friend or family member to your seminar. Second, on the bottom of all seminar feedback forms I always put, please add

these people to your next seminar invitation. I have received valuable referrals from this form information.

• Worksheets or handouts.

Verbal Messages:

• Up-front business referral. When I first heard this idea being presented by a top performing financial advisor from Vancouver, I loved it. It is something that you cannot decide to do when it seems right, but it should become part of every new client interview. I am referring to establishing the terms of how you do business. You would state to a new client that part of doing business with you is generating referrals for you so you can spend more time on managing client goals and less time marketing to new people. Up front, you tell the new client the profile of people you work with and that he or she should help you identify prospects, and tell you about these people. If the client agrees, you have a solid basis to regularly ask for referrals, and both of you are comfortable with this type of business practice. Remember it must be done up front each time a new client decides to do business with you.

• Competition target method. This method of referrals can be fun, especially if your target market is a certain segment of business owners. For example, let's say you do group benefits for engineering firms. After you deal with one firm, ask the representative about the competition. A firm will usually know its good competitors in town and may even know them well. Once you start asking about the competitors, ask if you can contact them giving the referring company's name. If they don't like their competitors, sometimes they will be reluctant to allow you to use their company name as a referral source, but the respect of competition usually makes it an interesting conversation. You can usually find a lot of information about a target group by asking for referrals to that group. The clients are usually more than willing to talk about their competition, positive or even sometimes negative.

• Clone your best clients. One of my best clients came to me as a result of asking a client to invite a friend to one of my meetings. My client tried to get his friends to come and see me for quite some time, although I didn't know that. When I asked for a referral, he mentioned this person's name and that he had tried to get them to come and talk to me. It was only when I asked for referrals that I found out that the client was trying to help me, but it wasn't working. Have a referral talk as part of your vocabulary. This is uncomfortable; asking for more business after the client has already given you business. However, once you do it 30 times for 30 days, it becomes a habit. It will be the best habit you pick up and by using that talk every day, over and over, you will go farther and faster than you ever thought possible.

• Have a worksheet or handout for clients. To remind you of the referral talk, use a cheat sheet to help you make it a habit. Use the Guerrilla Marketing Action Planning Worksheet at the back of this book.
• Centers of influence referrals–as discussed in Strategy 13.

Grant's Tip:

Try this exercise. Write down from memory the names of your top ten clients. Next to their names write the amount of assets or amount of insurance they bought, or both. Now write how they became clients–referral, seminar, etc. If it was a referral, write the name of the referrer beside the name. You should have 10 to 20 names down on paper. Now add up the total amount of assets that the referral sources have with you as well as your top 10 clients. From that list of 10 to 20 names, write down that total and multiply it by two. Would that make a difference in your business if you could do that? Would you have the best year ever? Now your task is to have coffee with these 10 to 20 people and ask for referrals, period. It's not as important as what you say but in the next 30 days make those calls, have some coffee, iced tea, latte, etc., and generate at least one or two referrals from the list. Sounds simple. Guess what? It is, this is a strategy I used to clone my top clients and it works. The key is to look for additional top prospects who are bigger than your top clients. You are now prospecting up, up, and up!

Create a points system and make it a game. If you need eight referrals per month, think of the sources that will generate them and how. When you know you will generate, by habit, one or two referrals a day to add to your database, it's exciting to know that you sometimes don't have enough time to keep up with them. One person with whom I have worked with knows how many referrals are usually generated during the course of the year and from whom; so at the start of each year, he has an estimate of the amount of business he will automatically generate through his referral networks. See Strategy 24.

Jay's Comments:

Guerrillas don't try to grow only in linear fashion by adding new customers. They grow geometrically by mining current customers. There are three ways to make a business more profitable and two of those ways lack something in the way of marketing wisdom. The first way and least likely to generate substantial profits but most likely to generate substantial heartaches is by waiting for word-of-mouth marketing to bring those clients and customers to you. An astonishing number of businesses follow this course and eventually learn that it leads directly over a cliff and into despair. This is called no-growth and it is very inexpensive but no fun.

A second way to make a business flourish is to market the business to the world and to your prospects. You can never stop doing this because it's a superb source of new customers, but if you follow this highway and no other, you'll find that it leads to a dead end. But even before you hit it, you'll run out of fuel or money because this method, known as linear growth, is very expensive, not to mention frustrating. Glamorous? Yes. High profile? Yes again. Profitable? No. Not profitable. It costs the linear growth people six times more to market their products and services than it costs guerrillas with the identical offerings—because guerrillas know a third and better way to beautify their treasuries.

The third way to create profits is to fully comprehend the remarkable worth of existing customers, then lean upon them for repeat business and referral business. This is called geometric growth because it has more dimensions than linear growth and greater magnitudes than no growth. In the quest for profits, it's the best way to fly. Guerrillas are sure to offer enough quality and service, enthusiasm and flexibility, to earn word of mouth recommendations hand over tongue. They are also assiduous about marketing their offers and benefits to attract prospects, even create prospects out of disinterested humanoids. And they are nothing short of awesome when it comes to converting those prospects into paying customers. But linear growth alone is not good enough for them.

Geometric growth is where it's at and guerrillas do it by focusing big-time on follow-up, which leads to repeat sales, and on referrals, which lead to referral sales. By combining good word of mouth, consistent linear growth and abundant geometric growth, they soon learn that marketing is easy, business is fun and life can be a dream. Of the three ways to grow, no growth is the cheapest because it costs absolutely nothing but faith, and linear growth is the most expensive because it costs absolutely nothing but money. Geometric growth, as all good guerrilla marketing, asks you to make an investment of time, energy and imagination. Spend actual time developing a follow-up plan, one which calls for you to stay in touch with existing customers about six times a year. Do it with snail-mail letters and postcards, email, faxes, phone calls, personal visits, gift packages, greeting cards and anything else your imagination can cook up. This is no time to be cool. This is when to be effusive. Grant talks about these ideas in Chapter 5 and 6.

After you've got a fully-loaded follow-up plan, ready to put into force within 48 hours of every sale you make—for that timing is part of superb follow-up—devote the time to create a referral plan. Many guerrilla financial advisors report that up to 70% of their business comes from referrals. And they don't just sit around and wait for those referrals, lighting candles and praying. They begin going for referral business right from the start. The guerrilla dentist receives a phone call to make an appointment and asks, "Is this appointment for you or for your entire family?" The guerrilla always asks new client "Who referred you to us?" and then mentions that referrals are a very important part of the business.

That same guerrilla probably brings up the gifts that he gives clients who refer new people. He writes to his clients at least twice a year asking for the names of people who might benefit from getting adding to his mailing list—asking only for the name of five people and enclosing a postpaid reply envelope to make everything easy. That guerrilla realizes that there are about ten good referral systems and he's using five of them. The more you market geometrically, the less you invest in marketing. Because it costs only one-sixth as much to sell something to an existing than a new client, follow-up is paramount. Referral clients bring down the cost of doing business as well because they come to you at no cost or very little cost.

You don't need me to herald the benefits of growing geometrically. You only have to talk to a guerrilla. Better yet, try implementing aggressive follow-up and referral plans for yourself. Be your own guerrilla. Then you won't need me to give you any geometry lessons.

Action Summary:

To add to my marketing plans: Yes _____   No _____

Additional information required: Yes _____   No _____

A single conversation across the table with a wise man is better than ten years' study of books.

- Chinese proverb

Character is made in the small moments of our lives.

-Phillips Brooks

STRATEGY 24
Creating a Referral System

Concept:

Question: Have you ever received a new piece of business and thought afterwards, "Oops, I forgot to thank the person who referred these people to me?" Then you think, you should do something special to thank the client for the referral. So you go out, spend an hour or so, and buy a gift. Then you mail the gift. Not a bad idea; however, it can be improved upon by creating a system to make it a habit. (Unless you don't receive many referrals, in which case you might as well throw this book away now.)

Objective:

As discussed in the strategy on gaining referrals, the goal is to gain valuable ones that match your ideal client makeup. First of all, use the worksheet and define your ideal client makeup. For example if I am seeking clients ages 55+ and investable assets of $250,000 plus, how many referrals do I need each week or month to reach my goal? If my goal is $6 million new assets each year, I will need three or four referrals per month to develop strategies and two per month to sign on as clients. Create a system so the client, the referrer, and you are involved in the process.

Strategy:

The goal is to get the communication flowing between yourself, your new client, and the referrer. Once the new client signs on, I ask if they can call the referrer to thank them for introducing me. Then I send a thank-you card or letter and a gift. If this is a first-time referral from somebody, you should make it so that it appears as if this is the biggest thing he or she could ever have done for you. After they would have received the gift, make a phone call to touch base thank him (or her) again for the referral. At that time, if you are comfortable doing so, you might ask if there's anyone else. The referrer received two phone calls and a gift, just for referring one person.

As always, the gift must be approved by your compliance department. One idea is to send a lunch gift certificate. A second idea to thank them both, your new client and the referrer, is to take both of them out for lunch. It's important that both people understand the system of appreciation for referrals, and that you appreciate these referrals. I always tell my sister, who is an actress, "It's not what they say about you that's important, it's important that they're talking about you."

Grant's Tip:

The follow-up system or process is the key. For a first referral, make sure a gift is sent. You don't have to send a gift every time, but for the first referral it's crucial.

The follow-up to the referrer, letting him know whether the people he referred became clients, is also very important. If I sent you three referrals and none of them became your clients, I would start to wonder why. But if you called me and explained that these three people are in the process of becoming clients, I would feel more comfortable. Feedback and tracking is key to all referrals.

I use the referral worksheet (see Referral tracking Review Worksheet on page 46) in several ways. First, to record the referral, the referrer, and the type of referral. Second, to make sure that the referrer was sent a thank-you card and/or gift. Third, to track during the calendar year where and what type of business was generated. I can go back each year and look at the referral sheets to see how many referrals, what type, and from whom I am generating them. For example, I may be receiving a lot from accountants, but not from lawyers; and I may want to pay more attention to the lawyers.

If you receive several referrals from one individual or source, such as an accountant, track the referrals received as well as those sent. It is also very important to receive feedback from the person to whom you sent the referral, to make sure you are helping reach your clients goals in a satisfactory way. On the form you would keep track of this, and periodically check back if you have not heard what happened with your referral. With referrals, if you give them, then you get them. Make it a goal in your client review planning and interviews to try to generate at least one referral. Imagine if you sent out 200 referrals this year. Do you think you might get a few back in return?

Jay's Comments:

Referral Program

An overwhelming majority of successful business owners will tell you flat out that obtaining referrals is the most powerful tactic for attracting new customers. They'll add that your best source of new customers is old customers. And all you've got to do is ask them. Simply review your customer list and your list of contacts, then ask these good people to recommend you to others. Testimonials are nearly as good as money in the bank, but referrals really are money in the bank.

To get the most, make it easy for people to give you referrals. One technique is to send them an email asking for the names of three people who might benefit from hearing from you. By keeping the number down to three, it will not be a daunting task for them to furnish names and email addresses to you. By doing it by email, you'll cut out the expense and time you need to devote to this.

Everyone who works for you should be trained in asking for referrals. They should say something like, "We're able to keep our prices in line by getting customer referrals rather than relying on expensive advertising. We'd be deeply appreciative if you could give us the names of just three people who you feel should be added to our mailing list." The leads that convert to sales at the highest percentage are referrals from current customers. As a guerrilla, you treat these people right, so they'll want to help you.

A referral program is a simply system that is set up for you to send letters asking for referrals automatically and on a regular basis—about twice a year. Thank those people who supply them. No other gift is necessary. I once participated in a teleconference with 300 chiropractors. We asked how many of them got 50 percent of their business from referrals and 100 of them did. We asked how many got 80 percent or more from referrals and only three did. When we asked how they did it, they told us that all their employees asked for referrals. Even the telephone operator was involved. When a person called to make an appointment, she would ask, "Is this only for you or do you also want to make an appointment for some members of your family?" Such an easy question! So many referrals came from it!

By having a referral plan and sticking to it, you'll begin to amass a list of new customers. And each one can give you another three referrals. Make it extra easy by having your referral email letters written and ready to send. Then get ready for a new influx of profits.

Examples:
Referral Tracking Review Worksheet on page 46

Action Summary:

To add to my marketing plans: Yes _____   No _____

Additional information required: Yes _____   No _____

Do what you do so well that your customers come back and bring their friends.

- Walt Disney

Imagination is more important than knowledge.

-Albert Einstein

STRATEGY 25

Be a Life Planner–Build a Life-planning Referral Network

Concept:

Be a resource to your clients by focusing on their lives as well as on their finances. If you had resources in several areas, then you would be seen as more valuable.

Objective:

This strategy has one main objective but several variations to achieve the main objective, which is: To be seen as a trusted resource to clients in more areas than just financial goals.

Strategy:

When I first heard of financial planners becoming more holistic in their approach, it sounded kind of strange. After all, we are here to help people financially, not become life coaches. But when you look at different ways to take a holistic approach, several ideas come to mind. One idea came from Barry LaValley of LaValley Communications in Nanaimo, BC. His concepts are the next wave for financial advisors to embrace.

Life planning is the process of helping people focus on the true values and motivations of their lives. It is in using these values, motivations, goals, and objectives to guide the planning process.

It is providing a framework for making choices and decisions in life that have financial consequences or implications, according to Steven Shagrin, Past president, International Society for Retirement and Life Planning.

To discuss this concept in one chapter is impossible. However, here are some ideas to get you thinking about becoming more holistic in your approach.

Build Your Own Yellow Pages:
1. Develop a list of potential contacts in other areas of peoples' lives.
2. Use the list to create a referral directory of services for your clients.
3. Circulate the list, with permission, to your clients once per year.
4. Eventually you will see the list expand because of your conscious effort to create your own yellow pages for clients–you will see that once people find that they are not on the list, they will want to be.

Build Your Own Holistic Planning Questions:

1. Start recording information about clients' lives and goals. This can include spiritual, physical, social, recreational, family, educational, or other pursuits in life.

2. Use this information along with your yellow pages to help people in other areas of their lives. For example, let's say you have a client who wishes someday to go on a cruise. You define her (or his) finances as how much she may plan to put aside on the cruise. Then ask her if she has a travel agent. You can then arrange a meeting with a travel agent you recommend to plan out cruise destinations and book the trip. The client takes a wonderful cruise holiday and returns thanking you for making things happen in her life. You get the satisfaction knowing that you were the catalyst in that person's life and helping to achieve more than just asset allocation.

Grant's Tip:

Have you ever been asked by a client "Who is a good doctor, dentist, mechanic, travel agent? If your clients come to you for recommendations, can you imagine the referral possibilities you are creating? Imagine your auto dealer sending you someone who just received a large windfall, bought a new car, and asked the auto dealer to recommended an advisor.

Can you imagine sending a retiree to a personal trainer and that person telling their friends about their financial advisor who helped them find a personal trainer? Will their friends not ask who is their financial advisor? The possibilities are endless when you start to take a holistic approach to your business.

A second way to becoming a life planner is to hire your own success coach. The growth of coaching is huge in North America, and for professionals what better way than to hire a coach or take a coaching program or certification.

All top actresses and actors, athletes, and top business people have coaches. Consider hiring a coach to help you in certain areas of your business such as marketing, business planning, or overall success coaching. Financial advisors who want the fast track often overlook the value of feedback. It's like Steven Covey says, "The law of the harvest—you must plant in the spring and harvest in the fall."

Many top advisors find themselves burning out amid all success. It is natural to want more and more success, but at what price. A coach can help you manage your growth while maintaining the lifestyle that you work so hard to enjoy.

If you want to become a guerrilla marketing coach, check out the program at *www.gmarketingcoach.com*.

Barry LaValley's work is revolutionary in helping advisors transition to becoming life planners to their clients. For more information, check out his web site at *www.lavalleycommunications.com*.

Jay's Comments:

The Amazing Growth Of Coaching
Every world champion has had a coach. Here's why the coaching industry growing so fast and how it can make you a champion, too.

I make a presentation and watch as the audience takes careful notes, nods in agreement with what I say, then rises to its feet with applause. But deep in my heart, I know that only 5 percent of the people in the audience will actually take action based upon what they have learned.

These are bright people, motivated people, but the vast majority of them are just too busy or too overwhelmed by day-to-day business matters to implement the changes they know they must make. They have everything it takes to succeed except for one thing—follow-up.

It's that lack of follow-up that has led to the explosive growth of the coaching industry. And "explosive" might be an understatement. Fortune magazine agrees: "The hottest thing in management today is the executive coach." Newsweek magazine chimes in with their take on coaching: "They're part therapist, part consultant—and they sure know how to succeed in business." The Harvard Business Review tells us, "The goal of coaching is the goal of good management: to make the most of an organization's valuable resources." And The New York Times expands on this by saying, "...other companies offer coaching as a prerequisite...in the understanding that everyone has blind spots and can benefit from a detached observer." Industry Week obviously goes along: "The benefits of coaching appear to win over even the most cynical clients within just a few weeks." Executive Female is even more specific: "Coaching is having a dedicated mentor; it's getting knowledgeable support and encouragement and a new way of looking at things when you need it."

Imagine closing the door to your office for 30 minutes and having your own private success coach right there. Or perhaps the perfect time is on your cellular phone during that tedious commute to and from work. In fact you can call from any state in the country.

It is clear that these days business coaching has been booming. It succeeds because it works. Consider this quote from D.A. Benton in "Secrets of A CEO Coach" :

"If high achievers like Tiger Woods and Donald Trump have one (or more) for their jobs, why shouldn't you have one for yours?...In today's competitive business market, having a personal coach is not a luxury, but a necessity."

To put my time and money where my mouth is, we're now offering coaching through Guerrilla Marketing. Your guerrilla marketing coach will help you create better, more-effective goals and then support you to reach those goals in a timely manner. He will encourage and help you to stay on track by helping you understand roadblocks to change and creating a solid support structure for you to stay motivated and proactive.

He will help you maintain a sharp focus, by focusing upon your goals and helping you overcome your problems. He will provide you with research-based tools including strategic exercises based on years of work with thousands of clients. His goals are the results you want. And he'll help you achieve them with one-on-one coaching.

The line at the bottom has "follow-up" written all over it. We've learned that guerrillas need follow-up and now we're offering it.

Success at marketing means you're part of a process and not merely engaging in an event. Have you ever attended an excellent training program, perhaps a full day or weekend seminar? The speaker is great, the information is valuable and you take eight pads full of notes. You come back to your business and you're lucky if you implement even one idea. Why?

Consider this analogy from the world of sports. Let's say you decide you want to become a tennis player. You take a tennis lesson. No matter how great that tennis lesson is, you do not become an overnight tennis champion. It takes a process to create a tennis champion, and it takes a process to create a profitable company. Coaching is a process training experience designed to have a dramatic impact on your business.

The entire design of a coaching program is to get you to take action and then to stay with you to assure the proper follow-up. If a coach is nothing else, he's a master of implementation, and if he's a winning coach, he'll impart that mastery to you.

When I write a book, I know it has only two parts: starting it and completing it. When you opened your business, you had the same two parts. Coaching exists to help you with that second part. Coaching exists to provide the objectivity and extra energy that champions possess.

If you're interested in learning more, just check out the explosive growth of the coaching industry as a whole, and if you're interested in participating, now you can do it as a guerrilla and gear up to be a champion yourself.

Examples:
• Life Planning Resource Worksheet.
• See Strategy 31.

Action Summary:

To add to my marketing plans:	Yes _____	No _____
Additional information required:	Yes _____	No _____

A mind, once expanded by a new idea, never returns to its original dimensions.

Oliver Wendell Holmes.

Life Planning Resource Worksheet

Specialty
Name
Phone
Fax
Email
Auto Mechanic
Bereavement Counselor
Bookkeeper
Building Supplies
Business Coach
Career Counselor
Caterer
Chiropractor
Communications Coach
Computer Consultant
Corporate Coach
Corporate Trainer
Dentist
Dog Walker
Education Tutor
Elder Care Specialist
Electrician
Event Planner
Florist
Gardening Expert
Golf Professional
Handyman
Health Food Entrepreneur
House Builder
House Painter
Housekeeper
Interior Decorator
Internet Consultant

Jeweler
Nutritionist
Pharmacist
Photographer
Property manager
Travel Agent
Veterinarian
Other

Our attitude towards life determines life's attitude towards us.

-Earl Nightingale

STRATEGY 26
The Ultimate Feedback and Idea Forum

Concept:

If I were asked to give only one idea upon which to build a dynamic financial planning practice, it would be this: Create a board of directors with your top clients and centers of influence. Ask them for feedback and ideas on every aspect of your business, from advice to marketing and client communications. Invite six to ten of your top clients, centers of influence, or referral sources. Hold these meetings three to four times a year and buy them lunch for giving you valuable feedback on all areas of your business (see agenda). Each year change the board to new clients or centers of influence to build relationships and gain insight, as well as referrals from influential individuals. Just like coaching and mentoring, it is invaluable feedback from the people that use your services—feedback you and your success coach, manager, or mentor may not see and understand. If I have not experienced being one of your clients for a period of time, how can I give you long-term valuable feedback on how your business is doing?

Objective:

Feedback from your top clients and centers of influence. A secondary objective is developing referrals and cloning your best clients by discussing the fact that you are looking for more clients like them to build your business. Make it clear though that this is not a referral session, but a genuine feedback session for your business.

Strategy:

Some advisors have used this as a referral meeting by bringing in their top referring clients, discussing their business plans, and asking who or what target market they should tackle next. The clients will tell them the clubs they're associated with, hobbies and activities, and where they might meet their friends in a casual setting to introduce their advisor. Advisors may have several types of focus groups they're working on. For example if you are looking to attract dentists, have a dentists' focus group or board of directors' luncheon. If you have more than one market, cluster together different types of groups and/or have several referral/focus group meetings.

Costs: Breakfast or lunch for six to ten participants: $60 to $150.

Time: One to four hours of preparing materials; one hour of confirmation phone calls; one to two hours for the meeting–total seven hours.

Potential results: Referrals, marketing ideas, clues to targeting your market, invaluable feedback–just like the *MasterCard* commercial–priceless.

Grant's Tip:

Make sure you discuss the ideal client you are seeking. Have an agenda for the meeting and be prepared to discuss and disclose your business ideas and plans. Depending on the group, you may also hand out a client communications plan, business plan, or your marketing plans for the coming year. Have at least one advisor with whom you are mentoring or working (and who earns more than you) at this meeting to give you feedback; he or she may be an excellent judge of your business plans. Don't reveal income numbers or sales targets to clients (you will come across as salesperson); rather, you are looking for constructive ways to help your clients and be the best in your field.

One example of a question and feedback received is, "How can I build better relationships and show appreciation for my top clients? I'm thinking of throwing a fancy client appreciation event." The feedback was that this was not the way to achieve that objective. One board member suggested calling these top clients this coming spring and dropping by with hanging baskets of flowers for their homes. The advisor thus had the opportunity to personally build the relationships, when he delivered the baskets, as well as to thank them with gifts. The spin-off was when family and friends asked the clients where they got the lovely hanging basket. Instant referrals through a strengthened relationship and a gift. The advisor's idea of client appreciation was dramatically different than the top client's idea.

Sample Agenda, Board Of Directors Meeting:
• Client statements format/recommended changes/timeliness of information/ do you want them hole-punched/suggestions for improvement.
• Client education/seminars format/topics of interest/speakers/suggestions for improvement.
• Web site–Format/content/additional stuff/future use/frequency of use/ suggestions for improvement.
• Client appreciation–Plans/lunches, golf days, books, gifts, spring promo (seeds and garden book?)/how to WOW clients/suggestions for improvement.
• Client service–Assistants/office/telephone/greeting/appearance/ perception/suggestions for improvement.
• Client communications–Email communication (Is it effective, interesting, or a waste of time; what do you think of the personalized emails?)/seminar

invitations/special bulletins/news articles/quarterly newsletters (quality, useful information, topics and ideas to discuss)/suggestions for improvement.
• Client tax planning focus–Tax efficient and planning focus/team of experts/resources/request for feedback/client perception.
• Client building–Typical sought client/working with other professionals/suggestions for additional team members/mailer ideas/database building/referral-generation ideas/performance feedback/suggestions for improvement.
• Target marketing–For example sponsorships such as lawn bowling, community events, other ideas/brochure or client intro kit.
• Advertising–Newspaper articles (Do you read them: Do they appeal to you?)/weekly ads in newspaper (Continue or change?)/suggestions for improvement.
• Professionalism–Interviews/feedback/knowledge, skills, commitment, etc./suggestions for improvement.
• Feedback and comments.

Jay's Comments:

Sometimes the student becomes the teacher. That's exactly what happened to me when Seth Godin, coauthor of three books with me, authored his own–Permission Marketing: Turning Strangers into Friends and Friends into Customers. It changed my entire outlook about marketing and can dramatically change the beauty of your bottom line.

Seth has enlightened me to the presence of two kinds of marketing in the world today. The first, most common, most expensive, most ineffective, and most old-fashioned, is interruption marketing. That's when marketing such as a TV commercial, radio spot, magazine or newspaper ad, telemarketing call, or direct mail letter interrupts whatever you're doing to state its message. Most people pay very little attention to it, now more than ever because there is so much of it and because many minds now unconsciously filter it out.

The opposite of interruption marketing is the newest, least expensive, and most effective kind. It's called permission marketing–because prospects give you their permission to market to them.

It works like this. You offer your prospects an enticement to volunteer to pay attention to your marketing. The enticement may be a prize for playing a game. It could be information that prospects consider to be valuable. It might be a discount coupon. Perhaps it's membership to a privileged group such as a frequent buyer club or a birthday club. Maybe it's entry into a sweepstakes. And it might even take the form of an actual free gift. All you ask in return is permission to market to these people. Nothing else.

Alas, you'll have to use interruption marketing in order to secure that important permission. And you'll have to track your costs like crazy, figuring how much it costs you to gain each permission—easily figured by analyzing your media costs divided by number of permissions granted.

Once you've embarked upon a permission marketing campaign, you can spend less time marketing to strangers and more time marketing to friends. You can move your marketing from beyond mere reach and frequency and into the realm of trust.

Once you've obtained permission from your prospects, your marketing will take on three exciting characteristics. It will be anticipated, meaning people will actually look forward to hearing from you. It will be personal, meaning the messages are directly related to the prospect. And it will be relevant, meaning you know for sure that the marketing is about something in which the prospect is interested.

Permission marketing is not about share of market, not even about share of mind. Instead, it's about share of wallet. You find as many new actual customers as you can, then extract the maximum value from each customer. You convert the largest number of prospects into customers, using the invaluable permission to accomplish this. You focus your marketing only on prospects and not on the world at large.

Let's use an existing coed summer camp as an example of permission marketing in action. The camp uses interruption marketing to run ads at camp fairs and in magazines that feature other ads from summer camps. But the ads do not attempt to sell the summer camp. Instead, they focus solely upon motivating prospects to send for a video and a brochure, thereby securing their permission to accept your marketing with an open mind.

Once the prospects receive the video, they soon see that it, too, does not try to sell the camp. It is geared only to get permission to set up a meeting. But having seen a video of the camp facilities, activities, happy campers, and attentive staff, the prospect is all set to say yes to a personal meeting. At the in-person meeting, the sale is closed. And once a camper attends the camp for one summer, chances are pretty darned good he or she will not only stay for several more summers, but also will bring along a brother, a sister, a cousin, a schoolmate or a friend—or all of these.

Notice that the only goal of each step is to expand permission for you to take another step rather than making the ultimate sale. Who uses permission marketing these days? Record clubs. Book clubs. Marketers who offer a free brochure. Even my own web site offers a daily marketing message for only $3 per year—in effect, gaining permission to market to all those who sign up.

The biggest boon to permission marketing is the Internet—but only by those who treat it as an interactive medium and not like TV. As clutter becomes worse, permission become more valuable. The moral: Since only a limited number of companies within a market niche can secure permission, get moving on your own permission marketing program pronto.

Additional Information:

• Web: *www.financialadvisormarketing.com* under client appreciation.
• Ask your top clients and centers of influence whether they are interested in being on your board of directors
• Ask your mentors or peer group about the Mastermind concept (see Strategy 6).

Action Summary:

To add to my marketing plans: Yes _____   No _____

Additional information required: Yes _____   No _____

I failed my way to success.

-Thomas Edison

The will to succeed is important, but what's more important is the will to prepare.

-Bobby Knight

STRATEGY 27
Gathering Millions of Assets by Tracking Them

Concept:

If you track your client's information (but may not manage his funds), you know ahead of time how to help him make investment decisions when opportunities or maturities arise. Have a software system that will allow you to track and consolidate assets and accounts for clients. Check with your compliance office and your company's technology department about tracking and reporting this information to your clients. At the very least, you should be tracking this information (also known as nonmanaged assets).

Objective:

There are four main objectives of the software.

• First, when nonmanaged assets are maturing, you have the opportunity to discuss investment options with clients; hence more assets under administration.

• Second, you are providing the client with a valuable service by tracking investments and seeing how they work with all of the client's financial plans and asset allocation.

• Third, if you were to sell your practice or retire, and you track millions of dollars in nonmanaged assets, your business would have added value in the form of future potential or, as I call it, inventory.

• Fourth, if you sell fixed-income investments and your firm doesn't have a system for tracking deposits and maturities, your solution is a complete fixed income tracking software program for managed and nonmanaged assets. As always, conform to your firm's compliance rules on software and its use.

Strategy:

How do you track nonmanaged assets now? Have you ever had a client say to you "Call me when this matures?" How do you record or track this information? Most advisors do not have any formal system of tracking maturities or nonmanaged assets. They just take over the assets they can and leave the rest up to their clients. There is a better way and it takes a systematic approach.

If your firm allows you to track nonmanaged assets with its software, do it now! If you do not have access to this software, find a solution. Some software allows you to track fixed-income investments and maturities and print maturity notices, statements, and consolidated reports. Just think, who will get the business next time your client has a maturity if you are the one who calls him or her to discuss options? This is a very powerful tool to help clients track all of their fixed income and maturities, since the average investor over age 50 has a good percentage of their assets in fixed income vehicles. Most retirees will love to have one person tracking their investments and helping them to consolidate holdings, thereby simplifying their lives. Usually most investors deal with three or more financial institutions, so if you can make their lives simpler, they will be happier clients. The other advantage of the software is for existing advisors using fixed-income options with their clients.

Grant's Tip:

As you gather information on clients, make sure you ask for copies of all of their investment holdings and offer to track any maturities on your system. As maturities come up, you can call or send letters outlining the maturity and offering options–a perfect asset-gathering opportunity. Depending on your compliance department (always check with it first), you may also be able to send out consolidated statements. You can also send out consolidated statements on a monthly, quarterly, semi-annual, or annual basis to stay in front of your clients and service all of their financial needs.

Wouldn't you like to know you have access to information for all assets for all clients? That way, all information, advice, and questions will automatically lead to your office. How many of your clients would enjoy this service?

Here is an opportunity to rise above your competition. A guerrilla marketer knows the competition. Find out how many of your competitors offer this type of service. Then find out all of the services your top three competitors offer and explore the possibility of enhancing your services and offering more. I know most people have a difficult time keeping track of their investments, especially if they deal with more than two financial institutions or advisors.

Jay's Comments:

Guerrillas know that it's easier to sell the solution to a problem than to sell a positive benefit. That's why they position themselves as problem-solvers.

A well-known axiom of marketing has always been that it is much simpler to sell the solution to a problem than it is to sell a positive benefit. For this reason, guerrillas position their companies to be ace problem-solvers. They home in on the problems confronting their prospects, then offer their products or services as solutions to the problems. In this case the problem is for clients to track all of their assets and keep it organized. How many of your clients have their assets organized and consolidated in one report? You job, as a right-thinking guerrilla, is to spot those problems. Ask questions, listen carefully to the answers, and keep your marketing radar attuned to the presence of problems. After learning them, you can contact the prospect and talk about the prospect's problems and your solutions to those nasty dilemmas.

As you already know, people do not buy shampoo; they buy clean, great-looking hair. That means selling a benefit. A way that some shampoos have achieved profits is by reassuring people that the shampoo cleans hair, then stressing that it solves the problem of unmanageable hair—a benefit and a solution to a problem.

Right now, products and services that are enjoying success are those that help people quit smoking, lose weight, earn more money, improve health, grow hair, eliminate wrinkles, and save time. These are problem-solving products and services.

Your biggest job is to be sure your products and services do the same. Perhaps you'll have to undergo a major repositioning. That's not bad if it improves your profits. Far more doors will be open to you if you can achieve it.

Maybe you know right off what are the major problems facing your prospects. Your marketing should highlight these problems. Then, it should offer your product or service as the ideal solution. If you don't know the problems, knock yourself out learning them. Regardless of the benefits you offer, realize that their importance is generally overshadowed by the problems confronting a prospect.

It's really not that difficult to position your offering as a problem-solver. But once you do, you'll find that the task of marketing and selling becomes a whole lot easier in a hurry. You'll have to examine your offerings in the light of how they affect your prospects. So what if they are state-of-the-art? That pales in comparison with their ability to reduce your prospect's problem of tracking and organizing their financial affairs and keep track of what's going on. Prospects don't really care about your company; they care about their problems. If you can solve them, then prospects will care a great deal about your company, and they'll want to buy what you are selling.

Guerrillas lean upon case histories to prove their problem-solving acumen. They make certain to include in their marketing plans both the problem and the solution—to guide those who create marketing materials from wandering off in the wrong direction.

Sales training in guerrilla companies involves a discussion of problems, problem-spotting, problem discussing, and problem-solving. Sales reps learn the nature of prospect problems from one another. Sharing their insights helps the entire company.

Amazingly, even though this all makes sense, many companies are unaware of the importance of problem-solving. They're so wrapped up in the glories of their product or *service that they are oblivious to how well it solves problems. So they sell features and neglect benefits. They sell the obtaining of positives instead of the eliminating of negatives.*

Keep the concept of problem-solving alive in your mind, your marketing materials, your sales presentations, and your company mission. Be sure your employees are tuned into the same wave length. Once this happens, I have a feeling that you're going to be one happy guerrilla.

Examples:
• See the Record-keeping Worksheet on the following page.
• Check out *www.financialadvisormarketing.com* and click on software for information on our software program developed for Canadian Financial Advisors who wish to track all of their clients assets.

Action Summary:

To add to my marketing plans: Yes _____   No_____

Additional information required: Yes _____   No_____

Great spirits have often encountered violent opposition from weak minds.

-Albert Einstein

Record–keeping Worksheet

Consolidate your investments on one easy-to-read statement.

If you have any additional items to be added to your statement, fill out the form below and send it to our office and/or enclose copies of your latest statements.

Name:

Phone:

Guaranteed investments (Please use mm/dd/yy for dates):

Institution:

Account number:

Deposit: $

% Rate:

Issue date:

Maturity date:

Mutual funds (Please use mm/dd/yy for dates):

Fund company:

Account number:

Number of shares:

Approx. market value:

Registered accounts/Annuities (Please use mm/dd/yy for dates):

Institution:

Account number:

Deposit: $

Issue date:

Maturity date:

High expectations are the key to everything.

-Sam Walton

STRATEGY 28
Great Ideas to Educate Your Clients and Prospects

Concept:
To help educate your clients and prospects and empower them together to make better financial decisions.

Objective:
The more a client understands what I do, the more trust I have with that client.

Strategy:
In your office, start to collect the best books on personal finance, tax investments, insurance, and estate planning. Then offer to loan them to clients. Have a bookshelf available for your clients to access anytime. Don't expect all of the books to be returned, as you can also suggest that if a client finds the book helpful to pass it on with your compliments. Make sure you put your name and business card in the front of every book.

Grant's Tip:
Call each one of your product suppliers and ask for recommended readings and ask if they have any books to offer to your client library. Also ask these companies for their very best brochures on selected financial topics. Some companies have great marketing departments that produce excellent client educational pieces that are never used by advisors. Make it a habit each quarter to talk to the head of marketing of the companies with which you deal. Ask what is new and request to be kept abreast of new marketing or educational material that would be useful to your clients. Each company has a large budget for this, so you might as well tap into it and make the best use of it. Your regional wholesaler can also be a valuable resource for helping you to build your library. One company I know has excellent tax bulletins that I share with accountants, and one has fantastic estate planning ideas that I share with my team of legal professionals.

One idea for generating new business is educating all of your clients on all of the services you provide, including referrals to other professionals. How many times have you heard a client say, "I just bought life insurance, I didn't know you did that?" Make sure you include, in your regular newsletters, a section called "New Ideas and Services." Although it may not be new, it generates excitement to announce it as such. Call your centers of influence and ask whether they provide a courtesy discount for referrals made through your office. For example: "NEW, Services to help you prepare taxes and wills. This new system of referral services will help you find professionals to help you prepare taxes and wills, and these professionals will provide a discount if you mention us."

Always make your marketing exciting and new. Always make your marketing stimulating enough to rouse people to pass it on. Interesting facts and stories are always shared. Financial magazines and subscriptions can also be effective for client and prospect education, but only if you are also reading them.

Costs: Go to your favorite bookstore and spend a few bucks. It will be worth it. Imagine if your accountant educated you on tax-planning ideas and books. How much more valuable would you see your accountant as a resource? How about buying the latest and hottest tax book and giving it to your favorite accountant? You can do the same with legal books for your centers of influence.

Jay's Comments:

Marketing is part art, part science and part business. Because it's such a subjective thing, there are few hard and fast rules. But here are five new ones to guide you in your quest to boost your profits with a minimum investment and avoid nasty surprises along the way.

1. The 10/30/60 Rule–All guerrillas know they have three markets. The largest of those markets and the one that represents the least profits to you is called your universe–everybody within your marketing area regardless of whether they match your customer profile. Guerrillas invest 10 percent of their marketing budget talking to their universe, attempting to move them into their second largest market, one that ranks in the middle for generating profits.

That market is called your prospects, those members of the universe who do fit your customer profile. Your job: invest 30 percent of your budget in an effort to nudge these people into your third market–your clients, easily your most lucrative source of profits.

Guerrillas invest 60 percent of their budgets marketing to their clients, knowing it costs them one-sixth as much to make a sale to an existing customer compared with marketing to a non-client. By investing the most in the market that produces the most profits, yet costs the least to reach, guerrillas maximize their total marketing investment.

2. The 1/10/100 Rule–Now that you know the value of clients, don't overestimate their importance even though it ranks very high. Other marketing investments are even more worthwhile. When guerrillas think of marketing, they know where the real power resides and invest accordingly.

A rule guides them to where they should be putting their time and money. It dictates to guerrillas that $1 spent communicating with their own staff is equivalent to $10 spent communicating with the trade and $100 spent talking to their clients. Clients are glorious and the trade very helpful, but never overlook the marketing power of your own people.

3. *The Rule of Thirds—Almost every sane small business owner is now marketing on line. Guerrillas have learned how to budget their on-line investments. They invest one-third of it in designing and posting their web site, making it look attractive and be very simple to find.*

They invest another third of that on line budget to attract people to that site, knowing that marketing that site offline is a key to succeeding with it. on line. The final third of their on line budget is used to improve and maintain their site, keeping it fresh and fascinating. By allocating their on line budgets realistically, guerrillas make the most of the Internet.

4. *The Rule of Twice—I hate to be the one to break the news to you, but even though the price of technology is dropping and will continue to drop, you've still got to face up to the reality that it will end up costing you twice what you think it will cost to remain truly competitive on line as technologies advance and evolve. And you've got to know that you're kidding yourself if you're not staying competitive in that arena.*

5. *The Rule of The Ruler—You may consider yourself just too busy to attend to run the marketing show. You may have followed in the footsteps of other guerrillas and delegated the marketing function to a designated guerrilla. Still, I think you should know that the very best CEOs in America are deeply involved in marketing and take full responsibility for it.*

While you can delegate the function, you can't really delegate the passion and the vision, making it necessary for you, as the ruler, to take command of the process and keep your eyes on it all along. Follow that rule and you'll never be lead down a garden path by well-meaning but misguided marketing types whose goals may not be quite the same as yours.

Action Summary:

To add to my marketing plans:	Yes _____	No _____
Additional information required:	Yes _____	No _____

It's amazing how much people can get done if they do not worry about who gets the credit.
-Sandra Swinney (This quote is said to have been framed on the desk of former U.S. President Ronald Reagan.)

I had no ambition to make a fortune. Mere money-making has never been my goal, I had an ambition to build.

-John D. Rockefeller

STRATEGY 29

Orphan Accounts–How to Find Them and How to Help Them

Concept:

Successful financial advisors have for years been able to get a pipeline of qualified accounts from several sources. How would you like to have new accounts on your doorstep every month? How do you find such a pipeline? Besides your marketing bringing in new accounts, having a regular flow of new accounts to service and cross-sell–the potential can be unlimited.

Objective:

Finding sources of orphan accounts. If you work for a career agency, brokerage, or independent firm, there are always sources of orphan accounts. Be advised, though, not all firms have orphan accounts, and if you decide to accept these accounts, you must service them appropriately. Since it may be difficult to pick and choose the orphan accounts you receive, you may not always get your ideal clientele.

Strategy:

Have a qualified lead list with which to make appointments to offer help with their financial goals. Sometimes a small lead can develop into a large client. The client may not have had a financial advisor contact them for years and may have all his or her accounts with one financial institution, which may not be giving the best possible service and advice. Here is a door-opening opportunity to turn an existing client into a top client.

Grant's Tip:

I know of top agents across the country receiving highly qualified leads from their companies because they are top producers. Wouldn't it be nice to receive a pipeline of leads? Most agents think of orphans as clients requiring lots of service and producing little money. Many millionaires have old life policies they have kept and need an agent to service. These accounts only cost you your time at this point, so they are cost-efficient. If you are building your book of business, try these sources for orphan accounts:

• Management within a company–branch manager, division managers, etc.
• Brokerage firms or insurance companies with which you do business.

• Investment companies that have retiring agents in their systems.
• Agents who are retiring or selling their practices.
• Company benefits departments who help executives retire.
• Companies who are laying off staff–look into helping them with severance packages.

Start making your own list here...

Jay's Comments:

Guerrillas are well aware that the highest form of public relations is human relations. They are able to blend warm relationships with sizzling profits.

No matter how good your marketing is, building referrals from orphan accounts can rarely bring customers back for more if they were disappointed with their first go-round with you. It cannot generate profits for you if your word-of-mouth marketing works against it. It can only get prospects to buy from you once. The rest is up to you–and up to your sense of humanity in marketing. One guerrilla truism is that people like to buy from friends. Another is that it is crucial to make the human bond before you can make a lasting business bond. To avoid the depersonalization that has been an unpleasant side effect of the digital age and endemic within the business community, several guerrilla marketing weapons may be employed to add more humanity to your marketing and more profits to your tiller.

Most of the marketing weapons I've mentioned cost very little money. They are attitudes that serve to warm up your overall marketing. They make doing business with you more of a pleasure than a chore. When your clients feel your caring, feel a sense of well-being because they're your customers, you have succeeded at one-on-one public relations. Who would ever think that a hallmark of the guerrilla is love? I hope you think it now.

Action Summary:

To add to my marketing plans:	Yes _____	No_____
Additional information required:	Yes _____	No_____

We can't solve problems by using the same kind of thinking we used when we created them.

-Albert Einstein

Chapter 4
Welcoming
New Clients

Whether you think you can or whether you think you can't...you are right.

-Henry Ford

STRATEGY 30

Client Introduction–Making Them Feel Welcome

Concept:

When a new client walks into your office, what is the experience like? Is it the same every time or is the first time special and then, after that, a client feels like she is at yet another appointment in her busy day? Your job is to capture the experience, from the first time and onward.

Objective:

A large photo finishing company has a slogan "Capture the Magic." When I walk into your office for the first time what is the experience like? First impressions speak volumes about your business. From the moment a client hears about you and meets you, your job is to prove the professionalism of yourself and your operation.

Strategy:

Here is a list of ideas for making a great first impression.

• Ensure they know your location and address and that there is visible signage. Also advise where to park and whether there is any cost for parking.

• Make sure your receptionist has a schedule of clients–for existing clients preferences should be noted in the system (e.g., coffee with sugar only). New clients they are offered a choice of drinks, such as coffee or juice. The receptionist is to greets clients by name and say, "Good morning Mr. And Mrs. Smith, Grant is expecting you; he will be with you in a minute. Coffee, black with one sugar, for both of you; is that correct?" It makes people feel important and cements the experience in your office.

• The reception area should have interesting magazines or books, non-financial related. Tasteful artwork from local artists always invites conversation.

• Pleasant and soothing music should be playing in the reception area if possible.

• Let new clients wait in the reception area to experience what your staff is like. Let them settle and get comfortable with the surroundings.

• Make sure you have a neat and/orderly office. Get rid of the clutter.

• Have your professional designations professionally framed and hung where clients can see them. Do NOT display sales awards. You could frame client thank-you letters and put them up alongside family pictures.

• If it is a client review, have a pad of paper and a pen with a copy of the agenda and/or review folder sitting on the desk in front of them when they walk in.

• Have a bowl of candy, chocolates, or mints on your desk so they can help themselves.

• Have a card holder on your desk with an engraved nameplate that says something like "The best compliment I can receive is a referral."

• Make sure your phone is on "do not disturb" and your computer noise is shut off.

• Offer additional goodies whenever possible. For example my office is near a bakery so we will have fresh-baked cookies on the desk or table when a client comes in.

• Display things you are very proud of (not your *Porsche*)—things such as accomplishments of other family members or artwork by your children.

Grant's Tip:

In the first two seconds, you can make a lasting impression and form an opinion about someone. That's right, research shows that in two seconds of meeting a person, you can tell if there is a connection. The old cliché, "You never get a second chance to make a first impression," is a true guerrilla marketing maxim. If you have ever read any books on NLP (neuro-linguistic programming), you will know body language accounts for about 50% of a conversation. Try a simple idea. Mirror your client. Mirror his voice tone, posture, and body language. During discussions make eye contact and write down the client's eye color. Eye contact is part of establishing one-to-one contact with your client and/or prospect. Try it. Next time you meet someone try mirroring him or her and finding out his or her eye color. It will help you connect in a very positive way. My other suggestion is obvious. Anytime you meet clients and prospects, smile and be enthusiastic. No one wants an unenthusiastic and uncertain advisor. Even if the market is down and the performance is poor, remember people want your confidence, so display it with your body language.

One additional idea is to make sure your prospects have a clear idea where your office is. For example, make up a document that you can mail, fax, or email that includes driving directions and a map to your office. You can also put a link on your web site to an on-line map service. This works well, especially in a large city (and your client may be a newcomer to the city). I have also seen advisors send out a menu of breakfast, lunch, or snack choices if they have a breakfast or lunch meeting or a choice of beverage such as coffee, tea, soft drink, water, etc.

You can include a list of items that the client needs to bring.

See the Financial Planning Documents Checklist at the end of Strategy 31.

Jay's Comments:

When you walk into another financial advisors office, does it feel warm? Does something grab your attention when your eyes wander? In other words, is there something or things interesting and unique? In Grant's office he has a neon cactus. Having something interesting and unique can always be a door opener to your new client learning something about you which is exactly what they want to do. Unconsciously they look around and may ask about something in your office to learn more. If you asked about the cactus, you would learn that Grant's family has been involved in the neon sign business for centuries. Family pictures are a must. Although your professional degrees are important, it really isn't a conversation piece. I don't care that my doctor graduated, I want to know more about him. Perhaps an item with an interesting story will let your client learn more about you. Anniversary pictures let clients know the meaning of long-term commitment that you have. Heck why not frame your children's art instead of your degrees, at least in your eyes they are probably equally important.

The whole idea of guerrilla marketing is to transform cold prospects into consenting partners. As with superb sex, marketers shouldn't be in a hurry, shouldn't direct their energies to disinterested people, and must realize that the consummation of a loving relationship won't take place without proper wooing, without knowing exactly what turns on the prospect.

When small business owners think less of marketing as an impersonal communication and more as a sexual journey, they will be far more able to market with success. In today's cluttered environment of marketing, instead of pondering numbers and demographics, explore instead the concepts of romance and love.

That means realizing that falling in love with the right person and keeping the relationship delicious and satisfying is not so much a single major event as a step-by-step process. It begins by playing the field and determining just who you want to date in the first place. During this step, guerrilla marketers concentrate upon the compatibility factor. They keep their radar attuned to the proper chemistry that leads to mutual understanding and eventual consent. Unfazed by superficial allure, they seek soul mates more than customers. Their taste and discretion helps reduce their marketing costs because their targets reflect quality over quantity.

The guerrilla marketer's next step is gaining "uncarnal" knowledge. He seeks information about prospects who have caught his fancy so they can satisfy their needs more than their wants—because guerrillas realize people often want what they don't need, and providing it is hardly the basis of a long-term relationship.

Guerrillas seek shared values in customers as they would in lovers, gaining information as they impart information, much in the manner of two people getting to know each other with romance on their minds. They treat all prospects differently, just as they want to be treated. They learn those ways with research and two-way communication.

It's at this point that guerrillas engage in flirting—taking that first step towards gaining consent. Marketing with personalized messages, treating advertising not as the way to make the sale but as the first step in gaining consent, they become attractive to those who have attracted them.

When the courtship begins, guerrillas pay very close attention and prove that they care. They enter into dialogues with those for whom they are lusting and know what to say for the lust to be returned. Any courtship is intensified with gifts of love, and it is no different in the guerrilla marketer's search for consenting partners. Gifts can be gift-wrapped or come in the form of prizes, memberships in loyalty groups, newsletters, booklets, regular email updates, etc. Each prospect knows that his or her individuality is recognized.

Next comes necking and petting, connecting even closer with prospects by becoming more intimate in marketing. By listening carefully to learn about likes and dislikes and specific problems, guerrillas learn to make promises they can keep. This penchant for taking action broadens even more the consent for which they strive.

The step in marketing that most relates to foreplay is when marketers give their partners the exact desired pleasure. They capitalize upon the interactivity afforded by on-line communications to become a part of their prospects' identities. They customize their messages to each prospect, not only making the prospect feel special but also proving devotion.

Guerrilla marketers and their prospects achieve consummation by closing the sale with mutual consent. Rather than having rushed, their timing is impeccable and their fulfillment implies a commitment. The marketer has consistently demonstrated empathy for the partner— with the goal of providing joy and satisfaction. The earth may not tremble, but a lasting bond has been created.

During the afterglow, the connection is solidified. This is accomplished with assiduous follow-up—proving, so to speak, that the marketer still respects the prospect in the morning. Statements of warm appreciation are made, resulting in prospects who are so delighted they just cannot help but relate their joy to other people they know.

The entire process involves a lot more than a mere sexual dalliance but is the start of a long and happy marriage. The devotion of the small business owner is unmistakable because it builds upon details that have been learned, the specific tastes of each customer, and their shared experience of sale, purchase, and use.

The more you view the marketing process as a mating ritual (as opposed to an economic ritual) the longer you will find your list of consenting and delighted partners.

Action Summary:

To add to my marketing plans: Yes _____   No _____

Additional information required: Yes _____   No _____

It's a funny thing about life, if you refuse to accept anything but the best, you very often get it.

- W. Somerset Maugham

You are the same today as you will be in five years from now except for two things—the books you read and the people you meet.

-Charlie "T" Jones

STRATEGY 31

The First Five Minutes—Key Questions to Ask Millionaires

Concept:

Besides your compliance department loving you for having complete information on your client, asking key questions will build trust and understanding of the client's point of view.

Objective:

When you have the biggest potential prospect walk through your door with millions of assets to invest with you, what's the first thing that goes through your mind? "Oh my gosh, what am I going to do or say to impress this person, what am I going to do differently to attract this client?" We get excited and wonder how the interview is going to go. The objective is sometimes not clear. Do you have a consistent framework for each interview structured in such a way as to build trust and gather all of the relevant information to help this person? Years ago as an advisor I was taught to probe for hot buttons and ask all kinds of questions. Then one day an advisor lent me a book by Bill Bachrach called *Values-Based Selling: The Art of Building High-Trust Client Relationships* (Bachrach & Associates Inc., 1996). I had never heard of Bill, but a book about prospecting always caught my interest. Soon after I heard another advisor talk about Bill's ideas. Bill's system is a way of asking key questions of millionaires. Find a system of gathering information beyond just a fact finder or a know-your-client form.

Strategy:

Whether you use Bill's system or not, having a system of gathering the client's goals and financial information, gaining trust, and getting commitment in less than one hour can be challenging. Here is an example of how Bill Bachrach teaches advisors to have a system for all new prospective clients (Courtesy of Bachrach & Associates Inc., Copyright 2003).

The Five Steps of the Perfect First Interview:

Extreme competence with the first interview means you follow the principle of 5/55: In a one-hour meeting, you're talking for a total of 5 minutes, and your prospect has the floor for the remaining 55. What's more, almost everything you say is a question, as the term "interview" implies. To complete the interview, a foldout color Financial Road map® is used to gather the information in front of the client.

1. The Values Conversation™ about 6 minutes/individual, 12 minutes/couple)

Key Question: "What's important about money to you?"

As people talk about what's important to them, they become emotional, and as you truly listen, you create trust. (For step-by-step instructions on the values conversation, see the Values-Based Selling Mastery System, *www.bachrachvbs.com*). The magic of the values conversation is the discoveries your prospects make, which are more important than what you learn. As people work their way up the "values staircase" with you, they articulate, perhaps for the first time, what will inspire them to implement the financial strategy your create for them.

2. Goals Conversation (20 to 25 minutes)

Key Question: "What are the tangible goals that will require you to have some money and planning to achieve?"

What makes this part of the conversation revealing for the other person is thorough examination of the goals, filling in the blanks on two previous unknowns: How much money will it take, and by when, specifically?

If someone says she wants to retire, you ask, "In what year?"

She may say, "When I'm 65."

"Okay, 65. What year will that be?"

Now the goal of retirement starts to feel more real to her as she replies, "Let's see, that would be 2030."

"All right, what day in 2030?"

It's interesting that even for someone who hasn't thought about the exact day before, it's no trouble to come up with one. As she does, she'll gain a profound sense of what is really possible–and that you're the one who can help.

After you've established an exact date, you can ask your prospect how much money per year it will take to have the kind of life he or she wants. Of course, they don't have to consider inflation, or make any other calculations. You just need an annual figure so you can do the rest.

3. All the money conversation (10 to 20 minutes)

Now that you've expanded your thinking into the realm of possibility, your dreams and goals for your financial future–it's time to evaluate your current situation.

It is not time to share with me the documents you brought with you. (Note: This is a simple math exercise and not designed to be a thorough analysis. Your thorough analysis would come after you get hired.)

A relevant fact finder roadmap has several different purposes including:

Finding out peoples values, goals, and dreams.

Understanding what they mean by their risk tolerance.

Their investing history.

Referrals to your team of advisors including accountant, lawyer, estate planner, insurance professionals, and realtor.

Complete financial planning.

Net worth and listings of assets, liabilities for future planning.

Retirement information such as pensions and retirement planning goals.

Tax planning and helping to identify possible tax solutions.

Estate planning and concerns.

Personal networking information such as their family, hobbies, recreation, and with whom they associate for future referrals.

This fact finder roadmap should also be accompanied by other relevant financial information such as investment statements, pension information, insurance information, tax returns and other relevant information.

This is where you separate yourself as being a true professional by finding out how you can help your client's financial situation

After completing the fact finder, tear off the last page or type a copy on letterhead to hand to the client along with a confidential envelope that they can drop off or mail to your office.

4. The commitment to hire you conversation (5 minutes)

What you are looking at is your Financial Roadmap for Living Life on Purpose. We're at the point in our time together for you to decide whether or not you want to hire me to create a written strategy/plan for you, before spending time doing a thorough plan.

What that means is that we will create a comprehensive, specific, written step-by-step plan of action that will tell you exactly what to do in these four areas.

We are going to tell you exactly the right amount of Cash Reserves to have and how to get it. Next is debt. We are going to tell you exactly how to go about eliminating your debt, or reduce it in a way that is prudent. We are going to examine all kinds of insurance that exists, compare that with what you have, and tell you exactly what kind of insurance you should have and how much. Now we are going to look at your assets and advise you on how to allocate them so that you have the highest probability of achieving your goals. (Now recap their goals)

It's knowing that you have achieved these goals that is evidence that you have made smart choices about your money. And for you, NAME, that means that you have more choices, sense of fulfillment knowing that leading your life with existence (recap this person's values). And for you, NAME, this means that you have (are…) more….. so that you feel connected with yourself… (recap this person's values)

The question on the table is, "Would you like to hire me to create this written plan for you and to be your coach?" Most advisors do it backwards. They create the plan and then ask for a commitment to a plan.

5. The commitment to implement the plan conversation

"Tell me about your commitment to implement your plan." This is a chance to find out how prepared and committed they are to the goals they have just described. It's one thing to have a plan, but it is useless unless it is implemented. As Roy Disney once said, "When your values are clear, your decisions are easy."

Another component to Bill's system is using his book, *Values-Based Financial Planning: The Art of Creating an Inspiring Financial Strategy* (Aim High Publishing; 2000). This book is for consumers to read and is given out by financial advisors to prospects and clients. One way to use the book is to ask your clients for referrals and let them know that you will send a copy of *Values-Based Financial Planning* to the referral. You also ask your clients to write notes asking their friend or family members to read the book and contact you, the advisor, to discuss the book. The note along with the book makes a statement to other clients about how important the interview process is. (Courtesy of Bill Bachrach, Bachrach & Associates, Inc. © 2003 Bill Bachrach, Values-Based Selling® *www.bachrachvbs.com*. All rights reserved)

Check out *www.bachrachvbs.com* for information on their interview system, or contact:

Bachrach & Associates Inc.
8380 Miramar Mall, Suite 200
San Diego, CA 92121
Telephone 858-558-3200 or 800-347-3707.

When you sign up for their free monthly e-newsletter, The Trusted Financial Advisor, you receive a discount on your initial order.

Grant's Tip:

Years ago I learned a technique for mastery on the phone. First of all ask questions that elicit a yes response. The questions should ask for something that will motivate the client. For example, if I called you up and asked the following question, what would be your response? "Mr. Prospect, are you interested in increasing your current retirement income?" If the answer is no, I am not interested in talking further with this person. Sometimes as financial advisors, we know we have to make contact with prospects by phone. Yet, we usually don't have a system for getting people excited about our ideas. We just assume they will want to come in and talk to us; yet when a prospect who isn't motivated says no to an appointment, we wonder why.

Another valuable lesson I learned is that if clients do not give you all their information, don't accept them as clients. I'm not saying you want all of their assets, but it is important to get all of their information. Otherwise, when are you going to gain their trust? When your one-pick stock or fund out-performs everything else they own, they are going to magically transfer their million dollars to you. How many accounts do you have that use you as a benchmark against another advisor? How can you honestly do the best job for the client if you don't know how those other assets are allocated? It is like going to the doctor's office and saying my foot hurts but not telling the doctor about your sore leg and arm. How can the doctor do a proper diagnosis without all of the information? Save yourself the headache and learning curve here; don't take on clients who won't give you all of their information. Your compliance department will also agree–full and complete disclosure is a hallmark of establishing and maintaining trust.

At the end of this strategy you will find a sample Financial Planning Documents Checklist form you can give to prospects. Use this to show your true professionalism and gain the attention of the client's personal advisor. Ask the client to sign a release of information for his or her accountant and lawyer to work with you to provide you with the necessary information. You now have two more people to contact who may be influential to the prospect. This automatically puts you into a team-oriented position, rather than a defensive position with the client who says, "I always run things past my accountant or lawyer." This way you can freely communicate with the advisor and the client sees you as part of the team.

Jay's Comments:

It's at proposal time that the rubber meets the road. To get the best ride possible, you've got to present a guerrilla proposal. Here's how.

There are poor proposals, which rarely get the business for you. There are good proposals, which might get the business for you. And then, there are guerrilla proposals, which usually get the business for you. If you present anything but a guerrilla proposal, it means that all the marketing you've done up till that time has probably been wasted. Sheer agony.

The companies that get the business realize that all the time and energy they've put into wooing a prospective customer has been mere groundwork for the dazzling display of business acumen that will be made apparent when they get down to the business of making an actual proposal. Guerrillas follow these ten steps to make sure that their courtship activities lead to a long-term business marriage–destined to flourish and prosper.

1. Guerrillas are always positive that they have qualified their prospects so that the marriage doesn't die during the honeymoon. Getting your prospect's attention is only a tiny part of assuring a lasting relationship. When your prospect shakes hands with you and says "Let's do it!"–you've got to be certain that both of you will gain. You must be right for them and they must be right for you. Chemistry counts in both people-to-people marriages and in business-to-business pairings.

2. Guerrillas start immediately to warm up the relationship by building rapport with their prospects. They never want to walk into a prospect's office or conference room as a complete stranger. That's why they see their job as forging a bond before making the proposal. They know well that it's much easier to do business with friends than strangers.

3. Guerrillas identify a real need that their prospects have and know in their hearts that they can fill that need better than anyone else. They keep foremost in their minds the truism that people give their business to firms that can help them solve their problems and exploit their opportunities.

4. Guerrillas make absolutely certain that the prospect to whom they are making their proposal can benefit from their advice right now, and not at some future date down the road. They present their proposals only to people who are the ultimate decision-makers and can give them the go-ahead immediately without having to check with higher authorities.

5. Guerrillas rehearse their presentation till they've got it down pat. They decide ahead of time exactly what they want to show and tell, then plan intelligently, back their chosen words with graphics, and always ask for the order at the conclusion of the proposal. Non-guerrillas may make a decent proposal, but usually fail to ask outright for what they want.

6. Guerrillas prepare a document to leave with their prospects right after the proposal has been presented. The document summarizes the high points of the proposal, is completely self-contained, and includes important facts and figures that might have bogged down the actual presentation.

7. Guerrillas design their proposals in a way that addresses their prospect's goals clearly and unmistakably. They are able to do this with a single sentence that proves they are directed and/oriented to those goals. They find ways to repeat that sentence several times during the presentation of their proposal—up front, in the middle, at the end, and in the written document they give to their prospect when the presentation is completed.

8. Guerrillas present their proposals in a logical manner so that one point flows naturally to the next, making the proposal very simple to follow. They know that the organization of their proposal is nearly as important as the content. Their proposals prove beyond doubt that they are qualified to get the business, and then that they are particularly qualified and deserving of the business right now.

9. Guerrillas speak and write in the first person, aligning everything they say with the prospect's business. They make it a point to talk about the prospect's business and not about their own. In fact, they only speak of their own business in terms of how it can help the prospect's business. This requires homework and guerrillas always do their homework before presenting any proposal.

10. Guerrillas are quick to reinforce their points visually, knowing that points made to the eye are 68% more effective than the same points made to the ear. They always try to visualize what they are saying, and they realize that if the visuals are shoddy or look home-made, they are sabotaging themselves.

Because guerrillas are ultra-keen about follow-up, they follow up their proposals with a thank-you note within 24 hours of the presentation. That follow-up also includes a phone call to be sure no questions are left unanswered, to see if there is anything else the prospect would like to know, and to establish a start date for doing business together. The follow-up should be directed to the person who has the authority to say "yes."

The more data you have about your prospect, the better your proposal will be and the more likely it is to land the business for you. The better you prove that you understand the prospect's competitive situation, the more likely that prospect will want your help. And the better the chemistry is between your people and the prospect's people, the more likely it is that you'll get exactly what you want.

Never fail to keep in mind the power of a personal bond. And never forget that when you're making a proposal, your three greatest allies are your knowledge of the prospect, your enthusiasm during the presentation, and the personal bonding you have already established.

Additional Information:
Visit *www.bachrachvbs.com.*

Action Summary:
To add to my marketing plans: Yes _____   No _____

Additional information required: Yes _____   No _____

Baseball is 90% mental–the other half is physical.

Yogi Berra

Financial Planning Documents Checklist

The first step towards increasing your personal wealth and financial security.

We require the following:

PORTFOLIO MANAGEMENT
- Investment Statements–including child savings plans, stocks, bonds, and mutual funds.
- GIC Maturities and Bank Statements.
- RRSP Statements.
- Retirement Planning Documents–including Pension Plan Statements, Group RRSPs.
- Net Worth Statement–See attached.

ESTATE PLANNING
- Life Insurance and Disability Insurance pPolicies.
- Group Insurance Policies.
- Wills/Inheritances.
- Lawyer's Release of Information Letter.

LAWYER'S NAME AND FIRM

INCOME TAX
- Personal Returns 1 to 3 years.
- Corporate Returns/Family Trust Documents.
- Accountant's Release of Information Letter.

ACCOUNTANT'S NAME AND FIRM.

OTHER
- Stock Certificates.
- Investment Real Estate.
- Company Information–Confidential to Grant Hicks.
- Limited Partnerships.
- Mortgage/Loan Information.
- Other _____
- General Release of Information Letter.

Note: All documents will be held strictly confidential and be returned to you.

You can observe a lot just by watching.

-Yogi Berra

STRATEGY 32
Adding Incredible Value

Concept:

This is a letter or package you would send out after your first transaction with a new client. I can't remember how many times I have heard clients say "Our last advisor invested our money and that's the last we heard of him for a long time." While there are a lot of things you can do when a new client signs on, how about an existing client with a large transaction?

Objective:

Follow-up is the key. Create a system of follow-up with new and existing clients after a transaction has occurred.

Strategy:

Here are some simple strategies to help you follow up.

• Client confirmation letter: The follow-up system. This is a letter you would send out after most financial transactions completed with your clients. Your assistant can easily save this document and customize for several different client transactions. It has several purposes including thanking your client for the business, confirming in the client's mind the transaction, noting future planning with the client, and asking for referrals. It is also a way to confirm a lengthy series of transactions and/or future planning and sets up a future timetable; and it covers off possible compliance, since a copy is placed in the client file for future reference. It is also a commitment to the client based on what he or she can expect and cements the relationship.

• Client commitment letter: It is more than a welcome-aboard letter. This letter or package sets up client expectations and outlines your commitment. It may also include a background of your company and its commitments. Examples are at the end of this chapter. Some companies automatically do this, so use your company's examples.

• IPS–Investment Policy Statement: If you're new to the business, having a set of investment guidelines clearly outlined may be difficult. But if you have been in the investment industry for seven years or more, you should work with a written set of investment parameters; otherwise, your business practices will be confusing (if your focus shifts from month to month). As Nick Murray says in his popular book, *The Excellent Investment Advisor* (The Nick Murray Company, Inc.; 1996), "When I believe, I am believed. Having a conviction and set of written investment policy statements is the cornerstone of a solid financial planning practice."

The example I use is courtesy of Deena Katz, who outlines in her book, *Deena Katz's Tools and Templates for Your Practice: For Financial Advisors, Planners, and Wealth Managers* (Bloomberg Pr, 2001), "The benefits of a solid IPS are clear. It builds trust, manages expectations, enforces the long-term message, and helps you and your client to follow the path to help them reach their goals." The IPS was developed by the pension industry to allow money managers to make a commitment to their pension clients on their roles and responsibilities. Adapting an IPS is not an easy task, but once you have one your framework for managing money becomes clearer to you and your client.

Next time you generate business from a client, send the letter out on your professional letterhead. You can also make up a series of letters such as:
• First-time client: See introduction package and letter.
• Thank-you-for-additional-business letter or milestone letter: A transaction for a certain client milestone such as assets under administration over $500,000.
• Send thank-you gifts with the letters. Mail something special or educational with the letters to reinforce the benefits.

You can use these letters to outline the many financial services you offer and to allow clients to sign up for your email program and your on-line account viewing options. It is also a chance to introduce your assistants and/or team as well as outside professionals. You should now schedule the client's next meeting or contact, or place him in your 90-day call rotation schedule.

Grant's Tip:

I recommend you call each client two to four weeks after opening an account. It is part of building trust in your integrity and lets the clients know they are important and that you have reviewed the transactions for accuracy. It also allows them to ask questions and set up the next meeting date. With regard to the follow-up thank-you letter, I would not use it for every little transaction; however, when there has been a series of different transactions, it confirms exactly what you discussed. I would send it out for more than five transactions and more than $50,000 in any single transaction. See the sample supporting documents that follow this strategy. Create your system of adding value.

Jay's Comments:

Most people have to admit, they don't have a well-defined service mission. No wonder they can't find the right people. They don't know who they are looking for. First off you should develop and communicate your service mission. You need to find out what matters to your clients. As you develop your service mission, keep in mind that you must deliver a difference to your clients and make yourself unique. The old saying, price, quality, service, pick any two, is outdated. You need to deliver all three but differentiate on one characteristic only. For example, Domino's Pizza differentiated years ago by stating that they will deliver your pizza fast.

You should differentiate based on what your clients want, which is less financial worry and more financial peace of mind. Check out all the ads the big financial companies market to us every day and you will see some companies focusing on their ability to take the worry away better than the competitor. Once you have your service mission, create a list of the qualities a person must have to help you deliver that mission effectively and consistently. As Grant stated, a clearly defined service mission is crucial to success as a guerrilla marketer.

Additional Resources:
See Strategy 39.

Examples:
• Client confirmation letter.
• Client introduction letter.
• Client commitment letter (Our Commitment to You).
• IPS–investment philosophy statement–From Deena Katz's Tools and Templates for your practice, © 2001 by Deena B. Katz. Reprinted by permission of Bloomberg press.

Action Summary:

To add to my marketing plans:	Yes _____	No _____
Additional information required:	Yes _____	No _____

When you sit with a nice girl for two hours, it seems like two minutes. When you sit on a hot stove for two minutes, it seems like two hours–that's relativity.

-Albert Einstein

Client Confirmation Letter:

Dear Mr. and Mrs. Client:

I would like to thank you for the trust and confidence you have shown in placing your business with our firm. I have briefly summarized your transactions for you. You will receive confirmation from the investment company in the next few weeks.

Date of Transactions: May 15, 2003.

Investment Details: Invested your cheque in the amount of $60,000 as follows:
• $30,000 into Balanced Fund A.
• $30,000 into Income Fund B.

Future Planning: We will review your estate planning, will, and insurance policies at our next meeting on July 15, 2003, at our offices.

Please feel free to contact me at 248-2824 should your records not agree with mine, or if you have any further questions.

Sincerely yours,

Grant W. Hicks,
Retirement Planning Specialist

Carol Hagel
Client Service Manager

P.S. I have enclosed two of my business cards. Keep one for your records, and I would appreciate you passing one along to a friend who can benefit from our professional Financial Counseling. Thanks again!

Client Introduction Letter:

Dear Mr. and Mrs. Client:

I would like to take this opportunity on behalf of everyone at Hicks Financial and Partners In Planning Financial Services, to express how much we are looking forward to working with you. We believe it's important for you to know what to look forward to in being our client.

Carol and I have been working together since 1996 and we encourage you to call us with questions or requests. If we are busy when you call, the entire staff at the Parksville office is always available to assist you with questions you may have. We work on a team basis. We access some of the best advice regarding tax and estate planning, so if you require the services of other professionals such as accountants, lawyers, real estate, or mortgage financing, we can gladly provide you with a professional referral in any of those areas.

Accessing the best products for you is part of the research. We access the best GIC rates, mutual funds, securities, life insurance policies, and annuities. If you come across any investment or insurance product that you would like more information on please let us know. We are independent and can help you find solutions to meet your needs.

Communication means everything to us. Aside from phone calls, we will complete quarterly reviews and mail you a summary with comments in our quarterly newsletter. You also have the opportunity to view your accounts on line. To sign up for this service, please email us a request at: *ghicks@pipfs.com*. Occasionally we hold educational events for our clients. If you would like to see a specific topic discussed, feel free to let us know. Your opinions and feedback are appreciated. We also have a library of books on various financial topics, free to loan at any time.

We want to be there for you. If at anytime we fall short, please let us know.

Sincerely yours,

Grant W. Hicks,
Retirement Planning Specialist

Carol Hagel
Client Service Manager

Client Commitment Letter:

OUR VISION FOR YOU: To help you achieve financial security and peace of mind through sound estate, retirement, tax, and financial planning.

OUR MISSION FOR YOU: To become one of the best retirement planners on Vancouver Island. We are only satisfied when you are.

OUR COMMITMENT TO YOU: When I accept you as a client, I personally make a ten-year commitment to helping you reach your financial goals.

I PERSONALLY MANAGE YOUR ACCOUNTS: The minimum account size I manage is $250,000 per family. This includes all family members.

WHO IS GRANT HICKS? Fourteen years' experience as a Financial Advisor and Retirement Planning Specialist. Shareholder of Partners in Planning. Branch Manager, Certified Investment Manager (CIM). Fellow of the Canadian Securities Institute (FCSI). I live in Parksville; I am married with two children and a golden lab.

WHO IS PARTNERS IN PLANNING? PIPFS, a national independent financial planning firm.

WHO IS HICKS FINANCIAL? Independent manager of GICs through more than 30 different financial institutions including banks, trust companies, and credit unions.

YOUR COMMITMENT: I use the ICE philosophy to help you–information, communication, and education.

YOUR INFORMATION: Full disclosure/independent and unbiased/no conflicts of interest exist/tax returns, wills, and other information.

COMMUNICATION TO YOU: Every quarter, communications regarding life-changing events.

EDUCATION FOR YOU: Our client Library, web site, emails, bulletins, and seminars.

TEAM APPROACH FOR YOU: Accounting, legal, estate, and trust experts on my team to help you, as well as real estate and mortgage financing specialists. If you are looking for a professional service please let us know (see our team worksheet).

COMPLETE PLANS FOR YOU: Tax plan or estate plan; in some circumstances I sit down with you and the professional to complete. With your permission, I will discuss tax planning with your accountant or estate planning with your lawyer.

MONEY MANAGEMENT FOR YOU: I have a structured approach to managing money with a written investment philosophy. Our research is completed through a 50-point questionnaire for all funds. All securities research is completed through XYZ Financial, a leading Financial Securities firm. I personally have a conservative retirement planning philosophy, since I work with retired clients every day (see Investment Philosophy).

KEEPING YOU ORGANIZED: Each client will receive a binder we both will use to keep your plans up to date. I have a copy of your binder in my files so we have the same information.

FEES (how I get paid.): I am part of the management expense ratio. No fees on GICs–see fee schedule for self-directed plans and securities.

ADDING VALUE TO YOU: If you decide to become a client, we will cover all transfer fees up to a maximum of $500.

REFERRALS FOR YOU: Following are clients you can call to ask about my services.
• Joe Client, 955-1234
• Mr. and Mrs. Smith, 955-1235
• Others available upon request.

In summary, together we will:
• Know everything about you and your retirement plans.
• Know when we will see each other and when you will hear from us.
• Know we have no conflicts of interest.
• Know we will be organized together.
• Know we can find the answers with our Financial Team.
• Know we use a philosophy towards money management.

Sincerely,

Grant W. Hicks, CIM
Retirement Planning Specialist

New FREE booklet reveals...

8 Secrets of Highly Successful Mutual Fund Investors...

Why do some people always make money in mutual funds? What are the secrets to their success? Which time-proven strategies will make you richer by $100s, $1,000s, $10,000s and more? What secrets will save you money?

Find the answers to these questions and more in a new 12 page booklet entitled 'Make Money in Mutual Funds! 8 Amazing Secrets.'

Written clearly and in detail this FREE BOOKLET explains how a $10,000 investment grew to $3,699,409 using an amazing simple strategy. Gives you straight-talk on when not to buy a mutual fund. Tells you 3 essential keys to building more consistently profitable returns. Helps you with simple tips to avoid investing at market tops. Plus much, much more.

We think you will agree with Phil Cunningham. President of Canada's 4th largest Mutual Fund Company when he states "All 8 reasons are exactly what most Canadians need to retire with dignity in the coming years."

This booklet reveals the secrets of today's most successful mutual fund investors. Secrets that will make you GROW RICH in mutual funds. Secrets that will help you avoid costly mistakes. You will want to refer to it often.

For your FREE BOOKLET call **Grant Hicks c/o AAI Financial Group at 248-2824.** Call today while copies remain in stock. Booklet sent via first class mail.

Benefits For My Clients

Ten Reasons To Consider Financial Planning With Grant Hicks:

1. The development of a comprehensive financial plan. This is the start of our relationship with you to help you achieve your long-term financial goals. As part of this plan, we cover the investment, insurance, tax, and estate planning aspects of each client's situation.

2. Monthly e-mail of investment opportunities and experts' views. I believe my best client is one who is fully informed. Each month, timely market and investment opportunities will be emailed.

3. Access to client seminars. Regular seminars ranging from fund managers to tax experts will give you opportunities to learn.

4. Access to our investment library. If you have a subject about which you are wondering, ask me—I probably have a book that will answer your questions. I maintain a library of some of the best books on personal finance, available for loan to all my clients.

5. Access to accounts on line. The easiest, quickest way for you to obtain up-to-date information on your investments. Log on at *www.ghicks.com.*

6. Quarterly personal newsletters and statements. Each quarter, all clients receive a portfolio update, personally reviewed before it is sent. If changes are necessary, you will be contacted by our office to complete a review and look at all current investment opportunities.

7. Personalized written annual review folder. Personal, face-to-face interviews where you can ask all the questions that are in your mind, as well as make any changes necessary to ensure your financial goals are accomplished.

8. Referrals to top accountants, lawyers, real estate experts, and mortgage experts. As your financial advisor, I coordinate the activities of existing professional advisors such as tax accountants and estate lawyers. If required, I also tap into my network of professional advisors.

9. Access to the best investment opportunities. I monthly publish the best GIC rates and mutual funds to buy. We have access to almost any financial product or service available in Canada from banks, trust companies, credit unions, insurance companies, mutual funds, and securities.

10. Regular communication. I believe my best client is the one who is fully informed—through quarterlies, emails, the web site, seminars, reviews and

contact with a team of professionals. I strive to be one of the best retirement planners on Vancouver Island.

(c) Grant W. Hicks, CIM, FCSI Retirement Planning Specialist

Deena Katz

From Deena Katz's Tools and Templates for your practice, © 2001 by Deena B. Katz. Reprinted by permission of Bloomberg press.

■■■■■■■■■■■■■■■■■■■■■■■ **INVESTMENT PHILOSOPHY**

The following summarizes our firm's core beliefs. These provide the basis for your Investment Policy. The entire staff of Evensky, Brown & Katz participates, at different levels, in the development of our philosophy. All members of the firm are committed to its consistent implementation. Policy design, implementation, continuous monitoring and, as necessary, modification, are integral parts of the wealth management process. Our success is measured not by performance statistics but rather by our clients' success in achieving their goals.

CLIENT RELATED ISSUES

Goal Setting
We believe that clients must set their own goals. It is our responsibility to educate them in the process and to assist them in defining, quantifying, and prioritizing their goals.

Cash Flow
We believe that clients need total return, not dividends or interest. The traditional concept of an 'income' portfolio is archaic and places unnecessary and inappropriate restrictions on portfolio design.

Expectations
We believe that 'conservative' assumptions are a dangerous myth. Return requirements should be based on real rates of return. An investment policy should not be prepared based on a client's unrealistic expectations. If necessary, we will refuse the engagement.

Risk Tolerance
We believe that a client's risk tolerance is a significant constraint in the wealth management process. Success can be measured by our clients' ability to sleep well during turbulent markets.

Tax constraints
We believe that tax considerations must be considered. However, the goal of tax planning should be to maximize after-tax returns, not to minimize taxes. Neither reported turnover nor holding period calculated from reported turnover is a useful measure of tax efficiency. Annuities should generally only be considered when asset protection is an issue (in those states where the law protects annuity assets).

Deena Katz

From Deena Katz's Tools and Templates for your practice, © 2001 by Deena B. Katz. Reprinted by permission of Bloomberg press.

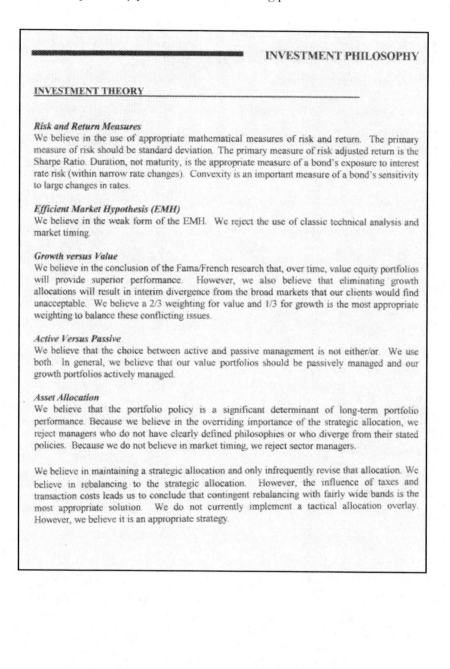

INVESTMENT PHILOSOPHY

INVESTMENT THEORY

Risk and Return Measures
We believe in the use of appropriate mathematical measures of risk and return. The primary measure of risk should be standard deviation. The primary measure of risk adjusted return is the Sharpe Ratio. Duration, not maturity, is the appropriate measure of a bond's exposure to interest rate risk (within narrow rate changes). Convexity is an important measure of a bond's sensitivity to large changes in rates.

Efficient Market Hypothesis (EMH)
We believe in the weak form of the EMH. We reject the use of classic technical analysis and market timing.

Growth versus Value
We believe in the conclusion of the Fama/French research that, over time, value equity portfolios will provide superior performance. However, we also believe that eliminating growth allocations will result in interim divergence from the broad markets that our clients would find unacceptable. We believe a 2/3 weighting for value and 1/3 for growth is the most appropriate weighting to balance these conflicting issues.

Active Versus Passive
We believe that the choice between active and passive management is not either/or. We use both. In general, we believe that our value portfolios should be passively managed and our growth portfolios actively managed.

Asset Allocation
We believe that the portfolio policy is a significant determinant of long-term portfolio performance. Because we believe in the overriding importance of the strategic allocation, we reject managers who do not have clearly defined philosophies or who diverge from their stated policies. Because we do not believe in market timing, we reject sector managers.

We believe in maintaining a strategic allocation and only infrequently revise that allocation. We believe in rebalancing to the strategic allocation. However, the influence of taxes and transaction costs leads us to conclude that contingent rebalancing with fairly wide bands is the most appropriate solution. We do not currently implement a tactical allocation overlay. However, we believe it is an appropriate strategy.

Deena Katz

From Deena Katz's Tools and Templates for your practice, © 2001 by Deena B. Katz. Reprinted by permission of Bloomberg press.

INVESTMENT PHILOSOPHY

Optimization

We believe that mathematical optimization is the appropriate method for designing a strategic asset allocation model. We also believe that an optimizer is simply a tool to be used by a knowledgeable wealth manager. The primary controls over the optimizer are the development of logical input data (expected returns should not be historical projections), an awareness of the optimizer's sensitivities to the input and other appropriate constraints. The final recommendations should not be based on the optimizer's unconstrained optimal solution but rather the optimal, sub-optimal solution.

Time Diversification

We believe that the relative risk of increasing equity exposure decreases as the time horizon of the goal increases. We do not believe that any 'investment' should be made for a goal with less than a five-year time horizon. Funds required in fewer than five years should be placed in money markets or fixed income securities (e.g., CDs, Treasuries) with maturity dates equal to or less than the goals' time horizons.

IMPLEMENTATION

Managers

We believe that professional money managers will generate results far superior to a client's or wealth manager's direct security selection and management. With rare exception, separate account management (including wrap accounts) is inefficient and expensive. The universe of public and institutional funds offers the best alternative for the superior management of multiple asset class portfolios.

We believe that managers should be selected and evaluated based on their philosophies, processes and people. Once selected, a manager should be allowed periods of poor performance if he remains consistent with his philosophy and process. He or she should be replaced immediately if their implementation strays significantly from the stated philosophy or process.

Evaluation of managers should entail a detailed review of all available pertinent information, including both fundamental qualitative and return factor analyses. However, the ultimate decision to hire or fire should be based on fundamental data. Performance measurement should be against appropriate benchmarks, not broad market indices.

On-going Management

We believe that there should be regular review of a client's situation to determine if he is continuing to move in the direction of achieving his goals. This includes revisions in strategic allocations as a result of revised assumptions or changing client circumstances or goals. We should continue to educate our clients, always remaining sensitive to the volatility of each one's expectations. Our responsibility is to assure that our client 'stays the course' and does so with a minimum of emotional pain. The focus should always be the client and the achievement of his goals, not the performance of the portfolio.

We are or believe those things which we repeatedly do. Therefore, excellence can become not just an event but a habit.

-Albert Einstein

STRATEGY 33

Your Dynamic Communications Department

Concept:

Constant and never-ending improvement of our professional image and client communications.

Objective:

When you are a professional, your image must be one of success. The little things mean a lot. People are paying attention, are you?

Think of all of the correspondence that leaves your office every day. You wouldn't want your product suppliers, such as mutual fund companies, life insurance, or others to have marketing materials with cheap printing, would you? From your business card to your statements, you should invest in professional-looking stationery. Personally, when I started writing quarterly newsletters, the content was useful to my clients and prospects, but the professionalism was terribly poor. Even seminar invitations were just a sheet of paper.

To be taken seriously and manage serious money, I have committed to constant and never-ending improvement of marketing and communication materials. I am always careful to ensure it is purposeful and not flashy. So many high-end brochures I read are beautiful brochures, with lovely pictures, but are not reflecting the message. Make sure yours matches your philosophy.

Strategy:

Look at the correspondence and marketing material your bank sends out (or your favorite fund company). Use that as a standard to follow. You should have personalized stationery, including your business cards, letterhead, and envelopes. For your mailers, use confidential-style envelopes if you mail statements. Client binders or life-policy wallets should be standard. For your proposals, how fancy are your client reviews and presentations? Could they be improved? Take a trip to your favorite printer or stationery store. Build a relationship with a professional printer who can work to improve your professional image. It will be worth the money in the long run.

Grant's Tip:

Use a color printer for better presentations and prepare professional financial plans bound in quality stationery. Develop a customized presentation folder with pockets. Take stock of your current communication tools and write a list of areas upon which to improve.

Look at all of your marketing pieces and circle the words "I," "we," and "us." Whenever possible change them to "you" and "your." Make sure all of your professional pieces are for the client's benefit and client's point of view. I hate to say it, but we are all greedy sometimes. Think of yourself as a greedy person—what do you want? Think for a second that you don't really care much about your company, but the benefits it provides. Now put yourself into a prospect's shoes. What would you want as a greedy person from this business? Now your perspective on marketing starts to take shape.

Jay's Comments:

Seven Steps For Creating Successful Marketing

1. Find the inherent drama within your offering. After all, you plan to make money by selling a product or a service or both. The reasons people will want to buy from you should give you a clue as to the inherent drama in your product or service. Something about your offering must be inherently interesting or you wouldn't be putting it up for sale. In Mother Nature breakfast cereal, it is the high concentration of vitamins and minerals.

2. Translate that inherent drama into a meaningful benefit. Always remember that people buy benefits, not features. People do not buy shampoo; people buy great-looking or clean or manageable hair. People do not buy cars; people buy speed, status, style, economy, performance, and power. Mothers of young kids do not buy cereal; they buy nutrition, though many buy anything at all they can get their kids to eat—anything. So find the major benefit of your offering and write it down. It should come directly from the inherently dramatic feature. And even though you have four or five benefits, stick with one or two—three at most.

3. State your benefits as believably as possible. There is a world of difference between honesty and believability. You can be 100 percent honest (as you should be) and people still may not believe you. You must go beyond honesty, beyond the barrier that advertising has erected by its tendency toward exaggeration, and state your benefit in such a way that it will be accepted beyond doubt. The company producing Mother Nature breakfast cereal might say, "A bowl of Mother Nature breakfast cereal provides your child with almost as many vitamins as a multi-vitamin pill." This statement begins with the inherent drama, turns it into a benefit, and is worded believably. The word almost lends believability.

4. Get people's attention. People do not pay attention to advertising. They pay attention only to things that interest them. And sometimes they find those things in advertising. So you've just got to interest them. And while you're at it, be sure you interest them in your product or service, not just your advertising. I'm sure you're familiar with advertising that you remember for a product you do not remember. Many advertisers are guilty of creating advertising that's more interesting than whatever it is they are advertising. But you can prevent yourself from falling into that trap by memorizing this line: Forget the ad, is the product or service interesting? The Mother Nature company might put their point across by showing a picture of two hands breaking open a multivitamin capsule from which pour flakes that fall into an appetizing-looking bowl of cereal.

5. Motivate your audience to do something. Tell them to visit the store, as the Mother Nature company might do. Tell them to make a phone call, fill in a coupon, write for more information, ask for your product by name, take a test drive, or come in for a free demonstration. Don't stop short. To make guerrilla marketing work, you must tell people exactly what you want them to do.

6. Be sure you are communicating clearly. You may know what you're talking about, but do your readers or listeners? Recognize that people aren't really thinking about your business and that they'll only give about half their attention to your ad even when they are paying attention. Knock yourself out to make sure you are putting your message across. The Mother Nature company might show its ad to ten people and ask them what the main point is. If one person misunderstands, that means 10 percent of the audience will misunderstand. And if the ad goes out to 500,000 people, 50,000 will miss the main point. that's unacceptable. One hundred percent of the audience should get the main point. The company might accomplish this by stating in a headline or subhead, "Giving your kids Mother Nature breakfast cereal is like giving your kids vitamins—only tastier." Zero ambiguity is your goal.

7. Measure your finished advertisement, commercial, letter, or brochure against your creative strategy. The strategy is your blueprint. If your ad fails to fulfill the strategy, it's a lousy ad, no matter how much you love it. Scrap it and start again. All along, you should be using your creative strategy to guide you, to give you hints as to the content of your ad. If you don't, you may end up being creative in a vacuum. And that's not being creative at all. If your ad is in line with your strategy, you may then judge its other elements.

Examples:

Check with an investment company that you hold as having a very professional image and use that as a standard.

Additional Resources:

Visit *www.financialadvisormarketing.com* for a full array of marketing and communications web site listings.

Action Summary:

To add to my marketing plans: Yes _____   No _____

Additional information required: Yes _____   No _____

In three words I can sum up everything I've learned about life. It goes on.

-Robert Frost

Chapter 5

Wowing Clients

The mark of a true professional is giving more than you get.

-Robert Kirby

STRATEGY 34

Wowing New Clients–Keeping Your Clients Organized

Concept:

Keeping yourself organized, and subsequently keeping your clients organized with an organizer/binder. There is actually one idea, getting organized, with three variations. First, keeping yourself organized with files, information, and reviews. Second, a binder organized for your clients to help them stay organized. Third, a professional-looking organizer for your clients.

Objective:

Getting organized. As Louis Pasteur said, "Success favors the prepared mind." Think of how organized a doctor's office is in regard to files and information. Is the file (or chart, as it is referred to in doctors' offices) system organized, or did they ever lose your history? When you received your will from your lawyer's office or your tax return from your accountant, was it in a presentable folder to keep all the documents organized? Keeping yourself and your clients documents organized shows your professionalism. Have client files and client documents organized in a very professional and presentable manner.

Strategy:

If I walk into your office right now, is it organized? How about if I am a client or prospect and walk out after a review? As a client or prospect, do I walk out of your office with a life insurance policy in a plastic bag? Or do I have a professional-looking organizer with all aspects of my financial plans in an organized fashion? Do I always have to search for documents and information? When a client has a review, do you have a well-organized file of information, updated and summarized, or are you scrambling to remember details? Have your files organized, whether paper or electronics, to give the impression of organization.

Are your files labeled professionally or scribbled on? Do you have systems for file preparation or is your system just throw-it-in-and-file-it-away? Set up your files so the access to information can be easy for anyone on your team. For example, paste client details on one side of the file folder, and personal details on the other side. Put color-coded file folders inside your legal-sized file folder (which I recommend) with relevant documents such as tax planning, insurance planning, or investment summaries where they are easily identifiable by your team. (Note, your compliance officer or department may have file procedures–check for guidelines. It will also help if you are audited or reviewed on a regular basis by your compliance officer.)

For your clients, do you have policy wallets (if you sell insurance)? Do you have client review binders or organizers? If you don't, I suggest you ask your company for organizers, or take a trip to your printer or stationery store and get binders and organizers for your clients.

Just imagine if I turn my portfolio over to you, and the last firm provided me with a client organizer, but you don't get one from me. What message am I sending? Some firms have customized material, which you may decide not to use for everyone but your top clients.

Grant's Tip:

You may be asking yourself at this point how this fits into your marketing plans. If you showed a prospect your personally prepared binder, organized with all the documents, tabs, and information on your financial plan and then said, "This is what you can expect," would they have a reason to do business with you? Would your image and professionalism be one notch higher than the advisor who handed them a cheap brochure? Have a client binder prepared with the following tabs, depending on your type of business.

Tabs: Financial Goals, Portfolio Summary, Portfolio Benchmarks, Annual Reviews, Financial Plan, Financial Planning Documents, Retirement Plan, Retirement Planning Documents, Estate Plan, Insurance Documents, Estate Planning Documents.

Under the tabs you can have listings of documents to put in each section; for example, estate-planning documents may include: Copy of Will, Copy of Power of Attorney, Copy of Health Care Directives, Copy of Instructions to Executor, Life Insurance Policies, Net Worth Statement, Pension Summaries, Investment Summaries, and Notes/To Do.

Have a client binder for accountants and tell them to keep it as a reference for the ideas that you send them. Your ideas are now seen as excellent reference material.

You can purchase leather binders with tabs in them from stationery stores, and customize the tabs for each client. You can also put a nice pen in the binder. The next time you meet, the client has the binder and is as well organized for the meeting as you are. Most clients receive all kinds of financial mail and sometimes are not sure what to keep. Ask them to bring it in and you will help them sort what's important for them to add to the binder.

A valuable estate planning strategy to help keep your clients organized is an estate organizer (personal financial organizer). I recommend that each client:
• Put his or her estate planning documents in order and pick a date where everything is current.
• Write to his or her estate administrator(s) stating that everything is up to date as of a certain date—the estate administrator doesn't have to go back any further when he or she uncovers documents after your client has passed away.

I will repeat that since it is very important to a client's estate plan. Have the client bring everything up to date and then write a letter to his or her executor stating everything is up to date as of that date. The executor who finds old papers and documents will NOT have to search these items out to see if they are valid; this saves hours of time for the executor.

It is a valuable exercise for your clients. Ask if they need help with it; you can do it together. You may uncover also hidden planning opportunities for your client, and the level of trust is heightened.

Imagine this scenario with new clients who transfer in. They have entrusted you with their life savings and goals. You have done all of the paperwork and completed all of the follow-up. They are happy and your next review is scheduled three to four months from now. You then call and say you have something for them. What is it? It is their personal financial binder, well organized with copies of all of their important documents, statements, etc. You give it to them and say thanks again for trusting us with your savings. I won't tell you what some of the reactions will be, just that you should experience that moment with clients for yourself.

One time, an advisor asked me, "What should be in the binder and what should it look like?" My answer for him will be my answer for you. Complete a binder for yourself. Get your own personal finances organized in a nice professional-looking binder or portfolio case. That is your standard for your clients. You can even have your own binder in your office to show prospects how you help organize people's financial lives.

Costs: Binders range from $5 to $100 each. Make up 5 to 10 binders with tabs in advance.

Jay's Comments:

As this section is called wowing clients, I thought I would include a summary of some fantastic Guerrilla Marketers and how they wowed their clients and prospects.

Add Memos to Your Marketing

Frank Pipia, Jr. of Pipia-Graphics & Advertising, Inc. of Wauwatosa, WI, has a timely reminder for all you busy Guerrillas.

Pipia suggests writing a brief personal note to each of your clients and prospects on a post-it or 1/4 page memo pad. Attach it to your business card and mail it off. Keep the message short and personal. Ask them how things are going. Thank them for their business or their interest. Mention any new products or services you are offering and how they might benefit. Finally, ask them to give you a call or offer to call them in order to chat soon.

Pipia claims that people will be gratified that you took the time to jot down a few personal lines. If you do this once a month you'll maintain a high profile. Even if they don't need your services presently, you'll be more likely to get their business in the future.

Business Card Does Double Duty

Carol Parenzan Smalley, owner of Small Business Consulting Services in Palmyra, PA, has a great suggestion for a variation on the old business card. She's created a bookmark that folds to the size of a standard business card. The front of the card contains her business information. and the back of the card lists her services as well as free resource information with phone numbers, library sections, government agencies, and web sites (such as Guerrilla Marketing Online).

Smalley's stationery letterhead compliments the bookmark, with her services listed down the left margin—subtly advertising all of her services with each and every correspondence.

Finally, Smalley reduced her costs by utilizing a great guerrilla tool: bartering. A client designed her stationery package in exchange for a marketing plan that Smalley wrote. Good going!

Autoresponder or URL?

When Guerrilla Jim Daniels of Smithfield, RI, created his web site, he made some changes to his classified ads. He replaced the autoresponders—which had allowed his prospects to receive sales letters almost instantly—with his URL in his classified ads. He assumed that people would prefer to visit the site and view the color, sound, and graphics.

When his response dropped, he realized that there are literally millions of people who use email but don't surf the Web. So out went the URL address in favor of the autoresponders. Daniels also had an email newsletter so he decided to do a little more experimenting. There, his newsletter ads contained both the autoresponder address and the URL.

Finally he had the perfect mix. His total inquiries (autoresponders plus page hits) went up by about 20% and remained there as long as his ad contained both contact methods. Along with these increased prospects came increased profits.

A valuable lesson learned.

Become a Marketing Matchmaker

Guerrilla Dana Burke of Mind Your Business, has a terrific idea that can be used by anyone with a box of labels and some ingenuity.

Burke maintains a supply of her clients' and associates' business cards in her office and distributes them to likely customers. Using return address labels, she's created a sticker that says "Referred by Mind Your Business." Placed on the back of other people's business cards, the stickers remind the recipient who she is and help them when they call on the prospect.

The customer is reminded of her business and her name is the first one the prospect hears. Quite the win-win-win situation.

Guerrilla Greetings

Troubled by the high cost of keeping in touch with your customers? Guerrilla Ron Foster keeps in touch with his customers year round using simple and inexpensive fax greetings.

Ron sends a fax greeting just before holidays, special events and personal events. His customers really appreciate the faxes and even call him back when the greeting is particularly creative. Either way, they enjoy the effort and remember him year round.

Fishing for Leads

Are you always looking for local leads? Guerrilla Cyndi Stout goes "fishing" for free leads all over town and you can too!

Many stores and restaurants have a glass bowl for business cards and they give away some kind of prize return for the cards people drop in. Cyndi simply asks these business if she can have the cards in exchange for something. Sometimes they give them to her for free and other times she pays for the incentive prize in exchange for the leads. You could even offer to type up the names and give them to the store in text and database form.

So far nobody has turned down her request to share leads!

Give a Web Page

Seems everybody with a web site is either trying to get people to visit it or trying to make more money with it. Guerrilla Thaddeus Frick did both when he started giving away web pages.

Thaddeus gave away personal pages on his site to his clients to promote themselves and this in turn brought traffic to his site and loyalty to his consulting practice.

Don't Give it Away!

Ever tried to give something away only to find few or no takers? Guerrilla Wayne Schulz discovered how to sell what he couldn't give away and gave his marketing a boost in the process.

Wayne used to advertised software demonstration seminars as freebies. Perhaps 4 people would sign up and of those, only one would actually show up. In frustration he decided to charge something for the seminars. Same content—only now people have to pay to attend.

Surprise! His enrollments went from 4 to 14! And because people paid, they valued the seminar more highly and more actually attended the seminar. Just think. Qualified prospects pay to get into your seminar. Check with your compliance office before using this one.

Do you find getting media attention more painful than giving blood? Guerrilla Charles Larsen gave blood instead marketing and got plenty of attention.

Charles hosted a blood drive for his community and alerted the media about the event. He got all kinds of attention from the local TV and radio stations. The blood drive was a success for both the blood bank and Charles. Now lots of people know about his business.

You could also try the same approach with many other charitable acts and get the same result. You'll do yourself and your community a favor.

If your business requires a little trust from your customers then you need great references! Guerrilla Ronald Smith develops new references with every new job using a customer satisfation survey.

Ronald's company sells and installs a skylight product for home remodeling. He knows that whenever people start work on their homes they are afraid of what might go wrong, so he lets his current customers put those fears to rest.

They send out a customer satisfaction survey after they finish a job and ask for permission to use comments in their marketing. They also offer a free dinner to anyone who refers a new customer to the company.

Nearly 70% of the surveys are returned and about 90% of those agree to use of their comments in marketing efforts.

Everyone has trouble getting the attention of a prospect at one time or another. So, when it counts, Guerrilla John Rowley attaches one half of a US $20 note to a simple mail pitch. He promises to give them the other half in exchange for 20 minutes time.

Most customer loyalty programs are expensive to set up and manage but Larry Gaynor's simple approach is the Guerrilla solution that turns it into a profit center.

Larry sends a Tootsie Roll Pop out with EVERY order and attaches a client survey card. Each week they get back hundreds of customer survey cards raving about the candy and good service. Over 80% respond with some kind of comment.

Guerrilla Thomas Kan got his Hong Kong Internet marketing firm off to a quick start with advertising specialties.

He sent out 3,000 promotional mouse pads just as he launched his company. Now he's getting lots of calls. The promotion worked because of three things: the mouse pads all had a phone number, he gave his pads away early and before most were thinking about the Internet, and they were interesting enough to keep on a desk.

Financial planner Michael Marteloni calls prospects and asks them for 43 seconds of their time. It's such an odd number that people are curious enough to say yes. In his 43 seconds, Michael introduces his firm, himself, and his objective: a 50-minute face-to-face meeting. Around 10% of people agree to the meeting and of those, 10% become clients. Michael talks to a lot of people.

Courtesy of Guerrilla Marketing - *www.gmarketing.com*

Action Summary:

To add to my marketing plans: Yes _____   No _____

Additional information required: Yes _____   No _____

There is no failure except in no longer trying.

-Elbert Hubbard

To finish first, you must first finish.

-Rick Mears, Indy Car Driver

STRATEGY 35

The Best Client Appreciation Ideas

Concept:

People don't care how much you know, until they know how much you care. The concept is simple. Make sure you thank your clients for the trust and confidence they have shown in allowing you to manage their financial affairs. As an advisor, you sell intangibles all day. You sell a feeling that the client gets about you, your team and your company. How do you create this feeling?

Objective:

I had a client walk into my office wanting to switch his portfolio to me. Since we were acquainted personally, he was comfortable dealing with me. When I asked the reason he switched, it made me rethink client appreciation. He and his wife went to a client appreciation event set up by their existing advisor. They received a quick hello from the advisor and that was it. For the rest of the event, the advisor and staff spent time talking to other clients. They felt they weren't important enough and felt uncomfortable. They decided to move their portfolio right after the event. Each year client appreciation dollars are wasted in an effort to impress clients and say thanks.

Strategy:

It is critical to say thanks. How you do it and how you budget it can dramatically vary your result.

First, look at the feeling you get from other businesses that impress you. How do they thank and appreciate you? Try to establish the feeling with which you want your clients to come away.

Second, talk to your top clients, mentor, and other advisors on what works for them. Ask them personal questions such as how they feel when they leave your office or how they feel about client appreciation.

Third, set out a budget for the year and a timetable for client appreciation events. For example, two times per year for all clients may be very costly if you have hundreds of clients.

Fourth, once you set out to do client appreciation, keep doing it consistently. You will lose integrity if you do it three times and stop. Your clients may feel there is no consistency to your business. For example, each year I send out Thanksgiving gifts. I don't do Christmas or other holiday times-only Thanksgiving. I send a small, personalized gift and a letter of appreciation. For example:

Around this time of year we give thanks for many things in our lives. I love what I do and I am thankful for individuals like you. I have enclosed a gift to express my sincere appreciation for our business and personal relationship. I hope you and your family have a wonderful Thanksgiving holiday. Many thanks again.

Fifth, once you know the feeling you want to engender and have a budget in mind, factor in the time it will take to complete.

Sixth, you will need to determine what type of client appreciation you will do. For example, if you have a clientele of young doctors and retired clients, a golf event may work. That is why you need to know their hobbies or interests. You can customize the event for different groups as well. Client appreciation examples:

• Lunch or dinner.

• Charitable events. You can use a charitable event and tie it in with client appreciation, such as charity golf events for which you buy a table for your top clients.

• Client appreciation gifts.

• Client appreciation events–golf or movie events. For example, you could rent a theatre and have only your clients attend.

• You can also send birthday cards; but once you start, NEVER stop.

The best client appreciation examples are stories from other advisors. Collect these stories in a file and start a client appreciation ideas file.

Seventh, remember the goal of client appreciation. Is it a sincere thank you? Don't use this to try to get referrals. The goal is the feeling the clients receive about you.

Grant's Tip:

Client Appreciation Don'ts:

• Don't mix prospects with clients. You are sincerely thanking your clients. Don't mix the two.

• Don't mix sponsorship with client appreciation. You may get your name advertised with a theatre event and have an evening for your clients; however, the clients will feel it is a marketing event for you and not a sincere client appreciation. Are you a sponsor or are you doing client appreciation?

• Don't spend an enormous amount of time and money only to try and top the event each year until it becomes outrageous. Keep it consistent year after year.

That's why you budget it out each year.

• Don't thank clients with whom you don't have a good relationship. It may not come across as sincere.

• Don't ignore anyone at your events. If you don't have enough time to talk to everyone, then make the list smaller.

• Don't forget to appreciate your clients for their trust, confidence and relationship.

More client appreciation ideas:

Letters–Ask your clients if you can publish quotes from their appreciation letters in your marketing materials. Ask for testimonials if you don't have any and add them to your marketing.

Client appreciation cards–Print thank-you cards with your company name and logo to send out.

Special occasion cards–Have several types of cards to send out for different occasions (graduations, retirements, etc.). When someone notifies a change of address, I always send a congratulations on your new home card, sometimes with a small gift.

Magazine subscriptions–Send a subscription to a magazine about a client's favorite hobby. If you purchased the *Hockey News* for me, you would have one happy client who gets reminded of you several times per year.

Each month pick two clients to receive appreciation gifts.

Start an after-hours program–Team up with a restaurant to print and send gift certificates for dinner. You can include a movie or a sporting event.

Send email cards that say thank you–E-cards are free and you can customize them for any type of client or situation. If you have zero in the budget, send e-cards.

Gift baskets–Sending gift baskets is a great way to say thanks. It's easy to do. Find a person or company in your area that has several different types of gift baskets, then it only takes a phone call from you or your assistant to arrange delivery. You can even order these on-line.

Have a client appreciation program. For example:

With our program, you will receive valuable information and will be contacted at least six times each calendar year. We want to be your financial advisors for life and the trusted financial advisor who can offer you one-stop shopping with our preferred partners. Our business is based on your referrals. We know that you will want to have all your friends, relatives, and coworkers receive the same service you did. When you think of someone who can use our services, just give us a call with their name and telephone number and we will follow up with them.

Building appreciation themes–Consider a monthly client appreciation theme. Look at specific holidays or seasonal times of the year. For example, I send a thanksgiving gift in the fall. I send seeds out in the spring. In summer you can send out a coupon to a local ice cream place. Simple gestures to say thanks don't have to be expensive.

Promotional items–Year-long marketing items such as calendars and note cubes.

Family gifts–Send a voucher for free portrait sitting for a family. If you do it for parents and grandparents, all of the family members will know who paid the bill. Next thing you know you are doing intergenerational wealth transfer for the family.

Team up–Try to team up with businesses that you know do client appreciation. A florist or restaurant owner with whom you do lots of client appreciation business may be a great source of referrals. They can also be great for client appreciation ideas.

Have your cake and eat it too–One client appreciation idea I found very interesting is sending a cake to say thanks. No one eats cake alone and everyone will always ask where the cake came from–could be a great source of referrals to friends, neighbors, and family.

Host a "Widow's Luncheon" once per quarter–The KEY for prospecting success is to encourage them to invite other widows they know. Avoid making this a sales event. Make the theme clear. It will be "all fun and NO finance" –have a program that is fun.

Remember to check with your compliance office on client appreciation. Also check with your accountant to make sure the expenses are tax-deductible.

Jay's Comments:

Develop client loyalty by sponsoring client appreciation events. Clients go where they are invited, and they stay only where they are appreciated. Think about how you can demonstrate to your clients how much they mean to you.

Successful events could be:
- *Sporting and recreational events.*
- *Rounds of golf or tennis.*
- *Tickets to college and/or pro-team events.*
- *Cultural happenings.*
- *Concerts.*

- *Art shows.*
- *Holiday music events.*
- *Charitable events.*
- *Participate in, and co-sponsor, a charity golf outing in your area. Invite your best clients to invite their best clients to play.*
- *Educational events.*
- *Invite clients to hear a guest speaker who is well known and is visiting your area.*
- *Create a series of quarterly or semi-annual client briefings where they can gain insight and information.*

Get your profits off to a rip-roaring start with client appreciation. To make every stamp and letter count, follow these seven steps and leave your competitors in the dust.

While competitors are sleeping, guerrillas are quietly working away. Preparing to launch a series of marketing attacks to capture clients and prospects and sequester profits. You can use client appreciation to get new clients, and warm the way for a sales call from a prospect.

How?

Simple. By following these seven guerrilla rules of client appreciation:

1. Before you write, do a couple hours of research. Ask a handful of your current clients to tell you in their own words what they like most about doing business with you.

Use those words when you ask them. What they will tell you will be the most important benefits they perceive. Use those benefits to start your letter.

2. Come up with a really dynamite reason for someone to respond to the letter. Make an extraordinary offer.

Find a new and appealing way to bundle together a number of your product or services.

3. When you start writing, use short words and short sentences. People can't, won't, and don't read long, complicated stuff. Not if they don't have to.

They won't read your letter unless it's EASY to read.

4. Count the number of "you's" and "your's" in the letter. Your letter should have at least twice as many "you's" and "your's" as "I's," "we's," "me's," "our's" and your company's name. A ratio of four to one is even better.

When they read your letter, your customers like it when you talk about their dreams, their problems, solutions you can provide to their problems, and the benefits they will receive. And they will show their appreciation—with sales!

5. Whatever you do, DON'T mail it out the minute after you write it. No matter how good a writer you are! Let it sit a day or two. Then, rewrite your letter to make it simpler, clearer, and more compelling. After that, read it out loud. Then, show your letter to some clients. If their reaction is "interesting" or "well written," you may have a loser on your hands. A sales letter isn't an essay. It's a sales piece, first and foremost. So, after reading, if your clients say, "How can I get one of those?"–they want to buy what you're offering–you've got yourself a guerrilla letter. The offer goes along with a new client appreciation offer. Typically reserved for your top clients, do this with your top prospects.

6. Check to see if it's clear what you're offering and how a reader can take you up on the offer. One great way to find out is to have a child read your letter. Children often see the obvious that adults–caught up in the more abstract problems and distractions of life–miss.

7. Do a test mailing and measure the results. Don't send out all your letters at once. Just send out a few dozen. Or a few hundred. When the results come in–when your mail is good, they'll come in fast–then do the math.

Did you make money? Did the letter get you more than you would have gotten if you had put the time to other use? If the answers are yes, then roll out it. And let the profits roll in.

Action Summary:

To add to my marketing plans:	Yes _____	No _____
Additional information required:	Yes _____	No _____

The world makes way for the person who knows where he or she is going.

-Ralph Waldo Emerson

Chapter 6

Mastering Service
For All Client Levels

For three days after death, hair and fingernails continue to grow but phone calls taper off.
-Johnny Carson

STRATEGY 36

Client Correspondence Designed for Them

Concept:

How do you correspond with your clients? These days mostly everyone has email, yet how often is it used and how effective is it?

Objective:

To produce a stimulus strong enough to trigger a response. Depending on the type of email database, you can easily communicate with clients and prospects 24 hours a day. The best part is that you can be at the ski lodge or beach resort in Hawaii and send everyone a message at no cost. I cannot think of a better way to constantly communicate and market to clients and prospects.

Strategy:

Emailing to the masses can be a positive or a negative. I sometimes hate email because I receive several meaningless messages, however, I always keep or print out interesting emails. Mass emailing, also known as spamming, is becoming commonplace.

First of all, if you were to become a client, what would you like to hear about on a regular basis? Some companies have programs for which you can sign up, and all you do as an advisor is forward your clients email addresses and they do the rest. I can't think of a better way to send the message that you don't care about your client, because it's obvious it is some service you signed up for.

How do you establish effective communication? When sending your email, make sure it is personalized and not a mass list. Always use a signature at the bottom so they can email you back easily or check out your web site and have a reply mechanism. Always put a forwarding mechanism to have your email forwarded to other interested investors. This can be a Monday morning or Friday afternoon strategy if your intent is to generate calls to your office.

Your message should be consistent with your strategy. If your strategy is more holistic, email messages on health, recreation, and travel tips may be appealing. If you focus on a certain market such as retirees, sending a message about daily stock price movements is ineffective. I would try to segment clients into email categories such as younger and older retirees. Then you can send out similar email messages with slight variations to each group. The message should also contain a personal element, just like you would in a phone conversation. Comments such as, "What a great weekend for golf or gardening. Isn't this weather great?" or WOW! Did you see the Canadian golfer win the Masters this weekend? Asking clients a question in the email makes it responsive when they're reading it.

How do you get your clients excited about reading your emails? Simple–just like you do in all of your other marketing, have a great headline. The headline should not be disturbing; however, if you're emailing to prospects, you want your headline to rouse them. Beyond a great headline keep it short, simple and personal.

If you're emailing to prospects, have a way for that person to unsubscribe, since there is nothing more annoying than getting constant emails from someone you don't know or don't care to know.

Grant's Tip:

If you're emailing prospects a rousing or catchy headline, such as, "What to do with money now!" your email may get read. For existing clients, collecting their email addresses is the first key. You might be surprised how many clients now have email. Ask your clients who in their households reads email. Ask, if they have more than one address, which address you should use. Ask if they can help you by forwarding interesting web sites, topics of interest, or items they enjoy receiving. If you sent me an email on fishing or golf tips along with some interesting web sites, I would be inclined to read your brief information on investing. Once in a while add personal notes or questions to clients with whom you want to touch base. Sometimes an email will save a lot of time trying to get in touch with someone.

Do you ever feel you could do a better job of communicating with your clients? If you haven't talked with certain clients for a while, sending them a quick email can help you avoid the anxiety of receiving a phone call from a client who says, "Gee, I haven't heard from you in a while."

Remember to have your compliance department review your email reviewed. Correspondence to two or more people usually needs to be reviewed by compliance first.

Jay's Comments:

Guerrillas are well aware that free marketing exists in its most free state as email, which is far more than merely letters with free postage.

Mark Twain said he never let his schooling interfere with his education. Regardless of your schooling, there's little chance it covered what technology makes possible today. If you took a course in how computers can aid your marketing, the first insight you would have gained would be into the profitability for you if you become savvy about email.

When you think of email, don't compare it with snail mail because it's considerably different. In fact, it is such an improvement on old-fashioned mail delivery that the U.S. Postal service now uses it, and today there is a lot more email being sent daily than snail mail. Soon, half of all bills and payments will be sent electronically. Two-thirds of Social Security checks, tax refunds, and other federal payments sent in 1999 went electronically.

In fact, the U.S. Postal Service is now in serious trouble because of the vast amount of information transmitted via the Internet. For much of this, guerrillas owe a tip of their propeller beanie to Ray Tomlinson who invented email in 1971.

You can use email in your marketing in ways that will make your customers delighted to be doing business with you. Guerrillas love email but hate junk email, known as spamming. Their affinity to email is because they can deliver their messages instantly and to anywhere in the world if the recipients are on line, as more and more of them are with each word I type. That means email saves you time in communicating and money that you used to spend on postage. It can also help save trees on the planet because it is so delightfully paperless.

Each recipient can read your email on screen or print and save it just as with a standard letter, which does use paper. But you don't have to print and save your email, saving you the cost of paper and the convenience of space. Save it in your computer. Make copies as you need them. All your files and memos can be kept in one convenient location. Each one is dated and timed. Many experts feel that for all the great things about being on line, email is the most valuable of all computer applications.

Email also helps you save on the cost of courier service and faxing. You can use it to send brief messages or long documents, to send black and white communications or colorful, beautifully-designed materials. It's easy for you and easy for the person who receives your email.

Who should that be? People who want to receive it, that's who.

Technology, for all the wondrous things about it, can also be a major distraction and a drain on your time if you focus on the technology itself rather than on the benefits it can bring to your business.

As "Net Benefits" author Kim Elton reminds us, "Business is life and life is messy. Like a kitchen sink full of dirty dishes, you know that when you're finally cleaned them up, someone will burn a tuna casserole and you'll be back in sudsy water up to your elbows with a Brillo pad in no time. But if the kids are growing up healthy and strong—and helping out with the dishes now and then—it's all worth the effort. Soon you'll get a dishwasher and you can shift the mess from the sink to the dishwasher. The dishes still have to be cleaned. The technology eases the labor and takes away some of the pain, but it doesn't relieve the duty."

That's the insight that I want you to take from this. Technology helps with the job but doesn't do the job. That's your task. In order for you to understand how technology can help you, it's not necessary for you to learn the technical jargon, the nerdy part of technology. But you must comprehend the impact of technology and the ways it can transform a squirt gun into a cannon.

To cash in on the transformation, you must be in close touch with your needs. Technology will help you meet them. You must know how best to utilize the technology in which you've invested to get the maximum benefit for the money you've put forth. You've got to recognize hype for just what it is and solid science for just what it is.

You wouldn't dream of running a business without using a telephone. The computer will be just as endemic as phones. Using technology will be as easy as making a phone call. It's already well on its way. Investment research company Robertson Stephens stated it this way:

"Communicating is becoming the primary role of computers after four decades of number crunching. We stand at a technology crossroads and are witnessing a technological metamorphosis...In our opinion, computers, originally designed for number crunching and applied to computing tasks for nearly 50 years, will be used in the future primarily for communicating."

The future is now the present.

An old adage reminds us that if you have foresight, you are blessed, and if you have insight, you are twice-blessed. Here are two insights to make you quadruple-blessed.

The single most important insight for the new millennium is to reach out for your client base. Ranking up there near the top is to engage in as much one-on-one marketing as you possibly can. Attesting to that is the hottest application for an Internet site—chat sessions. People love the one-on-one aspect of it, so that even though millions of people are on line, many of them are engaged in one-on-one conversations. That alone is probably the biggest reason for America Online's unparalleled success.

Although I've already written of the Internet in several books, I'm reminding you here of its unique ability in one-to-one communicating. With email, it's fast and easy to carry on a dialogue with your prospects and customers. Of course, you can also do it at trade shows, on the phone, when you are in person, and by mail. But faster and easier is the Net.

Guerrillas know in their hearts that every customer is an individual and wants to be treated as such. Client questionnaires let them learn of the individualities. They know that although there are tens of thousands of names on their mailing list, those people want to be serviced and sold to one at a time.

One-on-one marketing is akin to having somebody whisper in your ear rather than shouting across the street, as is the case with mass media marketing. It gives guerrillas a chance to cozy up to customers, customize their marketing, increase the delight factor of doing business with them.

The essence of the guerrilla's joy–long-term relationships–is found in one-on-one marketing. Guerrillas know well the enormous difference between their customers and their best customers. This enables them to treat their customers like royalty and their best clients like family.

To engage in one-on-one marketing, they must market with absolute precision. They must know their best customers from the rest, then market to them in ways that prove they care. Guerrillas tailor their relationships to helping their clients succeed at whatever they wish to succeed at. They do all they can to warm up relationships. And they play favorites.

Just keep in mind the true tale of the non-profit organization that increased its response rate 668 percent by treating its biggest donors in a special way–special but not expensive. They mailed to them a letter requesting funds, and enclosed the letter in a handwritten envelope using a commemorative stamp. At the end of the letter was a 25-word handwritten note. Hardly fancy, but astonishingly effective. It's not quite one on one, but it gives you the feel of one-on-one marketing in action. It's the wave of the future. And to guerrillas, it's the wave of the present. It's also an insight possessed by all guerrillas.

Another insight for this millennium and all the millennia to follow is to possess basic knowledge of human behavior. Human beings do not like making decisions in a hurry and are not quick to develop relationships. They certainly do want relationships, but they've been stung in the past and they don't want to be stung again.

They have learned well to distrust much marketing because of its proclivity to exaggeration. All too many times they've read of sales at stores and learned that only a tiny selection of items were on sale. They've been bamboozled more times than you'd think by the notorious fine print on contracts. And they've been high pressured by more than one salesperson.

That's why they process your marketing communications in their unconscious minds, eventually arriving at their decisions because of an emotional reason even though they may say they are deciding based on logic. They factor a lot about you into their final decision -- how long they've heard of you, where your marketing appears, how it looks and feels to them, the quality of your offer, your convenience or lack of it, what others have said about you, and most of all, how your offering can be of benefit to their lives.

Although they state that they now want what you're selling, and they do it in a very conscious manner, you can be sure they were guided by their unconscious minds. The consistent communicating of your benefits, your message and your name has penetrated their sacred unconscious mind. They've come to feel that they can trust you and so they decide to buy.

Any pothole in their road to purchasing at this point might dissuade them. They call to make an inquiry and they are treated shabbily on the phone? You've lost them. Do they access your web site for more information and either find no web site or find one littered with self-praise? You've lost them. They visit you and feel pressured or misunderstood? They're gone.

You've got to realize that the weakest point in your marketing can derail all the strong points. Excellence through and through, start to finish, is what people have come to expect from businesses and, these days, they won't settle for less. Marketing is a 360-degree process and you've got to do it right from all angles at all times. When it comes to marketing, people have built-in alarm systems, and any shady behavior on your part sets the bells to clanging, the sirens screaming.

It is very difficult to woo a person from the advisor they use right now to your advice. Although they are loath to change, they do change. And when they do, they patronize businesses that understand the psychology of human beings and the true nature of marketing. If you're the guerrilla I think you are, you understand both.

Action Summary:

To add to my marketing plans: Yes _____   No _____

Additional information required: Yes _____   No _____

I used to sell furniture for a living. The trouble was, it was my own.

-Les Dawson

Why don't they make the whole plane out of that black box stuff?

-Steven Wright

STRATEGY 37

Newsletters That Impact Your Clients' Lives

Concept:

Every financial firm on this planet tries to communicate with newsletters. How can you impact your clients' lives? By sending messages that will impact their lives. Motivation, positive attitude, and a focus on their lives and lifestyles through newsletters.

Objective:

Nearly 80% of financial advisors who use newsletters are not using them to full potential. What innovations do you have to think about in your newsletter that will impact your clients' lives?

Strategy:

To create effective newsletters, we must first answer a basic question. Why do financial advisors use newsletters? The five main reasons are:

• Consistent contact.
• Client education.
• Building relationships.
• Sharing ideas.
• Communicating future events.

When I speak to groups of advisors, I always bring up the major problem with newsletters. As financial advisors, clients come to us to solve their problems so they have less worry and more confidence in the plan we create together. Then we go and send out a newsletter that lists and identifies all of the things our clients should worry about. Hey, if you're my advisor, why send this out? If there is something for me to worry about, call me and we'll take care of it. Don't send out stuff we have already taken care of. Especially, don't make the mistake of sending out product ideas. Leave that mistake for the wholesalers. Instead, send me out lifestyle issues, coming events notices, motivation, or other information.

Grant's Tip:

I learned the hard way with newsletters, by trying all kinds from fancy to simple, from large to small. Becoming a guerrilla marketer, I learned that a one-page newsletter works best. It's simple, it can easily be glanced over or read, and people always turn it over. You can easily print this type of newsletter with desktop publishing.

Invite clients to read your latest newsletter via the Web. Then you can have clients and prospects register to receive it via email and save yourself some costs. Focus each newsletter on a single topic. For advisors who send out newsletters to prospects, take a different approach. Focus on being a problem-solver and illustrate this through case studies. Describe how you've helped others overcome similar problems and challenges. End your newsletter with a call to action.

Jay's Comments:

You know exactly what your company is, what it stands for, what it offers to its target audience and what it hopes to accomplish. But is that really your company?

Not really. In reality, your company is the marketing that people see. It's the big things such as your web site and your features and benefits, but it's also a combination of seemingly minor details—all anything but minor. Your company is the way your telephone is answered. It's the way you listen to customers and prospects. It's your ability to render superlative service. It's every letter you send, every phone call you make, every person you employ.

There is an enormous difference between reality and perception. You know in your heart the reality of your company, but chances are that your prospects and customers perceive you not by that reality but by the attitude and professionalism of your marketing. Their perception of your company counts for every bit as much as the reality of your company.

Your company is your involvement with the community, your willingness to provide speed and convenience in all your transactions. It's the regularity of your follow-up, the experience of other customers you've had, even the way you greet your prospects and customers.

One of your primary jobs is to make certain that the perception of your company matches the reality. You've got to realize that your long-time customers may know exactly what your company is all about, but your prospects only know you by your marketing—or lack of it.

Your web site, along with your other marketing, must convey your company identity because more and more people every day will be learning of your company on line and not off line. To them, you are your web site.

Your ability to tailor your offerings and service to the needs of your customers is your company. The quality of information you provide and the generosity with which you provide it—those also are your company.

Your newsletter and brochures, your fliers and promotions—they are your company. Today, more than ever, you can craft your marketing to reflect exactly what your company is. You can use your computer and a wide array of software to create dynamic marketing materials that communicate your company is professional, caring, unique, and covers all the bases. You can use customer questionnaires to learn about your customers so that you get a good bead on their perceptions of you, both good and bad. The information they provide shines a beacon on their opinions of you, allowing you to make the necessary changes to match their perceptions with the perceptions you want them to have.

Your company is the sum total of what it truly is—combined with the marketing you put out to the world—or the marketing you do not practice. That's why active and aggressive marketing is the hallmark of successful companies. That's why they measure their marketing to be certain it is hitting home and communicating the actuality of their firms.

Most owners of small businesses focus upon their company far more than they focus upon their marketing. The two should be inseparable. And the vast majority of the world who are not yet your customers know you only by your marketing. If it comes up short or isn't noticed by them, it makes no difference how superlative your quality and dedication may be.

Never forget that one of the tiniest groups of people on the planet are your customers. They know your company by what it really is. But the billions of people who have never purchased from you—they know your company only by your marketing efforts.

Guerrilla marketers pay as much close attention to their marketing as they do to their business. They do not delude themselves into thinking everybody knows about their excellence. Instead, they put out the word and continue spreading it, making certain that it accurately reflects their company. We've all had experiences when we were shocked to learn that a company was drastically different from its marketing. Never let that happen to your company. It never will when you always remember that your company is two things at all times: what it really is and what people think it is based upon your marketing.

Additional Resources:
• Visit *www.gmarketingdesign.com* and register for Roger C. Parker's newsletter marketing ideas.
• Sign up for the Guerrilla Marketing Association newsletter at *www.financialadvisormarketing.com*.

Action Summary:

To add to my marketing plans:	Yes _____	No_____
Additional information required:	Yes _____	No_____

If you cannot read this, please ask the flight attendant for assistance.

-Airline Flight Safety Brochure

Attitudes are more important than facts.

-Karl Menninger, M.D.

STRATEGY 38
Read With Scissors

Concept:

Communicating with your top clients and prospects. Remember all leaders are readers.

Objective:

How often do you read something and think one of your clients would be interested in it? Or how many times have you discussed something with a client and a day or two later you read an article or pull something off the web site about it? The objective here is to let your clients and prospects know you are thinking of them. Send the client the article; cut it out and send it to him or her with a handwritten note saying something like, "I thought you would be interested in this, talk to you soon." Make sure you do not photocopy the article. Sending the original has meaning and people tend to keep the original if it was especially sent to them for them. Anything personalized, meant as something special, makes the client feel special.

Strategy:

Think of all of the reading you do on a daily and weekly basis. Next time you read a newspaper, read with scissors in hand. The articles can be on markets, funds, selected securities, tax ideas, financial planning ideas—anything you think is interesting and a client may find interesting. Or it can be about a mutual personal interest, or both. The Internet allows you to email articles from news stories to selected people. While this is not as personalized, it can be an efficient way to send ideas and information out and show you are thinking of the client, as long as it is relevant and not just another mailer.

Grant's Tip:

Each Saturday I read the national business newspaper with scissors and try to send, on Monday, a few interesting articles to top clients, centers of influence, or prospects. Then the next time I see that person, I ask what he or she thought of the article. Since it was personalized and cut out, in every case he or she read the article and has a comment.

Then it can be a great icebreaker for your next meeting. If you really want to show you care, send articles of personal interests or hobbies such as golf magazine stories or recipes, etc., that caused you to think of the client when you read it. You may want to start reading or subscribing to things your clients are reading. For instance, to a lawyer who is interested in fly-fishing you can send interesting articles you read on estate planning or fly-fishing or both. It shows the clients they are special and you are thinking of them.

Costs: Half a dozen stamps per week, to show 6 people per week, 24 per month, that you care about them and are interested. This is a cost-effective high-touch process you can develop and enjoy while you read. You're reading anyway, so read with scissors.

Jay's Comments:

Why do most businesses lose customers? Poor service? Nope. Poor quality? Nope. Well, then why? Apathy after the sale. Most businesses lose clients by ignoring them to death. A numbing 68% of all business lost in America is lost due to apathy after the sale. Misguided business owners think that marketing is over once they've made the sale. WRONG WRONG WRONG. Marketing begins once you've made the sale. It's of momentous importance to you and your company that you understand this.

I'm sure you will by the time you've come to the end of this on-line column. First of all, understand how guerrillas view follow-up. They make it part of their DNA because they know it now costs six times more to sell something to a new customer than to an existing client. When a guerrilla makes a sale, the client receives a follow-up thank-you note within 48 hours. When's the last time a business sent you a thank-you note within 48 hours? Maybe once? Maybe never? Probably never. The guerrilla sends another note or perhaps makes a phone call 30 days after the sale. This contact is to see if everything is going all right with the purchase and if the customer has any questions. It is also to help solidify the relationship. The what? The relationship.

Guerrillas know that the way to develop relationships, the key to survival in an increasingly entrepreneurial society, is through assiduous customer follow-up and prospect follow-up. And we haven't even talked yet about prospect follow-up. Back to the client. Guerrillas send their clients another note within 90 days, this time informing them of a new and related product or service. Possibly it's a new offering that the guerrilla business now provides. And maybe it's a product or service offered by one of the guerrilla's fusion marketing partners such as an accountant or lawyer. Guerrillas are very big on forging marketing alliances with businesses throughout the community—and using the Internet, throughout the world. These tie-ins enable them to increase their marketing exposure while reducing their marketing costs, a noble goal.

After six months, the customer hears from the guerrilla again, this time with the preview announcement of an upcoming sale. Nine months after the sale, the guerrilla sends a note asking the customer for the names of three people who might benefit from being included on the guerrilla's mailing list. A simple form and postpaid envelope is provided. Because the guerrilla has been keeping in touch with the customer–and because only three names are requested–the customer often supplies the names.

After one year, the client receives an anniversary card celebrating the one-year anniversary of the first sale. Perhaps a coupon for a discount is snuggled in the envelope. Fifteen months after the sale, the customer receives a questionnaire, filled with questions designed to give the guerrilla insights into the client. The questionnaire has a paragraph at the start that says, "We know your time is valuable, but the reason we're asking so many questions is because the more we know about you, the better service we can be to you." This makes sense. The client completes and mails the questionnaire. Perhaps after eighteen months, the client receives an announcement of still more new investment ideas that tie in with the original purchase. And the beat goes on. The client, rather than being a one-time buyer, becomes a repeat buyer, becomes the kind of person who refers others to the guerrilla's business. A bond is formed. The bond intensifies with time and follow-up. Let me put this on numeric terms to burn it into your mind. Suppose you are not a guerrilla and do not understand follow-up. Let's say you earn a $200 profit every time you make a sale. Okay, a customer walks in, invests, and leaves. You pocket $200 in profits and that one customer was worth $200 to you. Hey, $200 isn't all bad. But let's say you were a guerrilla. That means you send the client the thank-you note, the one-month note, the three-month note, the six-month note, the nine-month note, the anniversary card, the questionnaire, the constant alerting of new offerings. The customer, instead of making one purchase during the course of a year, makes three purchases. That same customer refers your business to four other people. Your bond is not merely for the length of the transaction but for as long as say, twenty years.

Because of your follow-up, that one client is worth $400,000 to you. So that's your choice: $200 with no follow-up or $400,000 with follow-up. And the cost of follow-up is not high because you already have the name of the person. The cost of prospect follow-up is also not high and for the same reason as with clients. Prospect follow-up is different from client follow-up. For one thing, you can't send a thank-you note–yet. But you can consistently follow up, never giving up and realizing that if you're second in line, you'll get the business when the business that's first in line messes up. And they will foul up. You know how? Of course you do. They'll fail to follow up enough.

Action Summary:

To add to my marketing plans:	Yes _____	No _____
Additional information required:	Yes _____	No _____

Build a dream and the dream will build you.

-Robert Schuller

You cannot push anyone up a ladder unless he is willing to climb a little.

-Andrew Carnegie

STRATEGY 39

Promise Less and Deliver More–Client Review Systems

Concept:

Send annual review letters and/or statements (if possible with your firm) with annual review worksheets. If you have a lot of clients, stagger the mailings over the first four weeks. You can also carbon copy their accountant and/or lawyer if there is tax or estate planning to complete.

Objective:

Client annual reviews are a must. Develop a systematic approach to annual reviews. The objective here is clear, to review their plans and continue the ongoing client planning. Most clients think financial plans are static. Your job is to show them that, based on their goals and objectives, together you are on the right track. Tax laws may change, estate planning changes, and investment objectives or financial situations and goals may be different. You need to review them to make sure you are doing your very best for your clients. You owe it to them.

Strategy:

The main reason why clients leave advisors is not performance, but communication. Your annual review also addresses their financial plans, tax plans, and estate plans. It also gives you opportunities to look for more areas to cross-sell your services (such as insurance or other investments). It allows you to cross-sell your team of professional referrals, such as accountants, lawyers, etc., to make sure they understand you have a team approach and can help them in other areas. Have you ever had a client say, "Gee, I didn't know you sold life insurance, I just bought a million dollar policy with ZZ Top Insurance last week." Make sure the client understands ALL of your financial services.

Grant's Tip:

Send out the annual review along with your quarterly newsletter. Package your reviews in a large envelope labeled "annual review." That way, they know you do this on an annual basis and that it's important to both of you to have specific annual information. Not all your clients may be interested in a specific idea, so have your assistant stuff each client's envelope with customized information.

"Clients are looking for peace of mind and financial security through sound financial planning." I put this statement on the back of my business card. For your annual review, we tend to look at markets and returns and measure up versus benchmarks and indexes. While analyzing the numbers is important, it is not as important as measuring people's lives.

How are they doing for their retirement, do they have enough to live on? Are they going to be able to retire? Are their children going to go to university soon? In other words, are they achieving all the financial goals and dreams to which they aspire? This is a different approach from that of the salesman who has a new financial product to sell this year or the transaction-based advisor who suggests a whole list of changes to make based on some fancy benchmark or index measurement. Remember, people don't care how much you know, but know how much you care!

I also recommend you hole-punch the statements so your clients can add them to their client binders. You can also package the reviews in presentable folders, hole-punched so they can add these to their binders; and year by year they can look at their annual reviews and see their progress towards completing and reviewing their financial plans. Make it a system to which the clients become accustomed, and the experience will be an extremely positive one focused on the clients, not the markets.

Costs: It takes a lot of time depending on the number of clients you have, but if you want to WOW them, it's worth it. You are making yourself more referable and your business more saleable—now that you have this type of system, anyone can deliver it. The other cost is stationery, usually $1 through $5 per client including mailing, depending on how expensive your stationery is.

Jay's Comments:

All business owners care about their customers, but guerrilla marketers prove they care. Here are twenty ways that they prove it.

It's very easy to care about your customers, but unless you take steps to show them that you care, they might be wooed away by a competitor. Your marketing can say all the right words and tell customers how important they are to you. But you've got to prove your dedication to customers—and prospects—by taking concrete steps beyond mere words.

Guerrillas know that there's a world of difference between customer care and customer attention. Many companies lavish attention upon their customers, but only the guerrillas excel at caring and know how to make customers feel sincerely cared for. Here are twenty ways that they do it:

1. Prepare a written document outlining the principles of your customer service. This should come from the president, but everyone should know what it says and be ready to live up to it.

2. Establish support systems that give clear instructions for gaining and maintaining service superiority. They help you out-service any competitor by giving more to customers and solving problems before they arise.

3. Develop a precise measurement of superb customer service and reward employees who practice it consistently. Many will if you hire people who really want to render great service and don't just do it because they should.

4. Be certain that your passion for customer service runs rampant throughout your company and not just at the top. Everyone should feel it.

5. Do all that you must to instill in employees who meet your customers a truly deep appreciation of the value of customer service. They should see how this service relates to your profits and to their future.

6. Be genuinely committed to providing more customer service excellence than anyone else in your industry. This commitment must be so powerful that every one of your customers can sense it.

7. Be sure that everyone in your company who deals with customers pays very close attention to the customer. Each customer should feel unique and special after they've contacted you or been contacted by you.

8. Ask questions of your customers, then listen carefully to their answers. Ask customers to expand upon their answers.

9. Stay in touch with your customers. Do it with letters, postcards, newsletters, phone calls, questionnaires and, if you can, at trade shows.

10. Nurture a human bond as well as a business bond with customers and prospects. Do favors for them. Educate them. Help them. Give gifts. Play favorites. Take them out to the ballgame or the opera. Your customers deserve to be treated this special.

11. Recognize that your customers have needs and expectations. You've got to meet their needs and exceed their expectations. Always? Always.

12. Understand why successful corporations such as 3M define service as "conformance" to customer requirements. This means that true guerrilla service is just what the customer wants it to be. Not easy, but necessary.

13. Keep alert for trends, and then respond to them. McDonald's operates under the axiom, "We lead the industry by following our customers."

14. Share information with people on the front line. Disney workers meet regularly to talk about improving their service. Information-sharing is easier than ever with new communications technologies. Share information with customers and prospects by having a web site that is loaded with helpful data. More and more, this is becoming mandatory.

15. Because customers are humans, observe birthdays and anniversaries. Constant communication should be your goal. If you find an article in the media that will help a customer, send a copy of the article to that customer.

16. *Consider holding "mixers" so customers can get to know your people better and vice-versa. Mixers are breeding grounds for human bonds.*

17. *Invest in phone equipment that makes your business sound friendly, easy to do business with, easy to contact, and quick to respond. Again, technology makes this easier than ever. Along with phone equipment, let customers know they can contact you by fax and e-mail.*

18. *Design your physical layout for efficiency, clarity of signage, lighting, handicap accessibility, and simplicity. Everything should be easy to find.*

19. *Act on the knowledge that what customers value most are attention, dependability, promptness, and competence. They just love being treated as individuals and being referred to by their name. Don't you?*

20. *When it comes to customer service, Nordstrom is a superstar, though Disney gives them a run for their money and Micsosoft is doing a bang-up job with their web site. Find it at www.microsoft.com/smallbiz. The Nordstrom service manual is eloquent in its simplicity: "Use your good judgment in all situations. There will be no additional rules."*

Guerrillas send postage-paid questionnaire cards and letters asking for suggestions. They fix the trouble areas revealed and know well the relationship between proving their care and success.

Examples:
See the following Annual Review Discussion Checklist.

Action Summary:

To add to my marketing plans:	Yes _____	No_____
Additional information required:	Yes _____	No_____

Seven out of ten people suffer from hemorrhoids. Does this mean that the other three enjoy it?

-Sal Davino

Annual Review Discussion Checklist:

In the weeks before our meeting, it would be helpful to gather the following information:

_____Annual net worth statement (see reverse to complete)

_____Most recent tax return/Notice of Assessment/RRSP contribution limits

_____Income tax summaries with capital gains or loss information

_____Annual income verification or summary including pension plans

_____Life insurance policies–life/group/mortgage

_____Charitable gifts information

_____Children's/grandchildren's education plans and documents

_____Other investment statements or summaries to discuss

_____List of major financial goals/dreams

For a productive and informative meeting, check off the items you wish to discuss:

_____Your overall retirement plan, including assumptions regarding inflation, life expectancy, and investment returns

_____The performance of your investments

_____Changes in your financial status

_____Changes in your retirement goals

_____Your retirement budget

_____Your annual RRSP contribution

_____Borrowing to invest

_____Income-splitting and spousal RRSPs

_____Generating income in retirement

_____Asset allocation

_____Portfolio rebalancing

_____Investing outside of Canada

_____General financial market and economic conditions

_____Tax minimization strategies

_____RRIFs and annuities

_____Individual securities/stocks or bonds

_____Retirement income options, including after-tax income maximization

_____Life Insurance review

_____Estate planning review

Utilize our team of professionals to help in the following areas:

_____Help with completing income tax–tax professional

_____Help with wills, trusts, or Powers of Attorney–legal professional

_____Help with mortgages–lending or borrowing to invest–mortgage lending specialist

_____Help with real estate planning–real estate professional

Notes/Comments/To Do

If you aren't fired with enthusiasm, you'll be fired with enthusiasm.

-Vince Lombardi

STRATEGY 40
Have Great Client Meetings–Use Agendas

Concept:

To ensure all areas of the financial plan are covered and discuss hidden areas that may have been forgotten, such as life insurance, tax planning, or other financial planning ideas.

Objective:

This will uncover planning opportunities and keep you and the client on track during the meeting. Have you ever done an interview and forgotten to talk about something, such as additional investment opportunities for the client and sales opportunities for yourself?

An agenda should be part of every interview and a copy given to the client at the start of the meeting. Once your meeting is over, you can note items on which you and/or the client need to take action. Put these items on the agenda for the next meeting, and so on.

Strategy:

Set up an agenda document in your word processor. Keep the same document or one or two versions. Then each time you see a client, it only takes a minute to change the agenda around for the meeting.

Another key part of the planning process is to plant two seeds in the clients minds.

First, when they will hear from you next. Just like a dental office assistant is trained to "book" you in for your next appointment before you leave the office, we should be trained to do the same thing. Schedule a review three or six months from now. Write it down for them and say, "Mr. and Mrs. Client, I have scheduled our spring review on May 15th at 2 p.m. We will call you and remind you a week in advance. Please let us know if this doesn't work for you. I look forward to seeing you in the spring." The clients then don't worry about when they will hear from you.

Second, the need to know which agenda items need further clarification, discussion, and/or planning. For example, the client is doing some tax planning; once that is resolved he will bring in additional funds to invest or buy additional insurance. There are always parts of the plan you are helping him to build, while planning future business.

Grant's Tip:

Keep the agenda simple. Have a bulleted list of items to discuss. Ask the client before you begin if there is anything to add. Then direct the meeting by starting at the top of the list, asking the client where he would like to begin.

The agenda should contain three parts. First, the list of items to discuss. Second, a summary of recommendations. Third, an action plan to complete. Without an action plan, clearly defined with a sense of urgency, the client may stall and "think" about it. When a client says they want to "think" about it, you know you have not created a sense of urgency and a need to complete the plans.

Another part of the review process is to complete the client contact log.

Jay's Comments:

Because we're smack dab in the middle of The Information Age and because time is so darned important, guerrillas do not waste the time of their clients. Is your current marketing distinctive because of its style or substance? The ideal answer is both. With its style, it conveys your identity and captures the attention of your targeted audience. With its substance, it makes essential points and motivates that audience. Well-informed marketers see to it that both their style and substance are obvious but that their product or service always has the starring role in their marketing. We've all had the experience of viewing a TV spot or reading an ad and wondering what the heck they were talking about, so you know what I'm getting at. Many web sites are more confusing than they are enlightening. In the early days of marketing, nobody needed special effects. When Harley Procter and his cousin, James Gamble, churned their soap too long and it floated, they came out and said Ivory is the soap that floats. Later, stressing its purity, they said it was 99 and 44/100ths percent pure. People knew exactly what they meant. But now the creative revolution is upon us. In the name of creativity rather than the less glamorous but more accurate name of selling, billions of dollars are being wasted each year. That's a conservative estimate. You can be sure that the top salespeople in the world don't begin their presentations with a tap dance or a cartwheel. They succeed because of the style they use to provide substance, not because of the style itself.

The overriding concept should be to present substance and do it with style. That means the emphasis is on the substance. Your clients will remember the substance. Checks get written because of the substance. Substance consists of both facts and opinions. It communicates both features and benefits. It is as specific as it can possibly be, as specific as 99 and 44/100th percent pure. And it effectively utilizes both words and pictures. What substance isn't is fun—and you shouldn't try to make people think that it is unless you sell video games or bicycles. It's style that's fun. Style makes it more enjoyable to read and hear. Or at least it makes your presentation digestible. Remember that your competition isn't Hollywood. It's that company that's been selling to your clients and attracting your prospects. But most businesses should not even think of selling with style at the expense of substance. Many have tried. Most have failed. Your task: stress your substance but do it with style. Fancy charts and graphs have style, not substance. Make your agendas with substance and support it with substance and style.

Examples:

Financial Planning Agenda–Prepared For: Mr. and Mrs. Client, by Grant W. Hicks:
• Review Existing Accounts
• Review Fixed Income Maturities
• Open Investment-Stock Account
• Estate Planning Review And Discussion
• Life Insurance Review
• Income Tax Planning
• Recommendations Summary
• Implementation Plan

This is substance; your support documents (and your charts, graphs, illustrations, and pictures) make up the essence of your style.

Action Summary:

To add to my marketing plans:	Yes _____	No _____
Additional information required:	Yes _____	No _____

I really didn't say everything I said.

-Yogi Berra

Great spirits have often encountered violent opposition from weak minds.

-Albert Einstein

STRATEGY 41

Guerrilla Marketing Ideas for Wholesalers

Concept:

Whether you're new to the business or a well-traveled road warrior, marketing ideas are just as important as product ideas to wholesalers.

Objective:

Most wholesalers are well-versed on product, sales, and relationship building. However, if you want to help advisors with their marketing, you need to upgrade your marketing education.

Strategy:

As a financial advisor (Retirement Planning Specialist) I have the opportunity to see the good, the bad, and the ugly of wholesaling from the financial advisor's side. Let's start off with a few questions.

First, why should I do business with you? Not your wonderful firm and all of its products–you? What do you personally bring to the table? As an advisor, we look at a new wholesaler sometimes the way a life insurance policy owner does when he receives a tenth phone call in five years to review his policy. What are you going to do differently (because I usually know who your company is)? Sell yourself and your team of people first.

Second, how do you intend to make yourself more valuable? In other words, are you going to be here in the future and are we going to grow together?

Third, do you eat your own cooking? In other words, where do you personally invest your family's money? This may seem like an unfair question, but if you believe in your products, answering this question will establish trust in the financial advisor's eyes.

Busy financial advisors these days will want to set an agenda with wholesalers. Simply dropping by for a visit is a waste of everybody's time. Having a pre-established agenda faxed or emailed to your advisors will show you respect them enough not to waste their time.

Grant's Tip:

Here is a list of marketing ideas to consider in the next year.

• Learn more about marketing and not markets–next time you go to your company meetings, find out what percentage of the agenda will be spent on marketing (versus product).

• Find representatives' hot buttons and excitement buttons–build your database based on them. For example, if a wholesaler came in to talk to me, he should know I am keen on tax planning for retirees. He should also know I love hockey and fishing. If a wholesaler sent me a magazine on fishing or hockey, he would get my attention faster than an article on a super small capital equity fund or even a sleeve of golf balls (although I can always give the golf balls to clients).

• Be known for the best communication strategies in the industry. Just as financial advisors develop a communication strategy for their clients, book your next meeting with an advisor before you leave. Save everyone a lot of time, even if it is three or four months from now. Ask your advisors what they expect of you for communications and develop your systems to help advisors.

• Sell holes not drills–case studies. If fund companies' marketing departments can put together typical case studies to which their products apply, advisors will have a better understanding of how to use those products. Be a problem solver. If I need holes drilled though a piece of wood, I want a drill to solve my problem. I ask the sales representative at Store A for a drill and he talks about drills or product. But at Store B, the sales representative asks me what size of holes I am drilling, how often, and through what type of material. Store B gets my business. What problems do your financial advisors face with their clients?

• Pictures and stories–tell me a story about the fund manager or a company in a portfolio and I begin to understand the manager's thinking. Tell me you have the best performance numbers, the lowest MER, and the best beta, and I'll never remember. Tell me stories or show me pictures to illustrate your points.

• Be a marketing agency–start by reading and collecting some of the best ideas on marketing. Be known as a resource. If you are known as a person to see for marketing ideas, your phone will be ringing.

• Be a coach to your top clients (teacher)–this is the next wave of wholesaling. Become coaches to advisors and take a coaching role in helping them manage and grow their businesses. How many top clients would you like to be coaching?

• Build a top client peer group–as an advisor I enjoy helping wholesalers. In fact put together a group of top advisors and sponsor a luncheon. Just like Strategy 26, have a board of directors to give you feedback. If I was a top advisor and you put together a peer group for me with other advisors, I would gladly show up to network with peers and learn from the best, just like in Strategy 6.

What the heck, hire me! If you want me to work with wholesaling groups, I will be glad to share the latest marketing ideas. My contact information is at the back of this book.

Jay's Comments:

The main idea can be clearly stated by stating one simple fact about marketing to financial advisors. If you spend your money to give them a copy of this book, it will have a greater support to their business than spending $25 for golf balls.

The Process of Marketing

Marketing is not an event, but a process. How long does the process last?

An insight for you to embrace is that a guerrilla marketing attack is never-ending. It has a beginning, a middle but never an end, for it is a process. You improve it, perfect it, change it, even pause in it. But you never stop it completely.

Of all the steps in succeeding with a guerrilla marketing attack, maintaining it takes the most time. You spend a relatively brief time developing the attack and inaugurating it, but you spend the life of your business maintaining, monitoring, and improving your attack. At no point should you ever take anything for granted. At no point should you fall into the pit of self-satisfaction because your attack is working. Never forget that others, very smart and motivated competitors, are studying you and doing their utmost to surpass you in the marketing arena.

Guerrillas thrive and prosper because they understand the deeper meanings of the phrases "customer base" and "long-term commitment." This enables them to reinvent their marketing–just as long as they are firm in their commitment to their existing customers and prospects. An attack without flexibility is in danger of failing. But that flexibility does not allow you to take your eyes off the needs of your customers.

Keep alert for new niches at which you can aim your attack. Large companies don't have the luxury of profiting from a narrow niche. No matter how successful your attack, never lose contact with your customers. If you do, you lose your competitive advantage over huge companies that have too many layers of bureaucracy for personal contact. Guerrilla marketing is always authentic marketing and never acts or feels to be impersonal, by-the-number marketing. It never feels like selling.

"Marketing Management" author Philip Kotler says "Authentic marketing is not the art of selling what you make but knowing what to make. It is the art of identifying and understanding customer needs and creating solutions that deliver satisfaction to the customers, profits to the producers, and benefits for the stakeholders. Market innovation is gained by creating customer satisfaction through product innovation, product quality, and customer

service. It these are absent, no amount of advertising, sales promotion, or salesmanship can compensate."

Your attack must be characterized by a very strong tie with your own target audience. You know them. You serve them. They know it. Guerrilla attacks do not suffer from your lack of resources, but instead prosper because lack of capital makes them more willing to try new and innovative ideas, concepts ripe for guerrillas but not for huge companies.

Your attack will succeed in direct relationship to how narrow-minded you can be. Guerrillas have the insight that precision strengthens an attack. They know the enormous difference between their prospects and their prime prospects. They are aware of the gigantic chasm separating their customers from their best customers. This perspective enables them to narrow their aim only to the best prospects that marketing money can buy and the finest customers ever to grace their customer list.

They are fully cognizant that it doesn't take much more work to sell a subscription to a magazine than to sell a single issue. That's why their marketing attack is devoted to motivating people to subscribe to their businesses mentally.

Once they have a customer, they do all they can to intensify the relationship, and they do not treat all customers and prospects equally. Consider the menswear chain with a database of 47,000 names. Mailings are never more than 3,000 at a time. Who receives the mail? Says the owner, "Only the people appropriate to mail to." When he received trousers of a specific style, he mailed only to those customers to whom he was certain they'd appeal—and enjoyed a 30% response rate.

The cost of his mailing was a tiny fraction of the size of his profits. There's not a chance of reveling in a healthy response like that unless you're targeting your mailing with absolute precision. It's something you're going to have to do in a world where postal charges and paper prices are both slated to increase. Unless you're hitting the bullseye, you're wasting your marketing investment. And unless you're treating your marketing as a continuing process, you're wasting everybody's time, including your own.

Action Summary:

To add to my marketing plans: Yes _____   No _____

Additional information required: Yes _____   No _____

There is little difference in people, but that little difference makes a big difference. That little difference is attitude. The big difference is whether it is positive or negative.

- W. Clement Stone

Chapter 7

Taking Your Business
To The Next Level

Taking Your Business to the Next Level

The karate master learns everything necessary to slam his hand through the wooden boards. He doesn't even think about the boards, only about seeing his hand on the other side of them. The shattering of the boards is not part of his vision. The board is merely an illusion. His hand beneath the cracked boards is the only reality the karate master will accept. Theory is what helped him earn his black belt, but he never would have earned it if he had not taken action.

Any obstacles he encountered on his way to mastery were merely illusions. All the successes he achieved were reality. As a master, he is aware of the illusion but focused upon the reality. And he realizes his insights into karate and energy, into force and concentration, are the power behind his action. Insight plus action equals success.

Mastering guerrilla marketing is not merely learning without doing, for the mastery of guerrilla marketing has action at its very core. Without action, there can be no mastery. Without action, there is only the illusion of mastery and never the results, never the fruits of having mastered what others only flail at.

Guerrillas understand there are two realities in life. The major one is illusion. The minor one is reality. The closer the two in your own life, the wiser you are, the better primed for success.

A key to mastery is to recognize each reality for what it is. Buying into illusion and mistaking it for reality is delusion. That delusion is no illusion. Now that you have the insights to master guerrilla marketing, you can change the illusion of mastering it into the reality of mastering it. Taking concrete action is how to do it.

Guerrillas know they can change reality just as they can change illusion. To most people on earth, illusion is reality. Shall I repeat that because it is so pivotal to your understanding, because so few people understand it? Then I will: To most people on earth, illusion is reality. In fact, to them, it's the only reality.

But guerrillas who have mastered marketing are blessed with the perception to separate illusion from reality and the wisdom to control both. Unless there is action, there can be no control. Ask the karate master.

Both karate master and guerrilla will tell you karate and marketing exist first as a state of mind. Guerrilla marketing begins at the end, at the goals towards which guerrillas strive. Their minds upon those goals, the rest of their actions are foretold by the clarity of their focus on that goal.

Although guerrillas are famed for their patience, they never wait too long, harking back to General George Patton's words: "A good plan implemented today is better than a perfect plan implemented tomorrow." They know perfection is merely the object of the quest and not something they will attain—at least not for very long. Rather than beginning with perfection, they perfect their activities as they attack.

Metamorphosing yourself into a guerrilla may seem to be a daunting task, but it really isn't. Mastering guerrilla marketing isn't something you do overnight, though the decision to do so happens in a flashing instant. Mastery of marketing is something so seemingly complex that you may not be sure where to start. Many business owners know the steps to follow, each one in order, but even the thought of taking all those steps sets some of them back on their heels. Not to worry.

Just realize that your task can easily be broken down into several small parts, each one simple enough for you to handle gracefully. Guerrilla entrepreneurs have learned that you should divide big tasks into smaller tasks, you should never underestimate the power of your own gut reaction, and your most valuable aid in hitting pay dirt with guerrilla marketing is your ability to prioritize the actions you must take.

You've also got to be able to dream, then to breathe life into those dreams. Henry David Thoreau said, "If you have built castles in the air, your work need not be lost; that is where they should be. Now, put the foundations under them."

The foundations begin with words. Guerrillas know well the enormous power of written words. The ancient Egyptians thought words were magic. They believed that if you write it, surely it will happen.

That's why a guerrilla marketing attack, a guerrilla marketing mindset, begins with you putting your plan into words. Success is not something that will happen to you. It will flow through you—to your staff, your customers, to future generations, and to the body of knowledge that comprises our small business wisdom of today.

The flow begins when you write those first words. Not a lot of words. A mere seven sentences, comprising a guerrilla marketing strategy, described in *Guerrilla Marketing Third Edition*, will contain all the words you need to begin. Those sentences are your first steps in the endless marathon. They will keep you on the right course.

Steps to Take You to the Next Level

• Develop your ten-year vision.

• Develop a plan of action for one-, three-, five-, and ten-year periods.

• Develop your marketing plan—use this workbook to start developing ideas that you can start implementing right away

• Turn intention into action—now that you have a plan, start working your plan and revisiting, revising, and improving every day—schedule time in your calendar for CANI—constant and never-ending improvement.

• Now that you have the time scheduled and an organized way to work on your plans and review your plans, be consistent. Plan your work and work your plan, over and over.

• Use the Guerrilla Marketing Action Planning Worksheet on page 271 - 278 to start your plan of action.

• Finally, reward yourself. Its great to set goals and plans, but along the way, as you improve and find more confidence, reward yourself. Remember, life is a journey, not a destination. Enjoy the ride.

Chapter 8

Marketing Principles
for
Financial Advisors

Marketing Principles for Financial Advisors:

This chapter has similarities to Jay Conrad Levinson's book *Guerrilla Marketing Excellence–The Fifty Golden Rules for Small Business Success.* It is not a workbook; rather it is a set of marketing commandments by which to live by as you develop your business. It contains principles learned over a decade of marketing.

Financial services and these principles, or golden rules, may seem obvious, but they allow successful financial advisors to separate themselves from the pack and allow them to "See the forest from the trees." Each principle is discussed in detail as it applies to the financial professional. A chapter excerpt follows:

Principle–Your career as a financial advisor is to "Market Financial Services"

When you ask most financial advisors what their job is you get statements like "To help people with their tax and retirement plans" or "to service and sell financial services." Most advisors don't understand that when they get into this business, they think of it as a sales job. Selling is only half the job, marketing is the other half. Selling does not occur without marketing. You need someone to sell yourself to, so how do you find that someone? By finding your marketing focus, and your ideal client profile, you can concentrate on selling. If we market to a set of clientele that we are looking for, it's like shooting fish in a barrel as opposed to spray and prey method of prospecting.

Principle–Practice what you preach and believe in it –"Own what you sell"

Establish your own written tax, estate, investment, and financial plan. Then put that plan into action. Most advisors know this rule yet often forget that the plan is the product. How can you sell what you don't own? How can you motivate investors or have enthusiasm for a product or service you don't believe in? Do you have your own organized plans for your estate, retirement, insurance, and investments?

Principle–Run your business like a franchise–"Develop your systems"

What differentiates you from other advisors? Why should I do business with you? What can I expect as a client? What is your approach to money management? Provide some examples of who you have helped, including names and numbers. How do you do what you do? How do you add value to the services you provide? What type of system do you have for managing new and existing clients? These are the types of questions clients are asking today. The cookie cutter approach doesn't differentiate you or your services. You must have systems for all aspects of your business. The systems are also part of your marketing statement that tell people why they should do business with you and then prove it. If I asked you these above questions, can you answer them in a format that makes you look organized and you have a plan for clients, or are you just winging it?

Principle—Earn the power of repetition—"Commitment to your marketing plan"

How many times have you stopped using an idea that worked well? Don't feel bad, most advisors do it all the time. The power of repetition can get boring. However, we eventually come back to what works. Marketing is sometimes a difficult measure because results can come down the road after months or years of trying. How long did it take for you to land your largest client? The persistent advisor knows that the best clients did not make decisions quickly, rather they need enough comfort to make a decision. What is enough comfort? Great question, why don't you ask your top clients what it was that eventually made them decide to join you and you will have incredible insight towards your marketing strategies. This will tell you what works and what doesn't. As an advisor I cannot tell you what works for your biggest clients, rather do your market research and gather your results. Maybe it was from a couple of seminars. Could it be that it was from more than one client referring your name to them, or finally it was that they found you had the systematic planning and teamwork approach that they were looking for? You won't know until you ask. Now if you were to have 10 or 12 more clients like your top ones, would you not be having your best year in the business?

Define your job
• *"Marketing Financial Services"*
• *Schedule time to make the calls*
• *Run your business like a "franchise"*
• *Help people who want to be helped*
• *What can you do for your company/dealer!*
• *Practice what you preach*
• *Re-invest 10-15% of your gross income back into your business to make it grow*
• *Take time off*
• *Be persistent—the 5-touch rule in marketing*
• *Nick Murray—What do you believe in?*
• *Success leaves clues!*
• *Provide excellent advice*
• *Activity drives production*
• *Brand yourself—What makes you unique?*
• *Love what you do*

Principle—Become effective

There is a world of difference between efficiency and effectiveness, and it's in that world that guerrillas flourish. They are well aware of the power and omnipresence of the 80/20 rule and have probably read Richard Koch's book, "The 80/20 Principle" because even its subtitle—"The Secret of Achieving More with Less"—is guerrilla through and through. It dramatically emphasizes the effectiveness that can be gained by simplicity.

Alas, even guerrillas don't hit the bullseye with all of their marketing, but at least they direct their energies towards learning which 20 percent of their marketing generates 80 percent of their sales. Just knowing this to be true is a compelling reason to learn where each of your customers learned of your existence, to recognize that all customers are not created equal and that 20 percent of them most likely account for 80 percent of your profits.

The 80/20 rule teaches you simplicity and applies to more of your business than marketing and more of your life than business:

- *80 percent of what you achieve at work comes from 20 percent of the time you spend working.*
- *20 percent of a company's products usually account for 80 percent of its sales and 20 percent of its employees contribute to 80 percent of profits.*
- *20 percent of criminals account for 80 percent of crimes.*
- *20 percent of motorists cause 80 percent of accidents.*
- *20 percent of your carpets get 80 percent of the wear.*
- *20 percent of your clothes will be worn 80 percent of the time.*
- *80 percent of traffic jams occur on 20 percent of the roads.*
- *20 percent of computer users purchase 80 percent of software.*

Your job? To find out which 20 percent of your marketing is motivating the most sales, to determine which 20 percent of your customers are producing 80 percent of your profits, to learn which 20 percent of your prospects are most likely to become customers.

One of the most fascinating definitions of entrepreneur comes to us from the French economist J-B Say, who coined the word, and said, "The entrepreneur shifts economic resources out of an area of lower productivity into an area of higher productivity and yield."

The underlying meaning of that definition and 80/20 rule is that there's a whole lot of wasted money and energy in life. The goals of the guerrilla are first to identify the area of lower productivity and do something about it, then identify the area of higher productivity and do something about it. It's the doing something about it that determines the real winners.

The actions you take to eliminate waste and double up on effectiveness may make you seem unreasonable. So take comfort in George Bernard Shaw's words: "The reasonable man adapts himself to the world. The unreasonable one persists in trying to adapt the world to himself. Therefore all progress depends on the unreasonable man."

When you discover which 20 percent of your customers are responsible for 80 percent of your sales, focus on keeping them happy, increase the amount of business you do with them, and tap them for their referral power because these are obviously satisfied customers. Paying more attention to them reduces your marketing budget because you can pay less attention to the 80 percent who motivate 20 percent of your profits.

Once your mind has absorbed the full implications of the 80/20 rule, consider applying it in other ways: celebrate exceptional productivity rather than raising average efforts. Look for shortcuts. Be selective more than exhaustive. Delegate and out-source as much as possible. Target a limited number of goals and focus like a laser beam upon them.

Because you're a guerrilla, don't do any of these things in a hurry. Patience will enable you to spot the areas that need changing, then to implement the changes so that humanity remains part of your modus operandi. Fast isn't beautiful. Big isn't beautiful. Small isn't beautiful. It's simple that is most beautiful if you're an 80/20 kind of guerrilla.

Memorize These 12 Words Then Live By Them
by Jay Conrad Levinson.

I'm giving you a memory crutch so that you'll never forget these words. All 12 words end in the letters "ENT". Run your business by the guerrilla concepts they represent and you'll be in marketing heaven.

1. COMMITMENT: You should know that a mediocre marketing program with commitment will always prove more profitable than a brilliant marketing program without commitment. Commitment makes it happen.

2. INVESTMENT: Marketing is not an expense, but an investment—the best investment available in America today—if you do it right. With guerrilla marketing to guide you, you'll be doing it right.

3. CONSISTENT: It takes a while for prospects to trust you and if you change your marketing, media, and identity, you're hard to trust. Restraint is a great ally of the guerrilla. Repetition is another.

4. CONFIDENT: In a nationwide test to determine why people buy, price came in fifth, selection fourth, service third, quality second, and, in first place—people said they patronize businesses in which they are confident.

5. PATIENT: Unless the person running your marketing is patient, it will be difficult to practice commitment, view marketing as an investment, be consistent, and make prospects confident. Patience is a guerrilla virtue.

6. ASSORTMENT: Guerrillas know that individual marketing weapons rarely work on their own. But marketing combinations do work. A wide assortment of marketing tools are required to woo and win customers.

7. CONVENIENT: People now know that time is not money, but is far more valuable. Respect this by being easy to do business with and running your company for the convenience of your customers, not yourself.

8. SUBSEQUENT: The real profits come after you're made the sale, in the form of repeat and referral business. Non-guerrillas think marketing ends when they've made the sale. Guerrillas know that's when marketing begins.

9. AMAZEMENT: There are elements of your business that you take for granted, but prospects would be amazed if they knew the details. Be sure all of your marketing always reflects that amazement. It's always there.

10. MEASUREMENT: You can actually double your profits by measuring the results of your marketing. Some weapons hit bulls-eyes. Others miss the target. Unless you measure, you won't know which is which.

11. INVOLVEMENT: This describes the relationship between you and your customer—and it is a relationship. You prove your involvement by following up; they prove theirs by patronizing and recommending you.

12. DEPENDENT: The guerrilla's job is not to compete but to cooperate with other businesses. Market them in return for them marketing you. Set up tie-ins with others. Become dependent to market more, spend less.

Chapter 9

Guerrilla Marketing Tools
and
Marketing Action Plan
Worksheet

100 Guerrilla Marketing Weapons:

These guerrilla marketing weapons should all be considered for promoting your product, service, or web site off line. Notice that more than half of them are free.

1. Marketing plan
2. Marketing calendar
3. Niche/positioning
4. Name of company
5. Identity
6. Logo
7. Theme
8. Stationery
9. Business card
10. Signs inside
11. Signs outside
12. Hours of operation
13. Days of operation
14. Window display
15. Flexibility
16. Word of mouth
17. Community involvement
18. Barter
19. Club/association memberships
20. Partial payment plans
21. Cause-related marketing
22. Telephone demeanor
23. Toll-free phone number
24. Free consultations
25. Free seminars and clinics
26. Free demonstrations
27. Free samples
28. Giver vs. taker stance
29. Fusion marketing
30. Marketing on telephone hold
31. Success stories
32. Employee attire
33. Service
34. Follow-up

35. Yourself and your employees
36. Gifts and ad specialities
37. Catalog
38. Yellow Pages ads
39. Column in a publication
40. Article in a publication
41. Speaker at any club
42. Newsletter
43. All your audiences
44. Benefits list
45. Computer
46. Selection
47. Contact time with customer
48. How you say hello/goodbye
49. Public relations
50. Media contacts
51. Neatness
52. Referral program
53. Sharing with peers
54. Guarantee
55. Telemarketing
56. Gift certificates
57. Brochures
58. Electronic brochures
59. Location
60. Advertising
61. Sales training
62. Networking
63. Quality
64. Reprints and blow-ups
65. Flipcharts
66. Opportunities to upgrade
67. Contests/sweepstakes
68. On-line marketing
69. Classified advertising
70. Newspaper ads
71. Magazine ads
72. Radio spots
73. TV spots
74. Infomercials

75. Movie ads
76. Direct-mail letters
77. Direct-mail postcards
78. Postcard decks
79. Posters
80. Fax-on-demand
81. Special events
82. Show display
83. Audio-visual aids
84. Spare time
85. Prospect mailing lists
86. Research studies
87. Competitive advantages
88. Marketing insight
89. Speed
90. Testimonials
91. Reputation
92. Enthusiasm and passion
93. Credibility
94. Spying on yourself and others
95. Being easy to do business with
96. Brand-name awareness
97. Designated guerrilla
98. Customer mailing list
99. Competitiveness
100. Satisfied customers

Final thoughts....

A note to advisors and my clients on very important things I have learned in this industry.

First, it is a relationship business. Form relationships.

Second, you must find a way to have fun in this business while working in good times and in bad. Keep a sense of humor and your enthusiasm will automatically be there.

Third, we manage feelings and emotions, not money.

Finally, people always worry about money. No matter how much or how little they have, no matter how safe or how risky they invest, people will always worry about money. If you can help them have less worry about money, you will have a very rewarding career. Grant W. Hicks - Parksville BC - September 2003.

Guerrilla Marketing Action Planning Worksheet

This worksheet is designed to build your Guerrilla Marketing Arsenal for attack in the next year. It lists all of the ideas presented in the book. Start by reading the chapters that you want to develop into your marketing plans. Then use the summary worksheet to start building your plan for the next year. Keep this book near your marketing files and use it as a resource to develop incoming ideas further. If you require further information, use the resources listed in the back of this book or log onto *www.financialadvisormarketing.com* for your source of information. It's all right here to start building your business today!

Ideas to build into my marketing plans:

Yes=Y; No=N; Additional info Required =A

Chapter 1 Building a Better Businees and Marketing Plan

1. Business Plan–Your 10-Year Vision

Does your business plan cover 1, 3, 5, 10 years?   _____

How big could your business become in 10 years?

---

2. Build a Marketing Plan Guaranteed to Increase Your Business

Do you have a written marketing plan?   _____

Is your marketing bringing you the results you desire or expected?   _____

3. Successful Franchise-like Production Systems.

Do you track your production results?   _____

Do you make month-to-month and year-to-year result comparisons and numbers?   _____

4. Secret to Rapid Business Growth

Are there any books of business you would love to purchase?   _____

Are there representatives considering retirement that you could take over?   _____

5. Success Secrets for Leveraging Your Time

How do you leverage your time now?   _____

Could you get more time?   ____

Do you use a handheld device to save time and stay organized?   ____

6. Learning From The Best

Do you have a mastermind group?   ____

Do you have a successful business model which you can copy or
emulate?   ____

Who could you invite to a mastermind peer group?

_____

_____

7 Marketing Team Builders

Who completes your marketing initiatives now?

_____

_____

Do they love marketing?   ____

Do you need to hire or train staff to improve your marketing?   ____

8. Finding Your Ideal Client

Do you have a detailed ideal client profile?   ____

Do you share this with clients and centers of influence?   ____

Do you have a target market?   ____

9. Secrets of Selecting Marketing Methods

How many methods do you use in your marketing?   ____

Which strategies are working now?

_____

_____

Which are not working?

_____

_____

What are you going to change?

_____

_____

10. What Sets you Apart From the Rest

Do you have a large list of prospects?   ____

Are they qualified?   ____

Are they ideal?   ____

Do you have a well-organized database and call system?   ____

Chapter 2 Getting New Clients From Outside Sources

11. Have Everyone Calling You!

How many times do you contact a prospect before deleting? ____

How long do you keep a prospect on your database? ____

How do prospects get to know you?

---

12. Who You Need to Call Now!

Do you have an organized approach for making calls? ____

Do you contact new prospects every day? ____

Do you schedule time to make the calls every day? ____

13. Building a Dynamic Referral Team

Do you have a dynamic referral team? ____

How many people are on your team? ____

Do your clients and prospects know about your team? ____

14. Centers of Influence Seminars

How do you educate your centers of influence?

Have you ever done cast study seminars with centers of
influence? ____

15. Finding Great Partners–Working with Wholesalers–Part I

Do you have individuals or a team of wholesalers who help you
grow your business? ____

Do your wholesalers help your business or push products onto
you? ____

Do you ask for an agenda before meeting with a wholesaler? ____

16. Strategies of Marketing With Your Partners–
Working with Wholesalers–Part II

What type of marketing can you do with your wholesalers?

Have you ever held seminars and meetings with wholesalers as
a panel discussion? ____

17. Your Media Advantage Part I–Radio and TV

Do you share your ideas through TV or radio? ____

Do you have relationships with people in the media that could help your business?   _____

18. Your Media Advantage Part II–Free Information

Does your advertising bring you the results you desire?   _____

Do you develop your own advertising or do you rely on company-written ads?   _____

What advertising do you see today that has an impact on you?

_____

_____

19. Build Money on the Web

Your web site strategy

Do you have a web site?   _____

Does your web site help market you?   _____

Does your web site help your clients?   _____

What is the purpose of your web site?

_____

What type of traffic does it get and from where?

_____

20. Ultimate Public Relations Part I–Writing Financial Columns

Do you use newspapers to help you build new clients?   _____

What do you use for your public relations?   _____

Have you approached publishers to write financial columns or news quotes?   _____

Do you have a list of contacts in the media to work with?   _____

21. Ultimate Public Relations Part 2–Your Slogan and Brand Image

Do you or does your company have a slogan that is branded into everything you do and communicate to clients and prospects?   _____

Do you have a brand image?   _____

What type of goodwill is associated with you and or your name?

_____

_____

22. Successful Seminar Strategies

Do you do successful seminars?   _____

Do you have groups of people or prospects you can target?   _____

Chapter 3 Getting New Clients from Internal Marketing

23. How to Double your Business by Cloning Your Top Clients–Referral Strategies Part I–The Getting-married Philosophy

Refer to the exercise in Strategy 23–List your top five clients and add up their total assets and annual revenue and now double it. How could you clone these top clients?

_____

_____

24. How to Double your Business by Cloning Your Top Clients--Referral Strategies Part II–Referral Systems

Do you have a referral system?   _____

What can I expect if I send you a referral?

_____

_____

25. Build a Life Planning Referral Team

Do you have a life planning referral team?   _____

Who else could be on your well balanced life planning team or referral network?

_____

_____

26. The Ultimate Feedback and Idea Forum–Your Board of Directors

Do you have a board of directors?   _____

Do you change them each year ?   _____

27. Gathering Millions of New Assets–Finding and Tracking Them

Do you track non-managed assets?   _____

Do you have software to track non-managed assets?   _____

28. Educating Your Clients

How do you educate your clients now?

_____

_____

What other strategies can you employ to educate your clients?

_____

_____

29. Orphan Accounts–How to Find Them and How to Help Them

Do you have a source for existing clients being referred to you?   _____

Is there someone who you could partner up with to gather and or service existing clients better?   _____

Chapter 4 Introducing New Clients

30. Making People Feel Very Welcome

When I come into your office, will I feel lost or welcomed?

_____

Is the atmosphere organized or frantic ?

_____

31. The First Five Minutes–Key Questions To Ask Millionaires

Do you have a system of fact-finding?   _____

Do you gather all of the relevant information from a client before proceeding with a plan?   _____

32. Add Incredible Value–What Sets You Apart

What sets you apart from the competition?   _____

Why should I do business with you?   _____

33. Your New Communications Company

Do you have a company that can help you with communications?   _____

Do your materials say "we," "I," "us," or "you" and "your"?   _____

Is it truly from the client's point of view?   _____

Chapter 5 Wowing Clients

34. Keeping your Clients Organized

How do you keep your clients organized?

_____

Do you use client organizers or binders? _____

Are your files organized _____

35. The Best Client Appreciation Ideas

How much do you spend on client appreciation per year?

Do you have a client appreciation system or program or schedule ? _____

Chapter 6 Mastering Service for All Client Levels

36. Client Correspondence Designed for Your Clients

How do you effectively communicate with your clients now? _____

Do you have a client and/or prospect email program? _____

37. Newsletters That Impact Your Clients' Lives

Do you successfully use a newsletter _____

Does your newsletter have an impact? _____

38. Read With Scissors

Do you ever send out interesting articles to clients, prospects and centers of influence? _____

39. Client Service–How to Deliver More

Do you have an annual review discussion checklist? _____

How do your clients know that you are completing reviews on their accounts? _____

40. Structuring Great Client Meetings

Do you use agendas for most of your meetings? _____

Are your meetings structured or overly time consuming? _____

41. Guerrilla Marketing Ideas for Wholesalers

Do you and your wholesaler discuss product or marketing? _____

What are the percentages for each category, product versus marketing?

Do you have structured meetings with your wholesalers or marketing companies? _____

Bonus questions:

What are the top activities that make up the majority of your business revenue each year?

_____

_____

What else can you do to make your business a success this year?

_____

_____

How can we help? Check out *www.financialadvisormarketing.com* for more ideas and support than you ever thought possible!

Bibliography

Allen, Robert G. *Multiple Streams of Internet Income.* John Wiley & Sons, 2001.

Ayling, Geoff. *Rapid Response Advertising.* Business & Professional Publishing; 1999.

Bachrach, Bill. *Values-Based Financial Planning: The Art of Creating an Inspiring Financial Strategy.* Aim High Publishing; 2000.

Bachrach, Bill. *Values-Based Selling: The Art of Building High-Trust Client Relationships.* Bachrach & Associates Inc., 1996.

Gerber, Michael E. *The E-Myth Revisited: Why Most Small Businesses Don't Work and What to Do About It.* HarperBusiness; 1995.

Katz, Deena. *Deena Katz's Tools and Templates for Your Practice: For Financial Advisors, Planners, and Wealth Managers.* Bloomberg Pr, 2001.

Koch, Richard, *The 80/20 Principle: The Secret to Success by Achieving More with Less.* Doubleday; 1999.

Lombardo, Franco. *Life After Wealth™.* Roper House Publising 2003.

Mackay, Harvey and Kenneth H. Blancard. *Swim With the Sharks: Without Being Eaten Alive: Outsell, Outmanage, Outmotivate, and Outnegotiate Your Competition.* Fawcett Books, 1996.

Murray, Nick. *The Excellent Investment Advisor.* The Nick Murray Company, Inc., 1996.

Peppers, Don, and Martha Rogers, PhD. *The One to One Future: Building Relationships One Customer at a Time.* Doubleday, 1996.

Stanley, Thomas J. *Marketing To The Affluent.* McGraw-Hill, 1988.

U2. *I Still Haven't Found What I'm Looking For.* From *The Joshua Tree,* Island Records, 1987.

Get The Complete Guerrilla Arsenal!

*MASTERING GUERRILLA MARKETING: 100 PROFIT-PRODUCING
INSIGHTS THAT YOU CAN TAKE TO THE BANK*
"No one knows how to use the weapons of the trade better than industry
expert Jay Levinson," said *Entrepreneur* magazine. And this is "the book of
a lifetime" from the man who has revolutionized small-business marketing
strategies.
0-395-90875-2

*GUERRILLA MARKETING: SECRETS FOR MAKING BIG PROFITS
FROM YOUR SMALL BUSINESS,* THIRD EDITION
The book that started the Guerrilla Marketing revolution, now completely
updated and expanded. Full of the latest strategies, information on the hottest
technologies, details about the fastest-growing markets, and management
lessons for the twenty-first century.
0-395-90625-3

GUERRILLA PERSUASION
Effective persuasion is half innate ability and half art. *Guerrilla Persuasion*
teaches readers how to realize their full potential by mastering five essential
concepts that will enable them to understand their argument, their audience,
any possible resistance, and themselves.
0-395-88168-4

*THE WAY OF THE GUERRILLA: ACHIEVING SUCCESS AND
BALANCE AS AN ENTREPRENEUR IN THE 21ST CENTURY*
An invaluable blueprint for future business success, *The Way of the Guerrilla*
includes advice on everything from preparing a focused mission statement to
sustaining one's passion for work. Entrepreneurs will discover the means to
achieving emotional and financial success.
0-395-92478-2

*GUERRILLA MARKETING ON LINE: THE ENTREPRENEUR'S GUIDE
TO EARNING PROFITS ON THE INTERNET, SECOND EDITION*
From building and maintaining a Web site to creating an on-line catalog and
encouraging users to shop on the Net, Jay Levinson and computer book
author Charles Rubin will turn entrepreneurs into Internet marketing experts.
0-395-86061-X

GUERRILLA MARKETING ON-LINE WEAPONS: 100 LOW-COST, HIGH-IMPACT WEAPONS FOR ON-LINE PROFITS AND PROSPERITY
From email addresses and signatures to storefronts, feedback mechanisms, electronic catalogs, and press kits, Levinson and Rubin's weapons will help any business define, refine, and post its message on line with ease.
0-395-77019-X

GUERRILLA MARKETING FOR THE HOME-BASED BUSINESS
Using case studies, anecdotes, illustrations, and examples, guerrilla marketing gurus Jay Levinson and Seth Godin present practical, accessible, and inspirational marketing advice and the most effective marketing tools for America's fastest-growing business segment.
0-395-74283-8

THE GUERRILLA MARKETING HANDBOOK
An essential companion to *Guerrilla Marketing,* this practical guide offers thousands of contacts, ideas, and examples that will help transform plans into specific actions, turning any business into a marketing powerhouse.
0-395-70013-2

GUERRILLA ADVERTISING: COST-EFFECTIVE TACTICS FOR SMALL-BUSINESS SUCCESS
Full of anecdotes about past and current advertising successes and failures, *Guerrilla Advertising* entertains as it teaches the nuts and bolts of advertising for small businesses.
0-395-68718-7

GUERRILLA MARKETING EXCELLENCE: THE 50 GOLDEN RULES FOR SMALL-BUSINESS SUCCESS
Outlining fifty basic truths that can make or break your company, *Guerrilla Marketing Excellence* takes readers beyond do-it-yourself marketing guides, explaining not just how to market but how to market with excellence.
0-395-60844-9

GUERRILLA FINANCING: ALTERNATIVE TECHNIQUES TO FINANCE ANY SMALL BUSINESS
The ultimate sourcebook for finance, *Guerrilla Financing* is the first book to describe in detail the many traditional and alternative sources of funding available for small- and medium-size businesses.
0-395-52264-1

GUERRILLA SELLING: UNCONVENTIONAL WEAPONS AND TACTICS FOR INCREASING YOUR SALES

Today's increasingly competitive business environment requires new skills and commitment from salespeople. *Guerrilla Selling* presents unconventional selling tactics that are essential for success.

0-395-57820-5

GUERRILLA MARKETING ATTACK: NEW STRATEGIES, TACTICS, AND WEAPONS FOR WINNING BIG PROFITS

Guerrilla Marketing Attack explains how to avoid running out of fuel by maximizing limited start-up resources and turning prospects into customers and investments into profits.

0-395-50220-9

GUERRILLA CREATIVITY

The guru of guerrilla marketing unveils his methods of optimizing originality and creativity for successful marketing. Levinson focuses on memes, simple symbols that convey complex ideas—how to generate them and how to disseminate them.

0-618-10468-2

Visit this website for the best marketing links on the website for financial advisors.

www.financialadvisormarketing.com

Join the Guerrilla Marketing Association at:

www.financialadvisormarketing.com

Check out Guerrilla Marketing and more at:

www.gmarketing.com

Book Order Form:

Please forward _____ book(s) to:

Name

Address

City

Province

Postal Code

I enclose cheque in the amount of $_____

I enclose Money Order in the amount of $_____

To order additional copies, log on to our website:
www.financialadvisormarketing.com.

Ordering books:

Trafford Publishing order desk
2333 Government Street, Suite 6E
Victoria, BC, Canada V8V 4K5
Toll-free 1-866-752-6820, fax 250-383-6804

Eastern USA:
Trafford Publishing, Inc.
301 South Front Street, Suite 8
New Bern, NC, USA 28560-2105
Toll-free 1-888-240-3723, fax 252-633-4816

United Kingdom:
Trafford Publishing (UK) Limited
Enterprise House, Wistaston Road Business Centre,
Wistaston Road, Crewe UK CW2 7RP
Local rate number 0845 230 9601
Phone 01270 252889, fax 01270 254983

Ireland and other European countries:
Trafford Publishing (Europe) Limited
former St. Mary's Church of Ireland building, Mary Street
Drogheda, County Louth, Republic of Ireland
Phone ++353 41 9831262, fax++353 41 9831206

Discounts available for orders of 100 or more books.

Index

Hire Grant to increase your companies revenue through marketing

Are you looking to increase your marketing of financial services, but don't have the time, expertise or money to develop a huge marketing campaign? Let Grant show you how to increase your revenue and develop proven marketing ideas for Financial Advisors at a fraction of the cost.

Grant's years of experience as a Financial Advisor and Retirement planning Specialist, manager and speaker are real and genuine. Most speakers are not financial advisors, but Grant is devoted to his clients in a meaningful way. He shares his unique marketing experiences, successes and mistakes and helps you take a dramatic shortcut on the road to financial Advisor success.

Here is a copy of an email response from Jay Conrad Levinson to Grant Hicks:

let's hear it for grant!

the book reads superbly, flows smoothly, and is going to be a life-changer for a lot of people. I looked for flaws and could only find gems. Unquestionably, you da man!

I'm proud to be associated with such a book.

Thank you, grant, for making me look so good and for being such an extraordinary Guerrilla yourself.

Jay Conrad Levinson- July 2003

The Benefits of Grant's Presentations

• Learn how to improve the quality and quantity of referrals from centers of influence

• Learn what your clients really want and how to deliver it.

• Learn how to develop an effective marketing plan in less than 30 minutes

• Learn how to think differently as a Top Financial Advisor

• Find ways of marketing that don't cost you a fortune to implement

• Learn why top Financial Advisors continue to prospect and how

• Learn how to leverage your marketing with wholesalers

• Learn time management secrets that speakers who are not financial advisors can never understand

• Learn principles of marketing exclusively for Financial Advisors

• Learn how accountant's lawyers and other professionals can improve their marketing

<u>Grant can speak at your next conference or meeting – contact us now to find out how</u>

How much time is allocated on your agenda to Marketing and Client Communication? Most seminars and conference planners NEVER schedule enough time in their agenda towards marketing.

How many hours is your conference ?_____

What percentage of time is spent on marketing ?_____

If your answer is not enough, then we have the solution for you. Book Grant to increase the time spent thinking about marketing to increase your companies bottom line. It's that simple. Call Grant's office today at 250-248-2824 or email him at *www.ghicks@financialadvisormarketing.com*

ISBN 141200399-7

9 781412 003995